Philemon

CLINTON'S BIBLICAL LEADERSHIP COMMENTARY SERIES

A Study in Leadership Style

J. Robert Clinton, D. Miss., PhD.

ISBN No 978-1-932814-09-5

Copyright © J. Robert Clinton Sep 2006
Editorial compilation work done by Jun Young Chung

Table of Contents

Page	Contents
v	**Abbreviations**
vi	List of Tables
viii	List of Figures
ix	Introduction to Clinton's Leadership Commentary Series
x	Preface
1	General Reflection on Philemon
3	Overview
5	**PHILEMON AS A SOURCE OF LEADERSHIP TOPICS:**
5	**1. INFLUENCE MEANS**
6	**2. MENTOR SPONSOR**
7	**3. RELATIONAL VALUE**
7	**4. PRAYER ENCOURAGEMENT PRINCIPLE**
7	**5. ISOLATION PROCESSING AND RESULTS.**
8	**6. SOCIAL ISSUE.**
8	**7. CRITICAL INCIDENT**
11	Philemon Commentary
17	For Further Study

Leadership Articles[1] (bold faced items appear in other commentaries as well):

21	*1. Figures and Idioms in the Bible*
28	*2. God's Shaping Processes With Leader.*
32	*3. God's Timing and Influence*

---

[1] Articles listed with numbers are included with this commentary. Some articles, without numbers (and boldfaced italic) occur in other commentaries. All articles are also available in one or more of the **Clinton Leadership Encyclopedia** Series. See Bibliography for listing of the Volumes of the **Clinton Leadership Encyclopedia**.

37	*4. Influence, Power, and Authority*
42	*5. Integrity—A Top Leadership Quality*
47	*6. Isolation Processing—Learning Deep Lessons From God*
54	*7. Leadership Act*
57	*8. Leadership Eras in the Bible—Six Identified*
61	*9. Leadership Genre—7 Types*
63	*10. Leadership Tree Diagram*
66	*11. Macro-Lessons—Defined*
69	*12. Macro-Lessons—List of 41 Across Six Leadership Eras*
71	*13. Mentoring—An Informal Training Model*
74	*14. Paradigms and Paradigm Shifts*
78	*15. Paul—And His Companions*
84	*16. Paul—Deep Processing*
90	*17. Paul—Developer Par Excellence*
92	*18. Paul—Intercessor Leader*
95	*19. Paul—Mentor for Many*
98	*20. Pauline Leadership Styles*
104	*21. Sovereign Mindset*
107	*22. Spiritual Authority—Six Characteristics*
110	*23. Starting Point Plus Process Model*
113	*24. Time-Lines—Defined for Biblical Leaders*
116	*25. Timothy A Beloved Son in the Faith*
118	Glossary of Leadership Terms
147	Bibliography

Abbreviations

Bible Books

Genesis	Ge		Nahum	Na
Exodus	Ex		Habakkuk	Hab
Leviticus	Lev		Zephaniah	Zep
Numbers	Nu		Haggai	Hag
Deuteronomy	Dt		Zechariah	Zec
Joshua	Jos		Malachi	Mal
Judges	Jdg		Matthew	Mt
Ruth	Ru		Mark	Mk
1 Samuel	1Sa		Luke	Lk
2 Samuel	2Sa		John	Jn
1 Kings	1Ki		Acts	Ac
2 Kings	2Ki		Romans	Ro
1 Chronicles	1Ch		1 Corinthians	1Co
2 Chronicles	2Ch		2 Corinthians	2Co
Ezra	Ezr		Galatians	Gal
Nehemiah	Ne		Ephesians	Eph
Esther	Est		Philippians	Php
Job	Job		Colossians	Col
Psalms	Ps		1 Thessalonians	1Th
Proverbs	Pr		2 Thessalonians	2Th
Ecclesiastes	Ecc		1 Timothy	1Ti
Song of Songs	SS		2 Timothy	2Ti
Isaiah	Isa		Titus	Tit
Jeremiah	Jer		Philemon	Phm
Lamentations	La		Hebrews	Heb
Ezekiel	Eze		James	Jas
Daniel	Da		1 Peter	1Pe
Hosea	Hos		2 Peter	2Pe
Joel	Joel		1 John	1Jn
Amos	Am		2 John	2Jn
Obadiah	Ob		3 John	3Jn
Jonah	Jnh		Jude	Jude
Micah	Mic		Revelation	Rev

<u>Other</u>

BAS	Basic English Version
CEV	Contemporary English Version
fn	footnote(s)
KJV	King James Version of the Bible
NEB	New English Bible
NLT	New Living Translation
N.T.	New Testament
O.T.	Old Testament
Phillips	The New Testament in Modern English, J.B. Phillips
TEV	Today's English Version (also called Good News Bible)
Vs	verse(s)

List of Tables

Page	Table-Article-Item
22	Phm 1-1. 11 Figures in the Bible Defined
23	Phm 1-2. 13 Patterned Idioms
25	Phm 1-3. 15 Body Language Idioms
26	Phm 1-4. 14 Miscellaneous Idioms
29	Phm 2-1. Early Shaping Processes Identified and Defined
30	Phm 2-2. Middle Ministry Shaping Processes—Identified and Defined
30	Phm 2-3. Latter Ministry Shaping Processes—Identified and Defined
33	Phm 3-1. 13 Bible Characters and God's Timing Across the Leadership Eras
39	Phm 4-1. Influence, Power, Authority Concepts Defined
44	Phm 5-1. Kinds of Integrity Check
46	Phm 5-2. The Ways that God Uses Integrity Checks
48	Phm 6-1. Isolation Results
48	Phm 6-2. Common Happenings in Isolation
49	Phm 6-3. Job and Type I Isolation
49	Phm 6-4. Moses and Type II Isolation
50	Phm 6-5. Elijah's Type I Isolation Experience, 1Ki 17:1-6—Some Observations
50	Phm 6-6. Elijah's Type II Isolation Experience, 1Ki 19—Persecution—Running For His Life
51	Phm 6-7. Nine Observations from Paul's Isolation Experiences
54	Phm 7-1. How To Study a Leadership Act
55	Phm 7-2. Lessons/ Principles Drawn from Joshua 3,4—Crossing the Jordan
59	Phm 8-1. Basic Questions To Ask About Leadership Eras
59	Phm 8-2. Six Leadership Eras in the Bible—Brief Characterizations
61	Phm 9-1. Six Leadership Eras in the Bible
62	Phm 9-2. Seven Leadership Genre—Sources for Leadership Findings
60	Phm 10-1. When Each Component Was In Focus in Leadership Eras
64	Phm 10-2. Elements of the Tree Diagram Described
67	Phm 11-1. Leadership Eras and Number of Macro Lessons
67	Phm 11-2. Top Three Macro Lessons in O.T. Leadership Eras
67	Phm 11-3. Top Three Macro Lessons in N.T. Leadership Eras
72	Phm 13-1. Nine Mentor Functions

List of Tables continued

Page	Table
72	Phm 13-2. Five Mentoring Dynamics
74	Phm 14-1. 10 Examples of Biblical Paradigm shifts.
77	Phm 14-2. Needed Paradigm Shifts; If Leaders Are to Impact the Post-Modern Era
78	Phm 15-1. Paul's Companions—Reflected in His Epistles
93	Phm 18-1. Paul's Prayer Concerns for the Churches
95	Phm 19-1. Nine Mentor Functions
96	Phm 19-2. Mentor Functions of Paul With Timothy
97	Phm 19-3. Five Features About Paul's Mentoring
108	Phm 22-1. Six Characteristics of Spiritual Authority
113	Phm 24-1. 12 Steps For Doing Biographical Study
116	Phm 25-1. Paul and Intimate Relationships

List of Figures

Page	Figure-Article-Item
22	Phm 1-1. 11 Common Figures of Speech
29	Phm 2-1. Some Major Shaping Processes Across The Time-Line
38	Phm 4-1. Leadership Influence Components—(Adapted from Wrong)
47	Phm 6-1. Three Types of Isolation Experiences
47	Phm 6-2. Isolation Sovereignty Continuum
58	Phm 8-1. Basic Questions To Ask About Leadership Eras
63	Phm 10-1. Graphic Display of Three High Level Generic Leadership Components
66	Phm 11-1. Leadership Truth Continuum/ Where Macro Lessons Occur
71	Phm 13-1. Three Training Modes
96	Phm 19-1. Paul's Mentor-Mix with Timothy
98	Phm 20-1. Influence Behavior Along a Continuum
111	Phm 23-1. Starting Point Plus Process Model-Marriage
114	Phm 24-1. The Apostle Paul's Time-Line

Introduction

This leadership commentary on Philemon is part of a series, **Clinton's Leadership Commentary Series.** For the past 17 years I have been researching leadership concepts in the Bible. As a result of that I have identified the 25 most helpful Bible books that contribute to an understanding of leadership. I have done fourteen of these commentaries to date and am continuing on the rest. I originally published eight of those leadership commentaries in a draft manuscript for use in classes. But it became clear that I would need to break that large work (735 pages) into smaller units. Philemon was one of those original eight and is now being done as a single unit by itself.

This is a leadership commentary, not an exegetical commentary. That means I have worked with the text to see what implications of leadership are suggested by it.

A given commentary in the series is made up of an *Overview Section*, which seeks to analyze the book as a whole for historical background, plan, theme, and fit into the Bible as a whole. In addition, I identify, up front, basic leadership topics that occur in the book. Then I educe leadership observations, guidelines, principles, and values for each of these leadership topics. This *Overview Section* primes the reader to look with leadership eyes.

Then I have the *Commentary Proper* I use my own translation of the text. I give commentary on various aspects of the text. A given context, paragraph size, will usually have 3 to 4 comments dealing with some suggestions about leadership things.

The *Commentary Proper* suggests *Leadership Concepts* and connects you to leadership articles that further explain these leadership concepts. The emphasis on the comments is not exegetical though I do make those kinds of comments when they are helpful for my leadership purposes.

The *Leadership Articles* in the series carry much of what I have learned about leadership in my 42 years of ministry. In one sense, these articles and others in the series are my legacy. I plan to publish all of the articles of the total series in a separate work, **Clinton's Biblical Leadership Encyclopedia Series,** which will be updated periodically as the series expands. I think a leader at almost any level of leadership can be helped greatly by getting leadership perspectives from these articles.

I also include a *Glossary* which lists all the leadership concepts mentioned in Philemon, plus more.

In an age of relativity, we believe the Bible speaks loudly concerning leadership concepts offering suggestions, guidelines, and even absolutes. We, as Christian leaders, desperately need this leadership help as we seek to influence our followers toward God's purposes for them.

My special thanks to Jun Young Chung, who has compiled the items for this Philemon commentary from the original 8 books of the original larger 735 page commentary.

J. Robert Clinton
Sep 2006

Preface

Every Scripture inspired of God is profitable for leadership insights (doctrine), pointing out of leadership errors (reproof), suggesting what to do about leadership errors (correction), and for highlighting how to model a righteous life (instruction in righteousness) in order that God's leader (Timothy) may be well equipped to lead God's people (the special good work given in the book Timothy to the young leader Timothy) .
(2 Timothy 3:16,17—Clinton paraphrase—slanted toward Timothy's leadership situation)

The Bible--a Major Source of Leadership Values and Principles

No more wonderful source of leadership values and principles exists than the Bible. It is filled with influential people and the results of their influence—both good and bad. Yet it remains so little used to expose leadership values and principles. What is needed to break this *leadership barrier*? Three things:

1. A conviction that the Bible is authoritative and can give leadership insights
2. Leadership perspectives to stimulate our findings in the Bible—we are blind in general to leadership ideas and hence do not see them in the Bible.
3. A willful decision to study and use the Bible as a source of leadership insights

These three assumptions underlie the writing of this leadership commentary series. **Philemon—A Study in Leadership Style**, is one of a series of books intended to help leaders cross the *leadership barrier*.

Leadership Framework
Perhaps it might be helpful to put the notion of leadership insights from Philemon in the bigger picture of leadership in the Bible. Three major leadership elements give us our most general framework (cross-culturally applicable as well) for categorizing leadership insights. The study of leadership involves:

1. **THE LEADERSHIP BASAL ELEMENTS** (The *What* of Leadership)
   a. leaders
   b. followers
   c. situations

   In Philemon we will see:
   a. leaders— like Paul, Timothy, Onesimus, Archipus, Philemon, Apphia, Epaphras, Mark, Aristarchus, Demas, Luke. Some are mentioned casually or in an off-hand way like the closing remarks mentioning Epaphras, Mark, Aristarchus, Demas and Luke. But Onesimus and Philemon along with Paul are featured in this book. As we watch this influence process in which Paul is exerting his influence on Philemon, we can learn much—especially about leadership style.
   b. followers— In this given leadership act, Paul is the dominant influencer—that is, the leader. Philemon (and the little church in his home including Apphia and Archipus and others of the household) are the folks being influenced—that is, the followers
   c. situations—This special situation involves Paul's plea on the behalf of a runaway slave who has become a Christian under Paul's ministry. Pau' is in prison in Rome. Onesimus, who ran away from Philemon's household some 10 yea , or so ago has been asked by Paul to return to Philemon and straighten up his situation. Paul very tactfully pleads with Philemon to receive back Onesimus (and forego the usually punishment for a run away slave—the death sentence).

Preface

2. **LEADERSHIP INFLUENCE MEANS** (The *How* of Leadership)
   a. individual means—this concept involves identifying leadership styles of individual leaders influencing the situation. The sub-title of this book is, *A Study in Leadership Style*. Philemon shows how a mature leader can influence a mature believer with whom there is a strong relationship. Paul exhibits 3 leadership styles in this book—with one being in focus: *father-initiator, maturity appeal,* and *obligation persuasion* More explanation on this will be given further on in this commentary as Paul's leadership style is in focus in this book. Leaders today need to be informed from this book—regarding leadership styles.
   b. corporate means—this refers to organizational structures or group pressures that influence followers in a corporate sense. Paul recognizes the importance of the Christians that make up the church in Philemon's home and mentions intentionally Apphia and Archippus, representatives of that local body of Christ. His plea for Onesimus most surely was read to the local church there. They as a corporate group would most surely give input into Philemon.

3. **LEADERSHIP VALUE BASES** (The *Why* of Leadership)
   a. cultural
   b. theological

With almost three quarters of the Roman empires' inhabitants in slavery, the cultural view of what to do about a runaway slave would certainly be exerting its subtle but powerful pressure. But in contrast, Paul is giving an underlying theological perspective—demonstrating the undercutting notion of love and forgiveness—Christian values that must permeate a local body, if it is to represent Christ as the pillar of truth in a community. In addition, Paul is modeling with Onesimus the concept of restitution—showing that believers must make right things that were done in the past—especially when they have on-going repercussions in the present. Onesimus courageously models one who is willing to make restitution, even though it may be costly for him.

It is through using these major leadership elements—leaders, followers, and situations—that we are able to analyze leadership throughout the whole Bible. Using these major notions we recognize that leadership, at different time periods in the Bible, operates sufficiently different so as to suggest leadership eras—that is, time periods within which leadership follows more closely certain commonalities than in the time preceding it and following it. This allows us to identify six such eras in the Bible.

Six Bible Leadership Eras

The six leadership eras include,
1. **Patriarchal Era**
2. **Pre-Kingdom Era**
   A. Desert Years
   B. The War Years
   C. The Tribal Years
3. **Kingdom Era**
   A. United Kingdom
   B. Divided Kingdom
   C. Southern Kingdom
4. **Post-Kingdom Era**
   A. Exilic
   B. A Foothold Back in the Land
5. **Pre-Church Era**
 6. **Church Era**

We are here when we study the book of Philemon.

For each of these major eras we are dealing with some fundamental leadership questions.[2] We ask ourselves these major questions about every leadership era. Usually the answers are sufficiently diverse as to justify identification of a unique leadership era.

Where does Philemon fit?

The book of Philemon fits in the sixth leadership era, *The Church Era* It is a pioneering time in which the Gospel is spreading to the Gentile world. Churches have been started in about 5 separate city/town locations in Asia minor, and Greece. The churches are new. The church in Philemon's home probably was started out of the church at Ephesus. It is a young church, perhaps 10 years or so old.

What does Philemon say?

Before we can look at leadership insights from Philemon we need to be sure that we understand why it is in the Scriptures and what it is saying in general. Having done our homework, hermeneutically speaking, we are free then to go beyond and look for other interpretative insights—such as leadership insights. But we must remember, always, first of all to interpret in light of the historical times, purposes of, theme of, and structure of the each of these epistles. Lets look at Philemon first in terms of Paul's organization of the book and his thematic intent and hoped for purposes.

Philemon is a very small book—one chapter in our English Bibles. I use the following structure to help me identify the flow of ideas being generated. Perhaps it is a bit over simplified yet it is helpful.

Structure

	I.	(Vs 1-7)	**Positive Lead In to the Plea**
	II.	(Vs 8-21)	**The Plea—Using Obligation/ Persuasion In a Powerful Way**
	III.	(Vs 22-25)	**Possible Follow-up of the Plea**

The overall thematic intent could be represented by a subject, which permeates the main overall thrust of all the sections of the book of Philemon and several ideas about that subject—each one flowing from one of the sections. Here is my analysis of such a theme.

Theme
Subject: **PAUL MAKES AN APPEAL TO PHILEMON,**
Major Idea 1 – based on a personal relationship with Philemon
Major Idea 2 – to receive back Onesimus, a runaway slave
Major Idea 3 – that contains strong persuasion without taking away Philemon's own freedom to decide or not decide.

Purpose

It is always difficult to synthesize statements of purpose when the author does not directly and explicitly give them. Here is my attempt to identify some of Paul's purpose for the book of Philemon.

- to appeal on Onesimus' behalf for Philemon to receive him back, forgive him, free him, and accept him,
- to model tact in dealing with Christians on important issues,
- to highlight the importance of Christian restitution,
- to show the power of the Gospel—life in Christ changes every relationship individuals have,

---

[2] The six questions we use to help us differentiate between leadership eras includes: 1. What is the major leadership focus? 2. What are the influence means used? 3.What are the basic leadership functions? 4. What are the characteristics of the followers? 5. What was the existing cultural forms of leadership? 6. Other? I comment on each of these in the **Clinton's Biblical Leadership Encyclopedia Series**.

Preface

- to show that our relationship to others, tests our relationship to Christ,
- to show how the Gospel impacts social institutions: social evils are to be ended willingly by individuals whose transformed lives can no longer tolerate them.

Having done our overview of the book, hermeneutically speaking, we can now focus on leadership issues seen in Philemon.

(This page is deliberately blank.)

General Reflections On Philemon

Approach To Philemon In Perspective

With this background in mind, we can now proceed to the leadership commentary including its *General Reflection, Leadership Lessons, Commentary Notes*, **Articles**, and **Glossary**.

Today, we live in the Church Leadership Era.[3] It is not difficult to place ourselves back hundreds of years into the 6th leadership era—Church Leadership. Though quite removed from us in time and certainly culturally, we can still identify with Paul and his church planting ministry. Most of us have studied well the New Testament. We are relatively familiar with the Acts and the Pauline epistles. So then, when Paul deals with church problems, such as the problems in Corinth, or Ephesus, or this situation in the Lycus valley where Philemon's house church was, we are eager to learn what we can about Paul's handling of it. We want to see how Paul dealt with them. We want to learn about his solutions. For we live in the church leadership era. We will be facing these exact same problems or some similar to them. Paul will model for us both how to deal with church problems and actually give us some answers—at least when we are dealing with the same problems. Paul is a mature leader at this point in his life. We are seeing a great leader, Paul, in the twilight of his ministry career. He leaves us with a beautiful example of how to use a relationship in order to solve a complex social problem.

Suggested Approach for Studying The Philemon Leadership Commentary

Read through the overview to get a general feeling for what Philemon is about. Note particularly the *Theme* of the book and its *Plan* for developing that theme, i.e., the outline for developing that theme. Then note the various purposes I suggest that the book of Philemon is seeking to accomplish. Then read through each of the leadership topics that I suggest are in Philemon. This is all preparation for the first reading of the text.

Read the whole text of Philemon, at one sitting, without referring to any of the commentary notes. Just see if you can *see what of the overview information* and the *leadership lessons* are suggested to you as you read the text.

Then repeatedly reread the one chapter book, Philemon, and note the comments I give.[4] In your repeated readings, take time to go back and read a leadership lesson again when it is brought to your mind as you read the text and the commentary. Also feel free to stop and go to the **Glossary** for explanation of leadership terms suggested by the commentary. And do the same thing with the **Articles**. The articles capture what I have learned about leadership over the years as I have observed it, researched it, and taught it. It is these articles that will enlighten your leadership understanding. Obviously, because of the uniqueness of the book, dealing primarily with an apostolic problem-solving issue in a local church ministry, there will be some hopefully helpful leadership articles.

Further Study

I have provided some *note space* at the conclusion of the textual comments, for both books, where you can jot down ideas for future study. Have fun as you work through Philemon and by all means learn

---

[3] See **Article**, *8. Leadership Eras In The Bible— Six Identified;* This is probably an important prerequisite for you before approaching the commentary.

[4] From time-to-time in the comments, we will use the abbreviation SRN. SRN stands for Strong's Reference Number. Strong, in his exhaustive concordance, labeled each word in the Old Testament (dominantly Hebrew words but also some Aramaic/Chaldean) and New Testament (Greek words mostly) with an identifying number. He then constructed an Old Testament and New Testament lexicon (dictionary). If you have a **Strong's Exhaustive Concordance** with lexicon, you can look up the words we refer to. Many modern day reference works (lexicons and word studies and Bible Dictionaries and encyclopedias) use this Strong's Reference Number. Many digital lexicons are available and referenced to the SRN.

something about *leadership styles*. Let this book inspire your own use of leadership styles to impact others. And also learn the important lesson of learning vicariously by studying other leaders' lives.[5] Three leaders are being highlighted—Paul, Onesimus, Philemon. Learn from them. Especially learn from Paul. Paul is exemplary in his modeling for church leaders. It was deliberate. And it was impactful then and can be impactful now.

The overview follows. It gives a summarized version of the hermeneutical background studies for Philemon.

---

[5] The old adage, *experience is the best teacher* is true, **if you learn from it**. Personal experience is a great way to learn. But in terms of leadership, you will never have enough time to learn, *by personal experience alone*, all you need to know for your leadership. I suppose that is why God gave us the leadership mandate—Hebrews 13:7,8. He emphatically reminds us that vicarious learning is crucial for our leadership. And we have three whole books (Job, Habakkuk, Jonah) in the Bible devoted exclusively to illustrating God's shaping of leaders. And that is their main purpose for being in the Bible. Paul's leadership is in view throughout the church leadership era. We can learn leadership practices vicariously from his model.

Overview	**PHILEMON**	**Author: Paul**

Characters People mentioned or involved: Paul, Timothy, Philemon, Apphia, Archippus, Onesimus, Epaphras, Mark, Aristarchus, Demas, Luke.

Who To/For Philemon, a fellow worker in the Gospel, probably the head of the church meeting in his home.

Literature Type A very personal letter which makes a special appeal to Philemon the recipient of the letter.

Story Line Onesimus, a run away slave from the household of Philemon, somehow made his way to Rome. There he got converted and came into contact with Paul while Paul was under house arrest. He grew in the Lord and became close to Paul. Paul sends him back to his master, Philemon to make amends. He sends along this letter (and the letters to the churches in Colosse and Ephesus). The letter asks Philemon to free Onesimus willingly. It is a strong appeal based on Paul's maturity and previous relationship with Philemon.

Structure
- I. (Vs 1-7) **Positive Lead In to the Plea**
- II. (Vs 8-21) **The Plea—Using Obligation/ Persuasion In a Powerful Way**
- III. (Vs 22-25) **Possible Follow-up of the Plea**

Theme **Paul's Special Plea To Philemon**
- was based on his special relationship to Philemon,
- was a request to receive back a former runaway slave, named Onesimus, and
- involved strong persuasion yet left the final decision to Philemon.

Key Words none

Key Events the past event—Onesimus running away is in view and a future event—the return of Onesimus and the reading of the letter with the appeal.

Purposes
- to appeal on Onesimus' behalf for Philemon to receive him back, forgive him, free him, and accept him,
- to model tact in dealing with Christians on important issues,
- to highlight the importance of Christian restitution,
- to show the power of the Gospel—life in Christ changes every relationship individuals have,
- to show that our relationship to others, tests our relationship to Christ,
- to show how the Gospel impacts social institutions: social evils are to be ended willingly by individuals whose transformed lives can no longer tolerate them.

Why Important

This book shows the power of the Gospel to transform lives and to transform society. It was written in the same time span as the epistle to the Ephesians and the epistle to the Colossians. Those lofty epistles, with great doctrinal truth, were companion letters being carried to churches in the same area. The three taken together serve to emphasize just how important this little epistle was. Its inclusion in the Scripture shows us how important the Gospel is in everyday life. Here is one illustration of three transformed lives, a very complex social problem, and how the Gospel requires love to be applied. We see Paul practicing what he taught others and asking them to do the same. This is a leadership book, par excellence. It is dealing with how one leader influences other leaders.

Where It Fits

This little book was written along with Ephesians, Philippians, and Colossians about two thirds of the way through Paul's ministry. It is vintage Paul and shows how a mature leader in the Church Leadership Era utilizes gentle yet powerful influence means to motivate and bring about change in a specific situation. This prison epistle shows how productive ministry can be, even in a major isolation period of Paul's life.

Philemon As A Source of Leadership Topics

The whole book of Philemon is in itself a leadership act (see **Article**, *7. Leadership Act*), one of the seven leadership genres. We have a leader in a leadership situation influencing a follower toward God's purposes in that situation (at least that is my opinion on it). It is a marvelous book that demonstrates the miraculous working of the Gospel in three lives. Without these three miracles this book could not have been.

One of the great miracles was the conversion of Paul. An almost greater miracle was the transformation of Paul's character over the years. This book was written further along in Paul's ministry. He was probably in his mid-fifties. God had mellowed this wonderful strong leader until he was a gentle leader. In his early days this strong (dare we say opinionated) leader would have simply commanded and confronted. But not so in this epistle. He is a living example of what it means to be shaped by the Holy Spirit into the image of Christ. Here is a leader in maturity dealing with a complex situation and yet doing it in a gentle manner which preserves the dignity of all concerned—Onesimus the slave, Philemon the slave owner and Paul himself the mature leader who, even as he writes, is suffering for the cause of Christ.

Philemon's story was the second important miracle. He had come to know Christ through Paul's ministry. He lived in a Roman Province in Asia just west of what is now Asiatic Turkey. Ephesus, was just inland from the coast, on the Aegean Sea. Further inland, about 75 miles away, was the Lycus Valley with its three towns within a few miles of each other: Colosse, Heirapolis, and Laodicea. It was in this valley that Philemon lived. It was the point at which the great routes from Sardis and Ephesus joined; a defensive place with an abundant water-supply. The area known for its volcanoes, chalk, dye—great Earthquake in Tacitus time. Philemon was most likely a wealthy person. He was a slave owner. Paul had an extended time of ministry in Ephesus, a two year Bible Institute. It was a result of his ministry there that Philemon was converted. If Christ had not entered this head of the household and slave holder and transformation of character had not happened no one could have asked him to take back a run away slave. The social pressures were immense for him to punish Onesimus, probably with death. But the Gospel was working in this life too.

Onesimus's story was the third miracle. Life as a slave, even for an educated slave, was still not much of a life. The bottom line, you were not your own and had very little control over major decisions for your life. One can almost not blame Onesimus for running away. And why not to the largest city in the world, Rome? What better place to get lost. But a miracle occurred there too. He met the imprisoned Paul and the Gospel message penetrated his heart. His conversion was genuine. No runaway slave would ever return to his master. But the Gospel brought about a Holy Spirit conviction concerning restitution. He was willing to go back and straighten up matters.

And so the stage is set for a leadership act of great import. It is not just these three leaders that are involved. We have here a model of how God breaks down institutions that are evil. We see how leaders can confront complex problems and work them out with Christian values in the forefront.

Leadership Topics/Lessons

1. Influence Means.[6]

This book demonstrates the importance of spiritual authority (see **Article**, *22. Spiritual Authority*) and three specific leadership styles as the essence of influence means with a mature follower.

Paul is attempting to influence Philemon to accept back a runaway slave, Onesimus. He uses three kinds of leadership styles to bring about that influence. <u>Leadership style</u> refers to the behavioral patterns that a leader exhibits when attempting to influence the attitude and actions of followers in a given leadership

---

[6] There are three over arching leadership categories: (1) *leadership basal elements* (the what of leadership—leaders, followers, and leadership situation); (2) *leadership influence means* (the how of leadership—the styles by which leaders as individuals and groups get things done); (3) *leadership value bases* (the why—the underlying philosophical reasons for doing things). This book reflects all of these. This particular lesson is dealing dominantly with influence means, the second category of the over arching leadership components. See **Article**, *10. Leadership Tree Diagram*.

act. How a given leader influences others depends upon several factors: personality-bent, toward task or relationship; the leadership function being attempted; the follower maturity; and the leader-follower relationship. Philemon is a mature believer. Paul has a very special relationship with him and others in his church. Normally Paul is a task oriented person (here he is too—the task to link Onesimus back into the situation); but here he is also very relationship oriented. The function is a delicate one. Discipline of run away slaves is expected and even demanded. Paul is trying to circumvent this normal social response with the hope of redeeming Onesimus for the Gospel's sake. Of the ten Pauline leadership styles identified in his epistles, three are seen here with one being in focus: *father-initiator*, *maturity appeal*, and *obligation persuasion* (see **Article**, *20. Pauline Leadership Styles*).

The *father-initiator* leadership style uses the fact of the leader as having founded or begun the work as a lever for getting acceptance of influence by the leader. The *maturity appeal* leadership style is a form of leadership influence which counts upon godly experience, usually gained over a long period of time, an empathetic identification based on a common sharing of experience, and a recognition of the force of imitation modeling in influencing people in order to convince people toward a favorable acceptance of the leader's ideas. An *obligation-persuasion* leadership style refers to an appeal to followers to follow some recommended directives which persuades, not commands followers to heed some advice. It leaves the decision to do so in the hands of the followers, but forces the followers to recognize their obligation to the leader due to past service by the leader to the follower; strongly implies that the follower owes the leader some debt and should follow the recommended advice as part of paying back the obligation. And finally it reflects the leader's strong expectation that the follower will conform to the persuasive advice.

It is this last leadership style that is in focus in the book. Persuasion is at the heart of this leadership style and is also at the heart of the notion of *spiritual authority* (see **Article**, *22. Spiritual Authority*). Spiritual authority is a power base from which a leader exerts influence. Leaders using spiritual authority as the power base for influence do so by modeling, persuading, and teaching and not by command or demand. They look for willing response from followers, not a forced response. Followers perceive spirituality in a leader and are thus open to that leader's influence. This spirituality is seen in a leader because of demonstration of supernaturally gifted power, deep experiences with God, and modeling of godly character. Paul here illustrates how a godly leader with spiritual authority dominant as the power base influences a mature follower toward an important life changing decision.

Leadership Principles/Values Suggested by this concept:
  a. Obligation-persuasion is a leadership style in harmony with spiritual authority and should be used with mature followers with whom a leader has a good relationship.
  b. An effective leader must learn to vary his/her leadership style to fit the situation and people being influenced.
  c. An effective leader should view spiritual authority as a primary power base but recognize that other bases will be needed to influence.

2. **Mentor Sponsor**.
Mentors frequently co-minister with mentorees in order to enhance the mentorees status and standing before followers.[7] (See Phm 1, 2Co 1:1, Php 1:1, Col 1:1, 1Th 1:1, 2Th 1:1) Mentors sponsor mentorees.

---

[7] Mentoring is a relational empowerment in which one person, called the mentor, empowers another person, called the mentoree in a number of ways such as building habits, helping learn skills, gaining perspective, maturing in spirituality, learning new concepts, imbibing values being modeled, being sponsored, being inspired to emulate a life, linked to resources, etc. Nine mentor types have been identified: discipler, spirituality mentor, coach, counselor, teacher, contemporary model, sponsor, divine contact. See **Articles**, *13. Mentoring—An Informal Training Model*; *19. Paul—Mentor for Many*; *15. Paul and His Companions*. Here sponsoring is occurring in three different ways: Timothy in terms of status and acceptance with Philemon, Onesimus in terms of being backed by Paul as to character and being accepted by Philemon, and other leaders being recognized (see Philemon 23). A further mentor sponsor function not seen in Philemon is the use of influence to link mentorees to resources, people and situations that will develop them.

One way is to co-minister with them. Mentorees tend to rise to the level of the mentor in the eyes of followers in terms of status and authority—though they must always eventually earn their own way. Co-authoring is a way of sponsoring and giving prestige and initial credibility to a mentoree.

Paul sponsors Onesimus. This illustrates how mentor sponsors use their influence on behalf of mentorees. It is interesting that church history makes note of a Bishop Onesimus in this region. It is also held by some New Testament scholars that Onesimus and Philemon were the gatherers of the Pauline epistles and thus helped facilitate the New Testament canon.

Leadership Principles/Values Suggested by this concept:
   a. Mentoring is a form of relational empowerment that any leader can use.
   b. Mentor sponsoring is needed in order to move potential leaders into opportunities and to connect them with resources which will aid their development.

3. **Relational Value**.
Paul believed that leadership selection and development and training should be done in a personal/relational manner. A *leadership value* is an underlying assumption, which affects how a leader behaves in or perceives leadership situations. One important value seen in Philemon and almost all of the Pauline epistles concerns personal ministry. Stated Generally—*Leaders should view personal relationships as an important part of ministry.* This dovetails with another Pauline leadership value: *Leaders must be concerned about leadership selection and development.* Paul constantly had about him people whom he related to very personally (mentor relationships) in order to train and release them into ministry. Notice even in this small very personal epistle to Philemon how Paul exudes personal relationships and how each are being trained: Timothy, Philemon, Apphia, Archippus, Onesimus, Epaphras, Mark, Aristarchus, Demas, Luke. See the **Article**, *15. Paul—And His Companions*.

Leadership Principles/Values Suggested by this concept:
   a. Effective leaders see relational empowerment as both a means and a goal of ministry.
   b. Effective leaders see leadership selection and development as a priority in ministry.

4. **Prayer Encouragement Principle**.
Leaders encourage their people by praying for them and telling them what they are praying for them. This *prayer encouragement principle*, seen in Jesus ministry (Lk 22:31,32), should be part of each leader's repertoire of influence means for development of followers. Here Paul demonstrates it as he so often does in his thirteen epistles. This little epistle also illustrates the *ministry prayer principle: If God has called you to a ministry then He has called you to pray for that ministry.* This is one of 41 macro lessons (see **Article**, *12. Macro-Lessons—List of 41 Across Six Leadership Eras*) identified in the six leadership eras (see **Article**, *8. Leadership Eras in the Bible—Six Identified*). This particular one surfaces in the Pre-kingdom Leadership Era in Samuel's ministry (1Sa 12:23) and then is seen thereafter—Jesus, being one of the prime examples of a leader operating with the value underlying this observation.

Leadership Principles/Values Suggested by this concept:
   a. A leader is responsible for prayer for his/her ministry. If God calls a leader to a ministry then He calls that leader to pray for the ministry.
   b. A leader can encourage followers by sharing with them that he is praying specifically for them.

5. **Isolation Processing And Results**.
Productive ministry is often rooted in isolation times (See *Isolation*, **Glossary**). For the most part isolation is a setting aside of a leader from normal ministry in order to develop a deeper relationship with

God. But here we see as in the other prison epistles how these times can be productive times in reflection, divine contacts, and production of lasting achievements (Pauline epistles). Productive ministry in the future is often rooted in these isolation times. Contacts, seed thoughts, and evaluation, which come in this time may lead to an expanded productivity in the future. Notice how Paul views his isolation situation sovereignly—a prisoner of Christ Jesus. He did not say a Prisoner of Nero or Prisoner of Rome or a Prisoner of Some Bad Circumstances. He was a prisoner of Christ. Four times in this short epistle, he reflects this sovereign perspective (1,9, 13, 15). That is, his perspective viewed his situation always from what God was doing in it. God was sovereignly intervening in the circumstances of Paul's life. See **Articles** *16. Paul—Deep Processing; 21. Sovereign Mindset; 6. Isolation Processing—Learning Deep Lessons From God.*

Leadership Principles/Values Suggested by this concept:
   a. A leader must recognize God's sovereignty in deep processing.
   b. A leader should seek, in deep processing, to ask what the Lord is doing in it both in a personal way and in the ministry, with a view toward the whole of life, not just the specific time.
   c. A leader in deep processing must be transparent and vulnerable enough to share with others in his/her community so as to garner support and prayer backing.
   d. A leader must be aware of the fact that his/her response to deep processing will be a model for those being influenced.
   e. A leader must, in deep processing, reevaluate life purpose and affirm it, modify it, or add to it, recognizing that God will often use deep processing to expand one's horizons as to life purpose.

6. **Social Issue**.
   Major wrongs in society can be changed by individuals. Paul attacks a major evil social institution, slavery, by hitting at its roots.[8] He stresses the transforming power of the Gospel, both to change a slave and a slave holder and himself. When the essence of the Gospel is understood it will cut at the root of issues like slavery. For the historical case study illustrating just this approach to changing slavery see John Woolman's story of ridding the Quakers of slavery (1961). Greenleaf (1977), gives a good descriptive vignette of Woolman's deliverance of slavery among Quakers. Notice also Paul's change tactics. See especially his tact and approach to getting a hearing—just a little bit of sugar makes the medicine go down, in the most delightful way (Phm 4-7). Notice also his gentle accountability threat (Phm 22). See the **Article**, *23. Starting Point Plus Process Model.*

Leadership Principles/Values Suggested by this concept:
   a. One means for overcoming a social evil is to undermine it at value level. Many Christian values speak to social issues.
   b. Major social change will take a long time to implement.

7. **Critical Incident**.
   This apparently simple little one chapter Bible book is much more complex than we at first glance realize. It describes a critical incident in the life of three Biblical leaders: Paul, Onesimus, and Philemon. Lets look at this incident through the framework of shaping of a Biblical leader. What was God accomplishing in these three lives through this incident, which was important to all, for very different reasons?
   Consider Paul. Paul was a mature Christian leader at the time of this incident. The timing is critical for him. He is in the latter stages of his ministry. Earlier in his ministry he could not or rather probably would not have been able to write Philemon with this request. His strong authoritarian conflictive approach to leadership would backfire in this kind of situation. But the numerous life shaping incidents over the years have mellowed him. He is a gentle leader. A powerful leader who with gentleness and maturity can lead

---

[8] In my opinion God is using this same kind of process today in gender issues in leadership. He is starting from a non-ideal position concerning women in ministry and moving toward a more ideal position based on giftedness and calling.

without demanding and yet see his influence effectively impacting others. This particular incident is first of all a major demonstration of the *Timing macro-lesson* (see **Article** *11. Macro-Lessons—Defined*). *God's timing is crucial to accomplishment of God's purposes.* This macro lesson was first introduced in the Patriarchal Leadership Era in Abraham's life. It was repeatedly highlighted in Joseph's ministry. In fact, it is seen in every leadership era following. It culminates with great force in Jesus Christ's ministry. Paul probably could not or would not have been able to write such a gentle yet powerfully persuasive letter earlier on in his ministry. And too, earlier, Paul was not as personally concerned with the slavery issue. Previously he had written about it; but more so from the view of maintaining harmony in relationships. But now, here, he became more deeply aware of the issues when he saw the Gospel penetrate the life of one slave, Onesimus, and turn him around. And Paul saw the leadership potential in this one man.

This also is a major step forward in God's elimination of slavery. (See the **Article**, *23. Starting Point Plus Process*). Heretofore, God has been working to eliminate the evil in this institution. He has addressed slavery all throughout the Old Testament, always working, to improve the status of these poor wretched beings. But this incident was a springboard for removing the institution itself. The major values of loving one's neighbor and love one another and the Golden Rule, treating someone like you would like to be treated, were values which cut at this social institution at the root. This incident placed clearly on the agenda the issue of abolishing slavery due to inherent Gospel values, which saw importance in every person created in the image of God. It would be another 1700 years before the institution was largely abolished in the World's social agenda. But this was the death knell for the abolishment of that institution. God works inexorably over time to accomplish His purposes.

This incident was life shaping for Paul, personally. It involved three kinds of shaping processes: an obedience check, networking power, and a word check (see the **Article**, *2. God's Shaping Processes With Leaders*). In writing to ask Philemon to receive Onesimus back Paul was simply obeying God. It was a logical response to what Paul knew about Gospel truth. It must be applied. It also illustrates the process of networking power. Many times in our leadership we will get things done because we have connections to people—people who can help us get things done. This incident illustrates networking power. Paul is one of the premier modelers of networking power. He ministry was personal. He related to so many people. Philemon, Archippus, and Apphia are simply examples of his personal relational ministry. A third process was that of a *word check*. Paul had boasted of the power of the Gospel to change lives. Now he was getting a chance to prove it by faith. Could the Gospel change the life of Philemon and enable him to make a right decision based on Christian value rather than one following social mores? Paul believed so. A real challenge to Paul's faith in the word and the power of the Gospel is involved in this incident.

Consider Onesimus. Onesimus had heard Paul's teaching on the Christian life. He knew that he was forgiven in God's sight for the sins of his past. But he knew too that he had responsibilities to make restitution for the wrongs done, where he could. And so for Onesimus two important shaping processes are in view: an *integrity check* and an *obedience check*. There are multiple kinds of Integrity checks, one of which involves restitution—having a conviction about having wronged someone in the past and doing what can be done to right the wrong. Onesimus had not only run away but had stolen from his master. He must make this right. For him it was a matter of integrity. And on such matters hinge future use of a leader by God. Onesimus complied. I believe Philemon accepted him. Later tradition describes a Bishop in this region, named Onesimus. I believe it to be this leader. And I believe this incident was pivotal to that future ministry. The issue was clear. Onesimus needed to go back to Philemon, willing to become his slave again and pay back what he owed. The decision was much more complex. Would Onesimus obey? It might mean death. Onesimus did obey and did take this letter, entitled the Letter to Philemon, to his former master.

Consider Philemon. For Philemon this was dominantly a *word check*. Word checks test a leader's ability to see truth and use it in life. Paul here really applies the law of love—a powerful biblical truth. Could Philemon see it? Would he recognize God's voice in it? Would he respond to it? What a test for Philemon. I believe he did. If not, I do not think we would have even seen the book of Philemon in the canon of Scripture. Tradition has it that Philemon and Onesimus were facilitators to collect the Pauline corpus of literature and see that it became part of the canon of Scripture. Whether or not this is so, it can be clearly demonstrated that this incident was a major test of Christian doctrine. Would the law of love work practically in real life in a tough social issue?

Leadership Principles/Values Suggested by this concept:
a. A critical incident in a life can be a pivotal point upon which the rest of ministry can depend.
b. Failure to recognize critical incidents and the proper Godly response to them can have long range ramifications in a life and ministry.
c. Sensitivity to God's shaping processes must be cultivated in a leader.

The Leadership Commentary

I. Positive Lead-In to the Plea (Vs 1-7)

1 Paul,[9] a prisoner of Jesus Christ,[10] and Timothy[11] our brother,[12] to Philemon[13] our dearly beloved, and fellow laborer. 2 Hello also to our beloved Apphia,[14] and Archippus[15] our fellow soldier, and to the church in your house.[16] 3 Grace[17] to you, and peace, from God our Father and the Lord Jesus Christ.

---

[9] Paul authored 13 epistles. See **Article** *24. Time-Lines-Defined for Biblical Leaders.*

[10] This is a prison epistle. (c.f. Eph, Php, Col, Phm, 2Ti). For sovereignty comments note also footnotes 25, 29 and 30. Paul omits his title, Apostle. His appeal must not be based on any formal authority. This will be a relational appeal. This is the only one of Paul's letters that is strictly a personal letter written to a person and not to correct some church problems. Two letters are written personally to Timothy but are really dealing with church issues at Ephesus. A leadership value is in view here. *Personal Ministry: Leaders should view personal relationships as an important part of ministry.* Paul will be using non-directive and highly non-directive leadership styles with Philemon. He recognizes that Philemon is mature. A leader can use less directive styles with mature followers. But with non-mature leaders more directive or highly directive styles have to be used. Contrast this approach in Phm with highly directive styles used in 1,2Co. Also, Paul is not dealing with a doctrinal heresy here but a very practical every day kind of problem on which Philemon can very well refuse. Heresy is not in view here, rather an appeal to a mature Christian conscience on a social matter. See also Php 1:1, 1,2Th, where omission is for other leadership reasons. *See leadership style, sovereign mindset, leadership value, deep processing, isolation,* **Glossary**. See **Article,** *16. Paul—Deep Processing; 2. God's Shaping Processes With Leaders, 21. Sovereign Mindset.*

[11] Timothy's name occurs 31 times in the N.T.—as a co-author six times. Timothy should be studied as an example of how a next generation leader is trained and transitioned into ministry. One transition technique involves co-ministering together to raise status for the younger leader. Timothy's last mention in Heb 13:23 is instructive. See **Article,** *17. Paul—Developer Par Excellence; 25. Timothy A Beloved Son in the Faith.*

[12] Paul here acts as a *mentor sponsor* for Timothy. People tend to see a lesser known leader as rising in status to the more well-known leader when the two co-minister together (e.g. write together, preach and teach together, etc.).The recipients would recognize that Paul thought highly of Timothy and would in turn respect him because of Paul's sponsorship. Paul includes Timothy, like the above, in six salutations: 2Co, Php, Col, 1Th, 2Th, Phm. But Philemon really knows this is Paul writing. See *mentor, mentor sponsor,* **Glossary**. See **Article,** *19. Paul—Mentor for Many.*

[13] The name Philemon occurs only here. But see final footnote on closing inscription.

[14] Apphia occurs only here.

[15] See Col 4:17 where Archippus is described as a church leader with a special calling.

[16] At this time all churches were in homes. Relationships were close.

[17] In his latter epistles Paul uses *grace* as the enabling presence of God in a life to cause that person to persevere in the Christian life. See also fn 2Ti 4:22. For a fuller definition, see *grace,* **Glossary**.

4 I thank my God, mentioning you always in my prayers.[18] 5 I hear of your faith in the Lord Jesus and your love for all the fellow Christians.[19] 6 I pray that you may communicate your faith[20] effectively with a good understanding of your resources in Christ Jesus. 7 For we take great joy and comfort from your love. Especially because you encourage the hearts of fellow Christians, brother.[21]

II. The Plea—Using Obligation Persuasion[22] (Vs 8-21)

8 So, though I might boldly order[23] you, in Christ's name, to do what I want you to do, 9 Yet for love's sake I rather appeal to you, as Paul an older mature brother, and now also a prisoner of Jesus Christ.[24,25] 10 I appeal to you for my son Onesimus,[26] who became my son while I was in prison 11 Formerly he was to you unprofitable, but now profitable to you and to me.[27]

---

[18] Paul illustrates here the macro lesson on prayer first seen in Abraham's ministry in the Patriarchal Leadership Era, in Moses' ministry in the Pre-kingdom Leadership Era and identified most strongly in Samuel's ministry (see 1 Sam 12:23). The macro lesson stated is: *Leaders called to a ministry are called to intercede for that ministry*. This macro lesson occurs in all six leadership eras in the Bible. For other Pauline expressions of prayer for churches see: Ro 1:8-10; 1Co 1:4; Eph 1:15-20; 3:14-21; Col 1:3; 1:9-14; 2:1; 1Th 1:3; 2:13; 2Th 1:3; 11-13; 2:13. See *leadership era, prayer ministry principle, macro lesson*, **Glossary**. See **Articles**, *11. Macro Lessons—Defined; 8. Leadership Eras in the Bible—Six Identified*.

[19] Literally—your love and faith toward the Lord Jesus and toward all saints. This is a rare figure of speech, *chiasmus*. Saints is used here meaning fellow Christians. See *figure, chiasmus, capture*, **Glossary**. See **Article**, *1. Figures and Idioms in the Bible*.

[20] Faith is here used as a figure of speech, metonymy—one word substituted for another to which it is closely related to give emphasis to the relationship. Here it means the truth of what he believes. *Captured: I pray that you may communicate effectively what you know and firmly believe about Christianity*. Here inner conviction about these truths is emphasized. See *metonymy, capture*, **Glossary**. See **Article**, *1. Figures and Idioms in the Bible*.

[21] Saints is here used in the sense of fellow Christians. One thing that touches the heart of any leader is to hear of others who are meeting the needs of followers in a deep pastoral way. Philemon was. This greatly encouraged Paul. He knew Philemon had a gentle heart and was counting on this as he made his own appeal for Onesimus.

[22] I have identified 10 Pauline leadership styles. Here *obligation persuasion*, vs 8-21, and *maturity appeal*, vs 9, is used. See *leadership style, obligation persuasion, maturity appeal*, **Glossary**. See **Article**, *20. Pauline Leadership Styles*. See **Key Leadership Lessons, Topic 1— Influence Means**.

[23] Strong words are at the heart of this appeal—an *obligation-persuasion* leadership style. *Boldly* (SRN 3954) is translated elsewhere by confidence, openness. It means frank communication. Command means an authoritative order. Paul could *command* (SRN 2004). But instead he *appeals* (SRN 3870). This same word is used for the spiritual gift of exhortation—the encouragement thrust. In 1,2Co Paul is more apt to use exhortation—the admonition thrust. See *exhortation, spiritual gift*, **Glossary**.

[24] In the *maturity appeal leadership style*, Paul counts upon his godly experiences gained over his many years in ministry. He wants Philemon's empathetic identification based on a common sharing of experience. The force of Paul's modeling will also convince and influence Philemon toward acceptance of his desires. Hey, Paul has earned the right to be heard. This is an highly non-directive leadership style. Philemon has a choice in the matter. See *maturity appeal, leadership style*, **Glossary**.

[25] Note Paul's strong indication of God's sovereignty— *A prisoner of Jesus Christ*, not Roman authorities. See also vs 1, 13, 15. A leader responding to life's situations this way will be shaped toward God's purposes. See *isolation, deep processing*, **Glossary**. See the **Articles**, *21. Sovereign Mindset; 2. God's Shaping Processes With Leaders*.

[26] Onesimus, meaning useful, was a common name given to a slave. Hopefully prophetic, I suppose. See vs 11 for a play on this meaning. See also: Col 4:9; inscription after Col 4:18; inscription after Phm 25.

[27] Paul here uses a play on words. Onesimus means useful; the verse uses the notions of useless and useful.

12 Whom I have sent back to you. Would you receive him, that is, my own heart?[28] 13 I would have liked to retain him with me. Then in your place he might have ministered unto me in the bonds of the gospel.[29] 14 But without your agreement I would not do this. I don't won't to force you to help me. I want you to do so willingly. 15 For perhaps he left you for a season, that now you should receive him for ever.[30] 16 Not now as a servant, but more than a servant, a brother beloved, specially to me, but how much more unto you, both in the flesh, and in the Lord.

17 If you count me your partner, receive him as myself. 18 If he has wronged you, or owes you anything, put that on my account.[31] 19 I, Paul, have personally written this. I will repay it! Though I do not need to say how you owe me even your own self besides. 20 Even so, brother, let me see the Lord's working in this. Refresh my heart in the Lord. 21 I confidently expect that you will obey. In fact, I wrote you, knowing that you would also do more than I have asked.

III. Possible Follow-Up of the Plea (Vs 22-25)

22 In addition, prepare me also the guest room. For I trust that through your prayers I shall be released and able to visit you.[32] 23 Greetings from Epaphras, my fellow prisoner in Christ Jesus and from 24 Marcus, Aristarchus, Demas, Lucas, my fellow laborers. 25 The grace of our Lord Jesus Christ be with your spirit. Amen.
[Written from Rome to Philemon, by Onesimus a servant.][33]

---

[28] This is a figure of speech, metonymy—one word substituted for another and emphasizing a relationship between the two. Here the meaning is *person dear to my heart*. Heart substituted for person dear to my heart and emphasizing how much Paul was attached to Onesimus. *See figure, metonymy, capture,* **Glossary**

[29] Again an indication of sovereignty. *Bonds of the Gospel* shows Paul's open understanding that he is in prison because he has taken a stand for the Gospel. But he could have used bonds of the Roman empire since outwardly they were the authorities holding Paul. Paul takes the divine perspective. See **Article**, *21. Sovereign Mindset*

[30] Again the sovereign perspective. Paul sees Onesimus' running away and most likely stealing from Philemon and his eventual imprisonment and contact with Paul leading to his salvation as all under the sovereign working of God. God has worked through even these negative circumstances to make Onesimus really profitable—to Paul, to Philemon, and to the Kingdom. Leaders need this kind of perspective in viewing emerging leaders. Tradition names a Bishop Onesimus in this region some time later after the writing of Philemon.

[31] This is not idle speculation. Paul knows Onesimus' story. He knows that Onesimus has taken some things. Otherwise he would not even say this. Imagine Onesimus' feelings at hearing this (see fn 33) and his resulting view of Paul as a mentor sponsor.

[32] The ministry travel verse. I frequently remind folks that they might get a postcard from me with Phm 22 on the back. If they do, get ready, I am coming to visit. This also put accountability into the appeal. Philemon would likely see Paul personally and would answer for his response.

[33] This note occurs on some manuscripts. One can imagine how Onesimus must have felt as Paul dictated this letter.

For Further Leadership Study

General

Philemon is dominantly one kind of leadership genre, a *leadership act*. It does however have limited biographical information in the lives of three leaders. It describes a critical incident. As a leadership act, the book is very helpful in understanding influence means—especially leadership styles.

Suggestions For Further Study

1. Study the Pauline leadership styles: apostolic, confrontation, father-initiator, obligation-persuasion, father-guardian, maturity appeal, nurse, imitator, consensus, and indirect conflict style. Paul exhibits styles all along the leadership style continuum which runs from highly directive to highly non-directive. The obvious implication of this was that Paul used a multi-style approach in his leadership influence depending on many factors including leadership function, relationship involved, and maturing of people being influenced. See the **Article**, *20. Pauline Leadership Styles*.

2. Study further the personal names listed in this epistle for any indications of other information about them or what might have happened to them.

    a. Paul, of course, is well known. His name occurs 217 times total in the New Testament, 186 times in Acts and 30 times in his 13 epistles. An interesting reference is made to him by Peter in 2Pe 3:15.
    b. Aristarchus occurs five times in Scripture (Ac 19:29, 20:4, 27:2, Col 4:10, and here in Phm 1:24).
    c. Epaphras occurs in Php 2:25, 4:18, inscription after 4:23, Col 1:7, 4:12; Phm 1:23.
    d. Marcus occurs in Col 4:10, Phm 1:24, 1Pe 5:13 and as Mark in Acts 12:12, 15:37, 39 and 2Ti 4:11.
    e. Lucas (or Luke) occurs 4 times: inscription after 2Co 13:14, Col 4:14, 2Ti 4:11 and Phm 1:24. He is the author of Luke and Acts and obviously was with Paul in the "we" sections seen in Acts.
    f. Demas occurs in Col 4:14, Phm 1:24, and with a negative comment in 2Ti 4:10.
    g. Philemon and Apphia occur only in the book of Philemon.
    h. Archippus occurs also in Col 4:17 with a leadership qualifier.

Special Comments

This is one of the five one chapter books in Scripture. It is small enough to be mastered and yet profound enough to challenge all leaders. This should be a core book for leaders who must influence largely by spiritual authority.

Personal Response

1. What is the most significant leadership insight you have gained from your study of Philemon?

2. What one idea from this study can you put into practice in your own leadership? How?

3. Immediate Application: List an idea from this study that you can share with someone today?

    a. Idea:

    b. Who to share with?:

Your Observations.

You may want to jot down important insights you want to remember. You may wish to note follow-up intents.

(This page is deliberately blank.)

Article 1

Relevance of the Article to Paul's Philemon Letter

Even in this short little epistle Paul uses several figures. Capturing of these figures adds emphasis to what Paul is really saying. See comments about figures in Phm verses 4, 6, 11, 12.

1. Figures and Idioms In The Bible

Introduction to Figures

All language is governed by law—that is, it has normal patterns that are followed. But in order to increase the power of a word or the force of expression, these patterns are deliberately departed from, and words and sentences are thrown into and used in unusual forms or patterns which we call figures. A figure then is a use of language in a special way for the purpose of giving additional force, more life, intensified feeling and greater emphasis. A figure of speech is the author's way of underlining. He/She is saying, "Hey, take note! This is important enough for me to use a special form of language to emphasize it!" And when we remember the fact that the Holy Spirit has inspired this product we have—the Bible—we are not far wrong in saying figures are the Holy Spirit's own underlining in our Bibles. We certainly need to be sensitive to figurative language.

Definition   A <u>figure</u> is the unusual use of a word or words differing from the normal use in order to draw special attention to some point of interest.

For a figure, the unusual use itself follows a set pattern. The pattern can be identified and used to interpret the figure in normal language. Here are some examples from the Bible. I will make you fishers of people. Go tell that fox. Quench not the Holy Spirit. I came not to send peace but a sword. As students of the Bible we need to be sensitive to figures and know how to interpret and catch their emphatic meaning.

Definition   A figure or idiom is said to be <u>captured</u> when one can display the intended emphatic meaning in non-figurative simple words.

One of the most familiar figures in the Bible is Psalm 23:1. The Lord is my shepherd. I shall not lack. *Captured*: God personally provides for my every need.

E.W. Bullinger, an expert on figurative language, lists over 400 different kinds of figures. He lists over 8000 references in the Bible containing figures. In Romans alone, Bullinger lists 253 passages containing figurative language. However, we do not need to know all of those figures for the most commonly occurring figures number much less than 400. Figure Phm 1 below list the 11 most common figures occurring in the Bible. If we know them we are well on our way to becoming better interpreters of the Scripture. In fact, you can group these 11 figures under three main sub-categories, which simplifies learning about them.

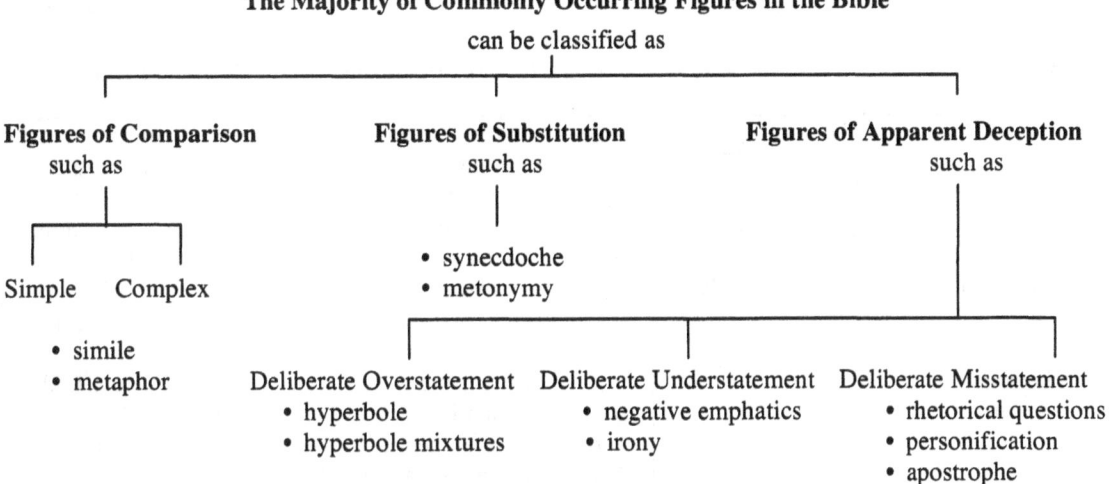

Figure Phm 1-1. 11 Common Figures of Speech

Table Phm 1-1 below gives these 11 figures of speech, a Scriptural reference containing the figure, and the basic definition of each of these figures.

Table Phm 1-1: 11 Figures in the Bible Defined

Category/ Figure	Scriptural Example	Definition
Figures of Comparison: 1. Simile 2. Metaphor	simile—Isa 53:6 metaphor—Ps 23:1	A simile is a stated comparison of two unlike items (one called the real item and the other the picture item) in order to display one graphic point of comparison. A metaphor is an implied comparison in which two unlike items (a real item and a picture item) are equated to point out one point of resemblance.
Figures of Substitution 3. Metonymy 4. Synecdoche	metonymy—Ac 15:21 Moses for what he wrote synecdoche—Mt 8:8 roof for the whole house.	A metonymy is a figure of speech in which (usually) one word is substituted for another word to which it is closely related in order to emphasize something indicated by the relationship. A synecdoche is a special case of metonymy in which (again usually) one word is substituted for another to which it is related as, a part to a whole or a whole to a part.
Figures of Apparent Deception— Deliberate Overstatement: 5. Hyperbole 6. Hyperbolic mixtures	hyperbole—1Co 4:14-16 ten thousand instructors hyperbolic mixture—2 Sa 1:23 swifter than eagles, stronger than lions	A hyperbole is the use of conscious exaggeration (an overstatement of truth) in order to emphasize or strikingly excite interest in the truth. Hyperbole is sometimes combined with other figures such as comparison and substitution. When such is the case it is called a hyperbolic mixture figure.

1. Figures and Idioms In The Bible

Figures of Apparent Deception—Deliberate understatement: 7. Negative emphatics	negative emphatics—Mk 12:34 not far = very near	A figure of <u>negative emphasis</u> represents the deliberate use of words to diminish a concept and thus call attention to it or the negating of a concept to call attention to the opposite positive concept (I have deliberately merged two figures, litotes and tapenosis into one because of the basic sameness of negative emphasis). My own very favorite litotes is Ro 1:16 not ashamed = completely confident.
Figures of Apparent Deception—Deliberate Misstatement: 8. Rhetorical questions 9. Irony 10. Personification 11. Apostrophe	rhetorical question—1Ti 3:5 irony—2Co 12:13 personification—Heb 4:12 apostrophe—1Co 15:55	A <u>rhetorical question</u> is a figure of speech in which a question is not used to obtain information but is used to indirectly communicate, (1) an affirmative or negative statement, or (2) the importance of some thought by focusing attention on it, or (3) one's own feeling or attitudes about something. 1 Co is filled with rhetorical questions. <u>Irony</u> is the use of words by a speaker in which his/her intended meaning is the opposite of (or in disharmony with) the literal use of the words. <u>Personification</u> is the use of words to speak of animals, ideas, abstractions, and inanimate objects as if they had human form, character, or intelligence in order to vividly portray truth. <u>Apostrophe</u> is a special case of personification in which the speaker addresses the thing personified as if it were alive and listening.

I have developed in-depth explanations for all of the above figures. I have developed study sheets to aid one in analysis of them. Further I have actually identified many of these in the Scriptures and captured a number of them.[34]

Introduction to Idioms

Idioms are much more complicated than figures of speech.

Definition   An <u>idiom</u> is a group of words, which have a corporate meaning that can not be deduced from a compilation of the meanings of the individual words making up the idiom.

What makes idioms difficult is that some of them follow patterns while others do not. For the patterned idioms, like figures, you basically reverse the pattern and capture the idiom. Table Phm 1-2 lists the patterned idioms I have identified in the Bible.

Table Phm 1-2. 13 Patterned Idioms

Idiom	Example	Definitive principle/ Description
Three Certainty Idioms: 1. Double certainty (pos/neg) 2. Fulfilled (promised/proposed) 3. Prophetic past	double certainty—1Ki 18:36 fulfilled—Ge 15:18 prophetic past—Jn 13:31	<u>double certainty</u>—a negative and positive statement (in either order) are often used to express or imply certainty. <u>fulfillment</u>—in the fulfillment idiom things are spoken of as given, done, or possessed, which are only promised or proposed. <u>prophetic past</u>—in the prophetic past idiom the past tense is used to describe or express the certainty of future action.

---

[34] See my self-study manual, **Interpreting the Scriptures: Figures and Idioms**.

4. Superlative (repetitive superlative)	Ge 9:25 servant of servants Isa 26:3 peace, peace = perfect peace 2Ti 4:7	The <u>Hebrew superlative</u> is often shown by the repetition of the word. Paul uses a variation of this by often using the noun form and a verb form of the same word either back to back or in close proximity. (2 Ti 4:7 the good struggle I have struggled = I have given this Christian ministry my very best effort).
5. Emphatic comparisons	1Pe 3:3,4	This takes three forms: <u>absolute for relative</u>: one thing (importance or focus item) is emphasized as being much more important in comparison with the other thing (the denial item). form not A but B really means A is less important than B. <u>relative for absolute</u>: One thing is positively compared to another when in effect it is meant to be taken absolutely and the other denied altogether. <u>abbreviated emphatic comparisons</u>: Half of the comparison is not given (either the focus item or denial items). Half of the statement is given. the half missing is an example of ellipsis and is to be supplied by the reader.
6. Climactic arrangement	Pr 6:16-19 Ro 3:10-18	To emphasize a particular item it is sometimes <u>placed at the bottom of a list</u> of other items and is thus stressed in the given context as being the most important item being considered.
7. Broadened kinship	Ge 29:5	Sometimes the terms son of, daughter of, mother of, father of, brother of, sister of, or begat, which in English imply a close relationship have a much wider connotation in the Bible. Brother and sister could include various male and female relatives such as cousins; mother and father could include relatives such as grandparents or great-great-grandparents, in the direct family line; begat may simply mean was directly in the family line of ancestors.
8. Imitator	Ge 6:2, 11:5	to indicate that people or things are governed by or are characterized by some quality, they are called <u>children of</u> or a <u>son of</u>. or <u>daughter of</u> that quality.
9. Linked noun	Lk 21:15	Occasionally two nouns are linked together with a conjunction in which the second noun is really to be used like an adjective modifying the first noun.
Indicator Idioms: 10. City indicator 11. List indicator 12. Strength Indicator	city indicator La 1:16, daughter of Zion list indicator Pr 6:16, these 6 yea 7 Strength indicator 1Sa 2:1,10	<u>city indicator</u>—idiomatic words, daughter of or virgin of or mother of. <u>list indicator</u>—2 consecutive numbers—designates an incomplete list of items of which the ones on the list are representative; other like items could be included. <u>strength indicator</u>—a horn denotes aggressive strength or power or authority.
13. Anthropomorphism	Lk 11:20	In order to convey concepts of God, <u>human passions, or actions, or attributes are used to describe God.</u>

In addition, to the patterned idioms there are a number of miscellaneous idioms, which either occur infrequently or have no discernible pattern. I have labeled 32. Their meaning must be learned from context, from other original language sources, or from language experts' comments, etc.

1. Figures and Idioms In The Bible

Table Phm 1-3: 15 Body Language Idioms

Name	Word, Phrase, Usually Seen	Example	Meaning or Concept Involved
1. Foot gesture	shake off the dust	Mt 10:14, Lk 9:5 et al	have nothing more to do with them
2. Mouth gesture	gnash on them with teeth; gnashing of teeth	Ps 35:16; 37:12 Ac 7:54 et al	indicates angry and cursing words given with deep emotion and feeling
3. Invitation	I have stretched forth my hand(s)	Ro 10:21; Pr 1:24; Is 49:22	indicates to invite, or to receive or welcome or call for mercy
4. New desire	enlighten my eyes, lighten my eyes	Ps 13:3; 19:8; 1Sa 14:29; Ezr 9:8	to give renewed desire to live; sometimes physical problem sometimes motivational inward attitude problem
5. Judgment	to stretch forth the hand; to put forth the hand	Ex 7:5; Ps 138:7; Job 1:11	to send judgment upon; to inflict with providential punishment
6. Fear	to shake the hand, to not find the hand, knees tremble	Is 19:16; Ps 76:8	to be afraid; to be paralyzed with fear and incapable of action.
7. Increase punishment	to make the hand heavy	Ps 32:4	to make the punishment more severe
8. Decreased punishment	to make the hands light	1SA 6:5	to make punishment less severe
9. Remove punishment	to withdraw the hands	Eze 20:22	to stop punishment
10. Repeat punishment	to turn the hand upon	Is 1:25	to repeat again some punishment which was not previously heeded
11. Generosity	to open the hand	Ps 104:28; 145:16	to generously give or bestow
12. Anger	to clap the hands together	Eze 21;17; 22:13	to show anger; to express derision
13. Oath	to lift up the hand	Ex 6:8; 17:16; De 32:40; Eze 20:5,6	to swear in a solemn; take an oath; an indicator of one's integrity

to consider worthy to be accepted; to accept someone or be accepted by someone |
| 14. Promise | to strike with the hands (with someone else) | Pr 6:1; Job 17:3 | become a co-signer on a loan; to conclude a bargain |
| 15. Accept | to lift up the face | Nu 6:26; Ezr 9:6; Job 22:26 | to consider worthy to be accepted; to accept someone or be accepted by someone |

Table Phm 1-4: 14 Miscellaneous Idioms

Name	Word, Phrase, Usually Seen	Example	Meaning or Concept Involved
1. Success	tree of life	Pr 3:18; 11:30; 13:12; 15:4	idea of success, guarantee of success, source of motivation to successful life
2. Speech cue	answered and said	Mt 11:25; 13:2 and many others	indicates manner of speaking denoted by context; e.g. responded prayed, asked, addressed, etc.
3. Notice	verily, verily	Many times in Jn	I am revealing absolute and important truth; give close attention (this is a form of the superlative idiom)
4. Time	___ days and ___ nights	Jn 1:17; Mt 12:40; 1Sa 30:11; Est 4:16	any portion of time of a day is indicated by or represented by the entire day
5. Lifetime	forever and ever	Ps 48;14 and many others	does not mean eternal life as we commonly use it but means all through my life; as long as I live
6. Separation	what have I to do with you	Jn 2:4; Jdg 11;12; 2Sa 16:10; 1Ki 17;18; 2Ki 3;13; Mt 8:29; Mk 5:7; Lk 8:28	an expression of indignation or contempt between two parties having a difference or more specifically not having something in common; usually infers that some action about to take place should not take place
7. Reaction	heap coals of fire	Ro 12:20; Pr 25:21	to incur God's favor by reacting positively to a situation in which revenge would be normal
8. Orate	open the mouth	Job 3:1	to speak at great length with great liberty or freedom
9. Claim	you say	Mt 26:25,63,64	means it is your opinion
10. Excellency	living, lively	Jn 4:10,11 Ac 7:38; Heb 10:20; 1Pe 2:4,5; Rev 1:17	used to express the excellency of perfection of that to which it refers
11. Abundance	riches	Ro 2:4; Eph 1:7; 3:8; Col 1:27; 2:2	used to describe abundance of or a great supply
12. Preeminence	firstborn	Ps 89:27; Ro 8:29; Col 1;15, 18; Heb 12:23	special place of preeminence; first place among many others
13. Freedom	enlarge my feet; enlarge	2Sa 22:37; Ps 4:1; 18:36	freed me; brought me into a situation that has taken the pressure off, taken on to bigger and better things
14. Reverential respect for	fear and trembling	Ps 55:5; Mk 5:33; Lk 8:47; 1Co 2:3; 2 Co 7:15; Eph 6:5, Php 2:12	describes an attitude of appropriate respect for something. The something could be God, could a person, or could be a combination including some process. Sometimes indicates confronting a difficult situation or thing with a strong awareness of it and possible consequences

Again I would recommend you refer to my manual **Figures and Idioms** to see the approach for capturing the patterned idioms.

Figures and Idioms should be appreciated, understood, and should be interpreted with emphasis. Hardly any passage which is any one of the seven leadership genre will be without some figure or idiom.

Article 2

Relevance of the Article to Paul's Philemon Letter

Even in this short little epistle several shaping processes are illustrated: possible life crisis for Onesimus; possible word check for Philemon; as well as learning about spiritual authority. This is a critical incident in the lives of three leaders—Paul, Philemon, and Onesimus. All feel the shaping hand of God in this critical incident. See **LEADERSHIP TOPICS 5. ISOLATION PROCESSING AND ITS RESULTS and 7. CRITICAL INCIDENTS.**

2. God's Shaping Processes With Leaders

Introduction

One major leadership lesson derived from comparative study of effective leaders states,

Effective leaders see present ministry in light of a life time perspective.[35]

This article deals with God's shaping processes with a leader.[36] It gives important aspects of perspective that all leaders need. Six observations of God's shaping processes with leaders include the following.

1. God first works in a leader and then through that leader.
2. God intends to develop a leader to reach the maximum potential and accomplish those things for which the leader has been gifted.
3. God shapes or develops a leader over an entire lifetime.
4. A time perspective provides many keys. When using a time perspective, the life can be seen in terms of several time periods, each yielding valuable informative lessons. Each leader has a unique time-line describing his/her development.[37]
5. Shaping processes can be identified, labeled, and analyzed to contribute long lasting lessons.[38]
6. An awareness of God's shaping processes can enhance a leader's response to these processes.

Figure Phm 2-1. Describes a generalized time line and some of the processes used by God over a lifetime.

---

[35] I have identified seven which repeatedly occur in effective leaders: 1. Life Time Perspective—Effective Leaders View Present Ministry In Terms Of A Life Time Perspective. 2. Learning Posture—Effective Leaders Maintain A Learning Posture Throughout Life. 3. Spiritual Authority—Effective Leaders Value Spiritual Authority As A Primary Power Base. 4. Dynamic Ministry Philosophy—Effective Leaders Who Are Productive Over A Lifetime Have A Dynamic Ministry Philosophy Which Is Made Up Of An Unchanging Core And A Changing Periphery Which Expands Due To A Growing Discovery Of Giftedness, Changing Leadership Situations, And Greater Understanding Of The Scriptures. 5. Leadership Selection And Development—Effective Leaders View Leadership Selection And Development As A Priority Function In Their Ministry. 6. Relational Empowerment—Effective Leaders See Relational Empowerment As Both A Means And A Goal Of Ministry. 7. Sense Of Destiny- Effective Leaders Evince A Growing Awareness Of Their Sense Of Destiny. See the **Article**, *Leadership Lessons—Seven Major Identified.*

[36] See also the **Article**, *Leadership Selection* which gives an overview across time of the major benchmarks of God's development of a leader.

[37] See **Article**, *24. Time-Lines: Defined for Biblical Leaders.*

[38] See **For Further Study Bibliography**, Clinton's **Leadership Emergence Theory**, a self-study manual which gives detailed findings from research on God's shaping processes with leaders. This manual describes 50 shaping processes in detail. This article touches on only a few of these shaping processes.

2. God's Shaping Processes With Leaders

I. Ministry Foundations	II. Early Ministry	III. Middle Ministry	IV. Latter Ministry	V. Finishing Well
• character shaping	• leadership committal • authority insights • giftedness discovery • guidance	• ministry insights • conflict • paradigm shifts • leadership backlash challenges	• spiritual warfare • deep processing • power processes	• destiny fulfillment

Figure Phm 2-1. Some Major Shaping Processes Across The Time-Line

Shaping in Early Ministry — In and Then Through

Most younger emerging leaders in their initial exuberance for ministry feel they are accomplishing much. But in fact, God is doing much more in them than through them. The first years in ministry are tremendous learning years for a young leader who is sensitive to God's working in his/her life. God works on character first, even before a leader moves into full time leadership. Table Phm 2-1 lists four major shaping processes dealing with character and four major shaping processes dealing with early ministry.

Table Phm 2-1. Early Shaping Processes Identified and Defined

Type	Name	Explanation/ Biblical Example
Character	Integrity Check	A shaping process to test heart intent and consistency of inner beliefs and outward practice./ Daniel 1:3,4.
Character	Obedience Check	A shaping process to test a leader's will for obedience to God. /See Abraham, Ge 22.
Character	Word Check	A shaping process to test a leader's ability to hear from God./ See Samuel ch 3.
Character	Ministry Task	A shaping process to test a leader's faithfulness in performing ministry./ See Titus, Corinth trip (references in both 1,2Co).
Foundational Ministry	Leadership Committal	A shaping process, part of Guidance, to recruit a leader into ministry and to continue to engage that leader along the ministry path destined for him/her. /See Paul, Ac 9,22,26.
Foundational Ministry	Authority Insights	A shaping process to help leaders learn how to deal with leaders over them and folks under them./ See Ac 13 Barnabas and Paul.
Foundational Ministry	Giftedness Discovery	A shaping process in which a leader learns about natural abilities, acquired skills, and spiritual gifts that God wants to use through that leader./ See Phillip, Ac 8.
Long Term Ministry	Guidance	A shaping process in which God intervenes in the life of a leader at critical points to direct that leader along the ministry path destined for him/her./ See Paul, Ac 16.

Shaping in Middle Ministry — Efficient Ministry

During middle ministry the leader now sees God working through as much as in the leader. Leaders identify giftedness. They learn how to influence; they are learning to lead. They gain many perspectives that channel their ministry toward effectiveness. Table Phm 2-2 lists some of the more important shaping processes that happen during this developmental phase.

Table Phm 2-2. Middle Ministry Shaping Processes—Identified and Defined

Type	Name	Explanation/ Biblical Example
Character/ Ministry	Conflict	A shaping process in which a leader learns perseverance, surfaces defects in character, gets new perspective on issues, and learns how to influence in less than ideal conditions./ See Paul, Ac 19 Ephesus.
Breakthroughs in Ministry	Paradigm Shifts	A shaping process in which God gives breakthrough insights that allow a broadening of perspective so as to propel the leader forward in ministry. /See Paul, Ac 9.
Character/ Ministry	Leadership Backlash	A shaping process in which a leader learns about follower reactions and about perseverance, hearing from God, and inspirational leadership./ See Moses, Ex 5.
Renewal/ Long Term	Challenges	A shaping process in which a leader is induced along the lines of new ministry; a part of the guidance process to take a leader along the life path. /See Paul and Barnabas, Ac 13.

Latter Ministry And Finishing Well—Effective Ministry

The essential difference between middle ministry and latter ministry has to do with focus.[39] In middle ministry the leader learns to be efficient in ministry—that is, to do things well. In latter ministry and the finishing well time the leader learns to be effective—that is, to do the right things well. There is a further deepening of character, which enhances the leader's spiritual authority. There is a growing awareness of spiritual warfare. The leader learns to minister with power. Table Phm 2-3 lists some of the shaping processes that take place in the latter part of a leader's lifetime.

Table Phm 2-3. Latter Ministry Shaping Processes—Identified and Defined

Type	Name	Explanation/ Biblical Example
Deep Processing	Crises	A shaping process in which a leader's person or ministry is threatened with discontinuation; an overwhelming time in which the leader feels intense issues which could torpedo his/her whole ministry./ See Paul, 2Co.
Deep Processing	Isolation	A shaping process in which a leader is set aside from ministry and goes through a searching time about identity and a deepening trust of God./ See Paul, Php.
Long Term Guidance	Negative Preparation	A shaping process in which an accumulative effect of a number of negative things in the life and ministry of a leader is used by God to release that leader from some previous ministry and give freedom to enter another ministry./ See Paul, 2Co.
Long Term Guidance	Divine Contacts	A shaping process in which God uses some person in a timely fashion to intervene in a leader's life to give perspective—could be directed toward personhood, ministry, or long term guidance./ See Paul and Barnabas, Ac 9:27.
Long Term Guidance	Double Confirmation	A shaping process in which God gives clear guidance by inward conviction and by external conviction (unsought)./ See Paul and Ananias, Ac 9.
Effective Ministry	Power Issues	A group of shaping processes including power encounters, gifted power, networking power and prayer power. The leader learns balance between own effort and God's enabling through him/her. The leader learns to minister effectively with God's power./ See Elijah, 1Ki 18 et al.

Conclusion

Awareness of these shaping processes allows a leader to combat the usually overwhelming attitude of *why me?* By seeing that these shaping processes occur in many leaders lives, leaders are affirmed that they are not way off base. It is part of God's way of developing a leader. A leader who understands what is

---

[39] See **Article**, *Focused Life*.

2. God's Shaping Processes With Leaders

happening in his/her life stands a better chance of responding to the processes and learning the lessons of God in them than one who is blindsided by these processes.

See *Integrity Check; Obedience Check; Word Check; Ministry Task; Leadership Committal; Authority Insights; Giftedness Discovery; Guidance; Conflict; Paradigm Shifts; Leadership Backlash; Faith Challenge; Leadership Challenge; Crises; Isolation; Negative Preparation; Divine Contacts; Double Confirmation; Power Encounters; Prayer Power; Gifted Power; Networking Power;* **Glossary**. See **Articles**, *21. Sovereign Mindset; 6. Isolation Processing—Learning Deep Lessons from God; 22. Spiritual Authority—Defined, Six Characteristics*. See **For Further Study Bibliography—The Making of A Leader; Leadership Emergence Theory;** *The Life Cycle of a Leader*.

Article 3

Relevance of the Article to Paul's Philemon Letter

God's timing is very evident in this book. Paul would not have been so diplomatic in his earlier ministry. Onesimus was ready to make restitution, something he could not have done before becoming a Christian. Philemon has matured in his Christian life and can now hear this plea favorably.

3. God's Timing and Influence

Introduction

What do these verses have in common?

Joseph's birth:
And God remembered Rachel, and God hearkened to her, and opened her womb. 23 And she conceived, and bore a son; and said, God hath taken away my reproach: 24 And she called his name Joseph; and said, The LORD shall add to me another son. Gen 30:22

Jesus Ministry:
But when the fullness of the **time** was come, God sent forth his Son, made of a woman, made under the law, 5 To redeem them that were under the law, that we might receive the adoption of sons. Gal 4:4

From John Quoting Jesus:
John: Jesus said unto her, Woman, what have I to do with thee? my **hour** is not yet come. Jn 2:4

Then Jesus said unto them, **My time** is not yet come: but your time is always ready. Jn 7:6

I am not going to the feast, yet; for **my time** is not yet full come. Jn 7:8

Then they sought to take him: but no man laid hands on him, because his **hour** was not yet come. Jn 7:30

These words spoke Jesus in the treasury, as he taught in the temple: and no man laid hands on him; for his **hour** was not yet come. Jn 8:20

And Jesus answered them, saying, The **hour** is come, that the Son of man should be glorified. Jn 12:23

Now is my soul troubled; and what shall I say? Father, save me from this **hour**: but for this cause came I unto this **hour**. Jn 12:27

Now before the feast of the passover, when Jesus knew that his **hour** was come that he should depart out of this world unto the Father, having loved his own which were in the world, he loved them unto the end. Jn 13:1

All have to do with God's timing. One of the major macro lessons first seen in *the Patriarchal Leadership Era* and then in every other leadership era thereafter states,

3. God's Timing and Leadership

God's timing is crucial to the accomplishment of God's purposes.[40]

Effective leaders are increasingly aware of the timing of God's interventions in their lives and ministry. They move when he moves. They wait. They confidently expect. Leaders must learn to be sensitive to God's timing. God's direction includes *What, How, and When*. All are important.

This is a leadership lesson that all leaders must learn. Strong leaders, such as apostolic leaders desperately need to learn this. Such leaders usually have a strong sense of destiny. Such leaders usually have a strong vision they want to accomplish. Often these strong leaders tie their vision to some prophecy or other revelatory word. While they may know the *what* and even the *how* of the vision they may well be off in the *when*. They often move ahead of God's timing. God's timing is crucial. Less bold and forceful leaders also need to learn about God's timing. Frequently, they lag behind God's timing. What can we learn from some Bible characters about God's timing?

Thirteen Bible Characters and God's Timing

Table Phm 3-1 lists thirteen Bible characters and implications about God's timing.

Table Phm 3-1. 13 Bible Characters and God's Timing Across the Leadership Eras

Character	Era	Timing Issue	Observations/ Lessons
Abraham/ Sarah	Patriarchal	Birth of Isaac/ Israel's deliverance 400 years later	Isaac: *The promises of God include what, how, and when.* Abraham and Sarah only knew what. The *how* they tried to manipulate. The *when*—they went ahead of God. God was true to his promise. The *what, how, when* all came together. God's timing was crucial. Israel's Promised Deliverance from Egypt: Sometimes God's timing is well beyond a leader's own lifetime. Such a promise can enable one to live with hope and faith though they may never see the fulfillment of that promise.
Jacob/ Rachael	Patriarchal	Birth of Joseph	Joseph's birth, as to timing was important. The birth order was necessary to God's purposes for him—both favored status and his brothers jealousy. The time of birth was important; he was to deliver in 39 years. *Manipulation of God's timing can bring problems. Manipulation begets manipulation.*
Joseph	Patriarchal	Fulfillment of Certainty Guidance—2 Dreams	Throughout the Joseph narrative timing is important (dreams at 17; caravan; in jail with two of Pharaoh's servants; God's dreams about drought, etc.) Most important lesson. *The way up is often down and may take a long time for God to accomplish.*
Moses	Pre-Kingdom	Deliverance of Israel from Egypt	Deliverance from Egypt: Moses was a strong leader who went ahead of God to deliver Israel from Egypt. He learned a major lesson that strong leaders often learn—The Death of a Vision. *A strong ego leader must surrender a vision and give it back to God. God will bring it about in his own way and timing. Don't move ahead of God. Make sure the how of guidance is God's how.* Crossing the Red Sea: *The when of God's guidance is crucial. It takes faith to believe in exact timing of God's intervention.* Failure to Enter the Land: *Failure to heed God's intervention time can bring long term ramifications— 40 years in the desert, loss of a generation* Going in to the land: *God's progressive timing has*

---

[40] See **Articles**, *11. Macro Lessons—Defined; 12. Macro Lessons—List of 41 Across Six Leadership eras.*

3. God's Timing and Leadership

			underlying reasons behind it. Development of an armed force takes time.
Joshua	Pre-Kingdom	Generational leadership/ Capture of Jericho/ Gibeon (flesh act)	Desert Wandering: *A leader often pays a price due to followership. A leader needs time to enculturate and be enculturated to a new generation of followers.* Crossing the Jordan: *They could have crossed in non-flood season without God's help. They needed this God intervention for courage and to give Joshua spiritual authority. The three days they camped beside the flood waters built anticipation and fearfulness.* Fall of Jericho: *The How and When must be obtained from God in a major achievement.* Gibeon: *Moving ahead of God, making a decision in the flesh with hearing from God and then asking God to approve your decision often results in major negative ramifications that you must live with.*
Caleb	Pre-Kingdom	Generational Leadership; Fulfillment of Promise	Desert Wandering: *Leaders who model whole hearted obedience to God can impact a new generation with the importance of believing God and obeying Him.* Land: *The promises of God will be fulfilled in His timing. Respond with courage.*
Samuel	Pre-Kingdom	Moving from decentralized leadership to a Kingdom	Sons: *The what of God's intervention is as important as the when and how. Samuel's sons were not God's answer to the leadership need.:* Saul: *Obedience to God's timing is necessary. Failure to obey God as to His timing may well imply lack of integrity and an eventual setting aside by God.*
David	Kingdom	Made King	Uniting the Kingdom: *Time is involved even when the what is known.*
Hezekiah	Kingdom	Sickness Unto Death/ Babylonian Envoy (flesh act)	Changing God's Timing: *Hezekiah's prolonged life brought ramifications he probably didn't foresee. The birth of Manasseh occurred in this time.* Babylonian envoy: *To move ahead of God, make a decision without consulting God, can bring ramifications (later Babylonian captivity). To be safe in one's own generation may well bode problems for future generations.*
Daniel	Post-Kingdom	70 Years Captivity Fulfilled	Learning Posture: *Daniel's maintaining a learning posture, studying the Scriptures, brought out the what and when and hints as to the how of God's plans. God's timing is exact. He will fulfill His promises on time.*
Jesus	Pre-Church	The Cross	World Scene: *The timing was perfect for Jesus' birth.* Sensitivity: *Jesus was sensitive to God's timing for his life, throughout his ministry. He never went ahead; he never lagged behind. Jesus models perfectly the whole notion of what, when, and how in following God's plans.*
Peter	Church	Impulsive Actions; Coming of Holy Spirit	Impulsive: *Peter's tendencies to move too quickly throughout the disciples training serves as a negative model. See Jesus' reactions and training of Peter.* Pentecost: *God's promise of power was fulfilled exactly on time. Waiting was involved.* Lagging Behind: *The church failed to expand. God brought persecution to get them to expand.*

3. God's Timing and Leadership

Paul	Church	Reaching of Gentiles/ Kings	Antioch Call: *A leader may be called upon to do something at a time (when is clear—release my Servants for the ministry to which I have called them). But the what and how are hazy. The what and when may be revealed over time.* Macedonian call: *God's timing may involve pre-preparation about the what and how. The move to Europe involved a pre-prepared receptive group ready to hear and respond.* The Book of Philemon: *This could not have been written earlier; it needed a mature gentled Paul, a relationship between Paul and Philemon, and a crossing of paths between Paul and Onesimus. All three of these had to converge for Paul to see and feel and write the appeal to Philemon.*

Reasons For Delay In Timing

In a number of the Biblical examples given above God delayed what He was going to do. Some possible reasons for delay include:

    a. **Dealing With a Strong Ego Leader**—The *Death of a Vision* as seen in Moses' case involved dealing with the right vision but the wrong motivation, wrong power base, and wrong timing.

    b. **God's Working out of other purposes**—In the promise to Abraham (400 years), God pointed out that He was dealing with the nations in the land and that their iniquity was not yet full. That is, He was giving them time to repent. That time wasn't up yet when Moses made his first attempt at deliverance.

    c. **Foundational Character Shaping**—Moses' isolation period brought about a humility in character (Nu 12:3) which made him a pliable vessel in God's hands. He would need this humility because God would reveal power through his ministry which could be dangerous with a strong unfettered ego leader.

    d. **Remedial Training**—God is doing remedial training. He is giving time for certain disciplines to be built in the life of the leader. Moses was a desert leader. He learned about desert disciplines as a shepherd wandering over desert land taking care of sheep.

Reasons To Move Fast in God's Timing

Just as some leaders have a tendency to move too fast and God has to delay their actions, some leaders move too slowly. Why should leaders move faster? Here are some reasons:

    a. **Windows of Opportunity**—God knows that sometimes the needed action must take place within a certain time period or an opportunity to accomplish something may be lost.

    b. **Networks/ onward guidance**—Sometimes the timing is such that obedience will connect to other things God has set up. The next piece of guidance will open up after obedience. To not move will be to miss it. Following an unusual, apparently hurried intervention may lead to a series of people or events and give guidance that would not previously have been dreamed of.

    c. **God's Doing**—Sometimes God moves a leader to action before things are apparently ready because He wants all to know that He alone is responsible and He alone will get credit for the results. That is, sometimes God has something happen fast because it would be impossib'e for it to happen unless God alone brought it about.

Four Implications of the Timing Lesson

Four observations can be drawn from a comparative study of God's timing with biblical leaders:

    1. **Ramifications.** Moving ahead of God's timing in guidance or in carrying out some aspect of ministry may accomplish the task, yet, it will most certainly bring ramifications which will require remedial training and the repetition of incidents to teach us the dependence lesson.

3. God's Timing and Leadership

2. **Guidance.** The *what*, *how*, and *when* are the major elements of guidance. We need clarity on all three. It is the *when* that is most in focus on the timing macro lesson.
3. **Sensitivity.** We must be sensitive to the Spirit in our lives. Timing can refer to daily interventions or long term guidance decisions. In either case we need to be sensitive to the Spirit. Seemingly small issues may turn out to be pivotal points. This implies that we as leaders especially need to develop the Spirit sensitivity component of the Spirituality model.
4. **Negative Preparation and Flesh Act.** We need to be thoroughly familiar with these two process items including the various illustrations of them in Scripture so we will respond more quickly and carefully to incidents which God is using for this kind of processing. A *flesh act* means making a decision based on fleshly wisdom and moving ahead without getting God's guidance. *Negative preparation* refers to numerous negative happenings in the life. These may well be used by God to move a leader out of a situation. Negative preparation refers to numerous negative happenings in the life. These may well be used by God to move a leader out of a situation.

Conclusion

Look again at the basic lesson.

God's Timing Is Crucial To Accomplishment Of God's Purposes.

Moses learned this lesson the hard way. But he learned it well. The latter stages of his desert leadership reflect his increased sensitivity to God's timing. The question is,

Are You Sensitive To God's Timing In The Little Things Of Daily Ministry As Well As The Big Things Of Major Guidance?

Some final advice should be noted, especially for major guidance decisions.

1. **Triple Confirmation.** Where possible never make a major decision unless you are clear on the *what*, the *how*, and the *when* of the issues. Should you be unclear on any, then it may be best to wait. Certainty guidance via double confirmation or divine contact should be sought on all three issues: what, when, how.
2. **Presumption.** Be careful of presuming to know God's intents on some aspects of ministry without clearing with Him first. Simply attempting to get His approval after the fact may prove fatal in the long run.
3. **Patterns.** Study the concept of timing in the Bible and identify patterns of sensitivity to God's timing. Note what to avoid as well as what to assert. Go back through the vignettes associated with the leaders given in Table Phm 3-1. Study them carefully and learn first hand what you need to know about God's timing and your leadership.

Let me repeat in closing. *Effective Leaders Are Increasingly Aware Of The Timing Of God's Interventions In Their Lives And Ministry.* They Move When He Moves. They Wait. They Confidently Expect God to reveal His timing. Leaders must learn to be sensitive to God's timing. God's direction includes *What*, *How*, and *When*. All are important.

See *flesh act; negative preparation; pivotal point; double confirmation; divine contact;* **Glossary**.

Article 4

Relevance of the Article to Paul's Philemon Letter

Paul is operating to the far right on Wrong's continuum. Persuasion is the dominant power form being used to influence Philemon. Spiritual authority and the voluntary reception of influence are highlighted. Philemon has the clear right to choose not to follow Paul's advice. Paul gives him that choice, while at the same time putting on great persuasive arguments for following his advice. It is clear that Paul is depending upon spiritual authority to pull off the major paradigm shift he wants to see in Philemon's response.

4. Influence, Power, and Authority

Introduction

A major lesson concerning how a leader ought to influence states:

Effective leaders value spiritual authority as a primary power base.

To understand this important principle we need to define some terms. The terms that are used to describe leadership make a difference in how we see leadership. Three important terms are influence, power, and authority. Sometimes these important terms are used interchangeable in leadership literature. I use a simplified adaptation of Dennis Wrong's[41] basic schema for relating these concepts—though I have adapted it to fit my understanding of spiritual authority. Influence is the most embracing of the concepts. Power is intended use of influence. And authority is one kind of power usually associated with tight organizations.[42]

Figure Ph 4-1, which follows, lays out Wrong's adapted taxonomy of influence, power, and authority forms. Notice for the book of Philemon, Paul is operating to the far right on this diagram.

---

[41] See Dennis Wrong, **Power--Its Forms, Bases, and Uses.** San Francisco, CA: Harper and Row, 1979. This is a brilliant treatment involving definitions of power concepts as well as recognition of how these forms change over time. His analysis gave a complicated taxonomy which I have simplified and adapted.
[42] Christian organizations operate on a continuum from tight to loose. The more loose an organization is the more it is characterized by voluntary workers who are not paid to do some job but do it because they want to. Therefore leaders in loose organizations do not have as much authority as those in tight organizations which are characterized by paid workers, structures levels of leadership, and supervisory responsibility (that is, people have bosses who can fire them if they don't submit to authority).

4. Influence Power and Authority

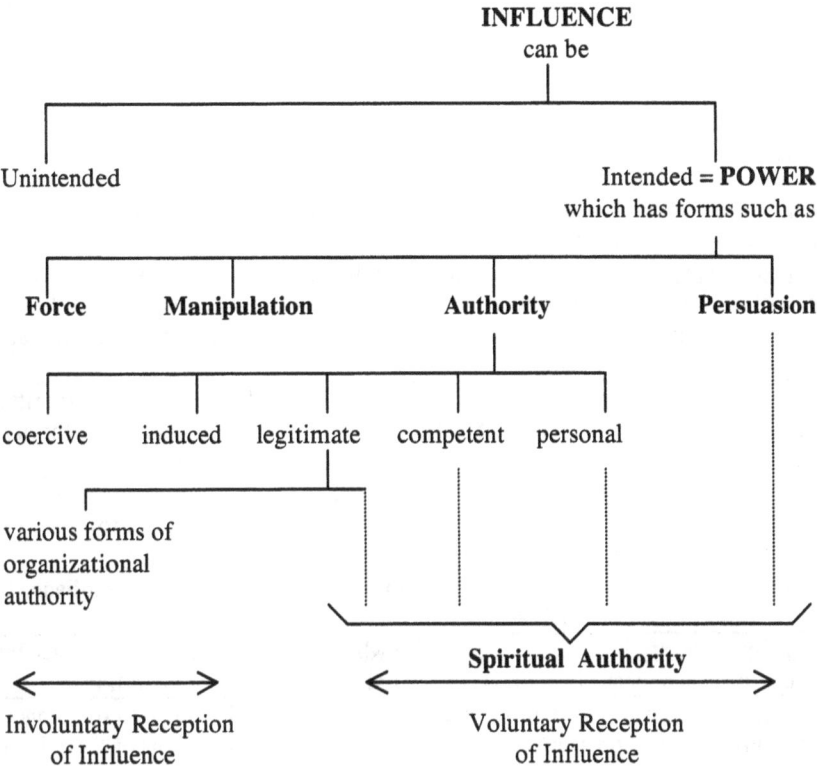

Figure Phm 4-1. Leadership Influence Components—(Adapted from Wrong)
Explanation

Leaders are people with God-given capacities and God-given responsibilities who are influencing specific groups of people toward God's purposes for them. They are intentional in their use of means to influence, meaning using deliberate power forms. When we describe such leaders we are coming down the right side of the diagram in Figure Phm 4-1. Leaders have a right to influence. The ability to influence comes through the control of power bases.

Definition — Power base refers to the source of credibility, power differential, or resources which enables a leader (*power holder*) to have authority to exercise influence on followers (*power subjects*).

Definition — Authority refers to the right to exercise leadership influence by a leader over followers with respect to some field of influence.

Power is manifested in power forms which bring about compliance. The four major power forms in our tree diagram include FORCE, MANIPULATION, AUTHORITY, AND PERSUASION. Authority is further sub-divided into coercive, induced, legitimate, competent, and personal. Spiritual authority is a hybrid combination of persuasion and legitimate, competent, and personal authority.

Power forms depend upon power bases. Bases come from power resources—those individual and collective assets such as organization, money, reputation, personal appeal, manipulative skills, interpersonal skills, kinds of knowledge, information, indwelling Holy Spirit, giftedness.

The central concept of authority is the right to exercise influence. That right is recognized both by leader and follower. It is based upon common assumptions about the *field of influence*. For a spiritual leader the *field of influence* has to do with God's purposes and His directions for accomplishing specific aims that He reveals. Morality, corporate guidance, and clarification of truth are three aspects within the *field of influence* which define the leader's range of use of authority.

Table Phm 4-1 details a number of important concepts that help clarify how a leader influences.

4. Influence Power and Authority

Table Phm 4-1. Influence, Power, Authority Concepts Defined

Influence, Power, Authority Concepts	Description
Power forms	Power forms refer to four general terms of influence means: force, manipulation, authority, and persuasion.
Force	A force power form refers to the use of physical and psychic influence means to gain compliance. This form is now rarely used by spiritual leaders though historically it has been used.
Manipulation	A manipulative power form refers to any influence means whereby a leader gains compliance of a follower where the follower does not have awareness of the leader's intents and therefore does not necessarily have freedom to exert moral responsibility in the situation.[43]
Authority	An authority power form refers to influence means such as: coercive authority, induced authority, legitimate authority, competent authority, personal authority and spiritual authority. See definitions which follow in this Table Phm 4-1.
Persuasion	A persuasive power form refers to any influence means such as arguments, appeals or exhortations whereby the leader gains compliance of the follower yet protects the freedom of the follower to exercise moral responsibility.
Coercive Authority	Coercive authority is the form of power in which a leader obtains compliance by using influence means such as threat of force or of punishment.
Induced Authority	Induced authority is the form of power in which a leader obtains compliance by using influence means of promise of reward or some gain for the follower.
Legitimate Authority	Legitimate authority is the form of power in which a leader obtains compliance by using influence pressure consonant with common expectations of the role or positions held by the follower and leader.
Competent Authority	Competent authority is the form of power in which a leader obtains or can expect (but not demand) compliance by virtue of acknowledged expertise in some field of endeavor. The authority is limited to that field of endeavor.
Personal Authority	Personal authority is the form of power in which a leader obtains or expects compliance (but can not demand it) by virtue of the follower's recognition of the leader's personal characteristics.

Machiavelli[44] posited two real ultimate motivations: fear and love. For him, fear was the stronger of the two and hence a vital part of effective leadership. Jesus advocated love as the stronger. On the power continuum, those forms to the left of inducement all utilize the motivation of fear—they are categorized by the notion of involuntary reception of influence. Those from induced authority to the right all have in essence love as the primary motivation. They are categorized by the notion of voluntary reception of influence.

Hersey and Blanchard[45] give terms which help us understand further the *competent* authority form. They use the term *expert* to indicate a person who has expertise, skill and knowledge about something so as to command respect from followers. In addition, they define *information* to indicate the leader's possession of information that is valuable to followers. Competent power includes this as well. From a Christian standpoint, giftedness—a God-given capacity—fits under competent power.

Two terms from Hersey and Blanchard help us understand further the *personal* power sub-form. *Referent* power is a type of power based on the leader's personal traits. Such a leader is usually liked and admired by others because of personality, sincerity, or the like. *Modeling* describes the Christian

---

[43] Manipulation in general usually has only negative connotations in western societies since it usually implies influencing against one's wishes. While it is true that manipulation is usually bad, it does not have to be so. The definition above is neutral. It is the motivation behind and the ultimate purpose of the influence that is the key.

[44] His views were published in the classic, **The Prince**.

[45] See Paul Hersey and Ken Blanchard, **Management of Organizational Behavior--Utilizing Human Resources.** Englewood Cliffs, N.J.: Prentice-Hall, 1977.

equivalent of this form. Follower are influenced by leaders they admire. They want to emulate them. *Connection* power refers to a type of power that arises because a leader has connections to influential or powerful people. In leadership emergence theory this is called networking power.

Leaders will need the entire range of power forms and authority forms in order to lead followers. It is helpful to know this as well as the negative and positive aspects of these forms.[46]

Understanding Spiritual Authority Via Influence, Power, and Authority Concepts

Now we can examine that major trans-Biblical lesson I stated earlier.

Effective Leaders Value Spiritual Authority As A Primary Power Base.

While it will take a whole range of power forms to accomplish God's purposes to take immature followers to maturity, it should be the goal of spiritual leaders to move people toward the right on the power continuum so that they voluntarily accept leadership and follow for mature reasons.[47] So, leaders who are concerned with developing followers should be continually using spiritual authority whenever possible. From our diagram in Figure Phm 4-1, spiritual authority is defined as a hybrid power form which includes influence via persuasion and authority, especially competent and personal. Legitimate authority frequently helps supplement spiritual authority but does not guarantee it. Notice the voluntary aspect of the spiritual authority definition.

Definition   <u>Spiritual authority</u> is the right to influence conferred upon a leader by followers because of their perception of spirituality in that leader.

An expanded clarification of this definition describes spiritual authority further as that characteristic of a God-anointed leader, which is developed upon an experiential power base that enables him/her to influence followers through:

1. Persuasion (a major power form),
2. Force of modeling (fits under the personal authority form) and
3. Moral expertise (fits under the competent authority form).

Spiritual authority comes to a leader in three major ways. As leaders go through deep experiences with God they experience the sufficiency of God to meet them in those situations. They come to know God. This *experiential knowledge of God and the deep experiences with God* are part of the experiential acquisition of spiritual authority. A second way that spiritual authority comes is through a life which *models godliness*. When the Spirit of God is transforming a life into the image of Christ, those characteristics of love, joy, peace, long suffering, gentleness, goodness, faith, meekness, temperance carry great weight in giving credibility that the leader is consistent inward and outward. Both of these sources of spiritual authority reflect themselves dominantly via the personal authority form. A third way that spiritual authority comes is through *gifted power*. When a leader can demonstrates gifted power—that is, a clear testimony to divine intervention in the ministry—there will be spiritual authority. This source of spirituality buttresses the competent authority form. While all three of these ways of getting spiritual authority should be a part of a leader, it is frequently the case that one or more of the elements dominates.

Conclusion

Some closing observations on spiritual authority are worth noting:

1. Spiritual authority is the ideal form of influence that should be used by leaders.

---

[46] See Dennis Wrong, **Power--Its Forms, Bases, and Uses**. New York: Harper and Row, 1979. He gives an excellent treatment of definitions as well as the dynamics of the forms. When certain forms are overused they tend to change to other types of forms.

[47] This is the model God uses with us as believers. He can force us to do things and sometimes does, but He always prefers for us to willingly obey.

4. Influence Power and Authority

2. Because of the responsibility of leaders, that is, they must influence—it will require more than just spiritual authority as a power base because of immature followers who cannot recognize spiritual authority.
3. Leaders must develop followers in maturity so that they can more sensitively see God's use of spiritual authority in a leader.
4. Leaders who do not develop followers in maturity will find they have to use the less ideal forms of power (coercive, inducive, legitimate) more often.
5. These forms tend to degenerate toward the left on the continuum becoming less effective over time. This in turn often drives a leader to abuse his/her authority because of the need to force influence.
6. Spiritual authority, like any of the authority forms, can be abused.
7. Mature leaders never abuse spiritual authority.
8. Spiritual authority is ideally used to build up followers and carry out God's purposes for them.
9. Leaders should treasure deep processing with God, knowing that God will use it to develop their spiritual authority.
10. Giftedness alone, even when backed by unusual power, is not a safe source of spiritual authority. Giftedness backed by godliness is the more balanced safe source of spiritual authority.

Jesus led almost totally by spiritual authority. Paul, having to deal frequently with immature believers, uses almost the whole range of authority forms. However, whenever Paul can he uses spiritual authority. Both of these models set the pattern for Christian leaders.

An awareness of what spiritual authority is and how it relates to the basic ways a leader influences forms a solid foundation upon which to move toward spiritual authority.

Effective Leaders Value Spiritual Authority As A Primary Power Base.

Do you value spiritual authority? Are you using it to influence specific groups of God's people toward His purposes for them?

See **Articles,** *20. Pauline Leadership Styles, 22. Spiritual Authority—Defined, Six Characteristics.*

Article 5

Relevance of the Article to Paul's Philemon Letter

Onesimus is faced with an integrity issue. Will he go back and face the music? His act of restitution shows that God has shaped his inner being. Paul demonstrates integrity in sending Onesimus back. He demonstrates integrity in his means of influence with Philemon. Philemon is faced with a new understanding of the Gospel and what forgiveness is all about. Can he go through the paradigm shift and experience the reality of forgiveness, especially under the social pressure he is facing about the slavery issue? Will the Gospel trait of love come through? All three leaders are dealing with character issues. Integrity is key for them and for us who would exercise leadership today.

5. Integrity—A Top Leadership Quality

Introduction

I have been repeating a number of times in the leadership commentary, for a number of books, a major leadership principle.

Ministry flows out of being.

Being is a term describing a number of factors which refer to the inner life and essence of a person. It refers to at least the following, but is not limited to them: (1) intimacy with God; (2) character; (3) personality; (4) giftedness; (5) destiny; (6) values drawn from experience; (7) conscience, and (8) gender influenced perspectives. The axiom, ministry flows out of being means that one's ministry should be a vital outflow from these inner beingness factors.

It is integrity, the rudder that steers character, that I want to highlight in this discussion. Consider the following two words:

1. deception — noun 1.The use of deceit. 2.The fact or state of being deceived. 3. A ruse; a trick. [adapted from The American Heritage Dictionary of the English Language, Third Edition, 1992.] **Synonyms**: trickery, gulling, lying, juggling, craftiness. **Antonyms**: sincerity, frankness, honesty, openness, truthfulness, trustworthiness, genuineness, earnestness, innocence, candor, veracity, verity, probity, fidelity.

2. integrity — The uncompromising adherence to a code of moral, artistic or other values which reveals itself in utter sincerity, honesty, and candor and avoids deception or artificiality (Adapted from Webster). **Synonyms**: honesty, virtue, honor, morality, uprightness, righteousness. Antonyms: deception, dishonesty, corruption, infidelity.

The words are opposite.

Few leaders finish well.[48] Most major failures in ministry are dominantly rooted in spiritual formation issues (spirituality) rather than ministerial formation and strategic formation issues.[49] Most of these failures

---

[48] Of the Biblical leaders for whom there is evidence about finishing well, about one in three finish well. Probably it is even less for contemporary leaders if anecdotal evidence means anything. What do I mean by finish well? I have identified six characteristics of finishing well from a comparative study of leaders who finished well. A given leader will not necessarily demonstrate all six but at least several. These six characteristics include the following: (1) They maintain a personal vibrant relationship with God right up to the end. (2) They maintain a learning posture and can learn from various kinds of sources—life especially. (3) They manifest godliness (especially Christ-like attitudes and behavior) in character as evidenced by the fruit of the Spirit in their lives. (4) Truth is lived out in their lives so that convictions and promises of God

can ultimately be traced to basic failures of integrity.[50] Leaders who fail often do not have integrity but instead have some sort of deception about at least some of their leadership. On the other hand, leaders who finish well, across the board are leaders of integrity.

Let me remind you of the definition of a Christian leader: A Christian leader is a person with a God-given capacity and a God-given responsibility who is influencing a specific group of God's people toward God's purposes for the group. You cannot influence a group very effectively if they don't trust you. And if you are suspected of trickery, gulling, mendacity, juggling, craftiness—they won't trust you and you won't lead them.

At the heart of any assessment of biblical qualifications for leadership lies the concept of integrity—that uncompromising adherence to a code of moral, artistic or other values which reveals itself in utter sincerity, honesty, and candor and avoids deception or artificiality. So if we want to be leaders who finish well we want to be people of integrity. What is integrity? How do we get it?

Definition   Integrity, the top leadership character quality, is the consistency of inward beliefs and convictions with outward practice. It is an honesty and wholeness of personality in which one operates with a clear conscience in dealings with self and others.

God develops integrity in leaders. It is at the heart of character. A repeated observation on leaders whom God developed and used for his purposes resulted in the following helpful definition.

Definition   An integrity check refers to the special kind of shaping activity (a character test) which God uses to evaluate heart–intent, consistency between inner convictions and outward actions, and which God uses as a foundation from which to expand the leader's capacity to influence. The word check is used in the sense of test—meaning a check or check-up.

I'll come back to this notion of an integrity check and give detailed information on it. But first think with me about Biblical leaders and the notion of integrity.

Biblical Leaders of Integrity

If I were to ask you to name the top two O.T. leaders who demonstrated integrity, who would you suggest? If I were to ask you to name the top two N.T. leaders who demonstrate integrity, who would you suggest?

My top two O.T. leaders who demonstrated integrity are Joseph and Daniel. My top two N.T. leaders who demonstrated integrity are Jesus and Paul (Barnabas is a close second behind Paul).

Both Joseph and Daniel exemplify leaders who were tested by God as to their integrity and passed with flying colors. Joseph in Gen 39 refuses to have an affair with Potiphar's wife. He sees this as wrong. In fact, he states that to do so would be sin against God. God honors this stand and later elevates Joseph to the top administrative post in Egypt (under the Pharaoh). Daniel in Da 1 is tested as to integrity with regard to eating food unacceptable to a Jew. He stands on his convictions. He too is blessed by God and becomes a high administrator under Nebuchadnezzar and eventually becomes the number one administrator under Darius. Jesus throughout his whole ministry demonstrates integrity, always showing unity between outward practice and inward conviction. (See especially the Satanic temptations in Mt 4.) Paul writes a whole

---

are seen to be real. (5) They leave behind one or more ultimate contributions. (6) They walk with a growing awareness of a sense of destiny and see some or all of it fulfilled.

[49] Spiritual formation is the shaping activity in a leader's life which is directed toward instilling godly character and developing inner life (i.e. intimacy with God, character, values drawn from experience, conscience). Strategic formation is the shaping activity in a leader's life which is directed toward having that leader reach full potential and achieve a God-given destiny. Ministerial formation is the shaping activity in a leader's life which is directed toward instilling leadership skills, leadership experience, and developing giftedness for ministry.

[50] Studies of leaders who have failed to finish well has identified six major barriers to their finishing well. These include: finances—their use and abuse; power—its abuse; inordinate pride—which leads to a downfall; sex—illicit relationships; family—critical issues; plateauing. At the very heart of most of these major barriers lies an integrity issue.

5. Integrity—A Top Leadership Quality

epistle defending his integrity. He was being accused of all kinds of deception: lying, craftiness, dishonesty, trickery. The book of 2Co reveals Paul's answers to the accusations of deception. A major Pauline leadership value emerges in 2Co.

Label	Statement of Value
Integrity and Openness	*Leaders should not be deceptive in their dealings with followers but should instead be open, honest, forthright, and frank with them.*

Paul, throughout 2Co, refutes the accusations of deception in his leadership and lays out for us many principles underlying integrity in a leader.

Paul's instruction to Timothy in 1Ti about leadership qualifications should be noted here. His qualifications for leaders includes character and conscience. Paul's list of qualifications focuses on integrity and deals mainly with character not giftedness. See his three lists[51] in 1Ti 3:1-7; 8-10; 11-13. All three lists emphasize integrity. And this integrity should be seen by those outside the church as well as those within.

Integrity Check Revisited

God uses life situations to test and build up the inner character of a leader. Integrity is one of the main qualities God shapes in a leader. The *integrity check* is a major way this happens. From comparative study (e.g. Daniel in Da 1,5; Shadrach, Meshach, and Abednego in Da 3; Joseph in Gen 39; Abraham in Gen 24; Jephthah in Jdg 11; Paul in Ac 20:22,23 and many others), a list of kinds of integrity checks can be identified. And their use by God can be suggested. Table Phm 5-1 gives the kinds of integrity checks. Table Phm 5-2 lists their uses.

Table Phm 5-1. Kinds of Integrity Check

Label	Explanation
temptation (conviction test)	An integrity check frequently is given to allow a leader to identify an inner conviction and to take a stand on it. Such a stand will deepen the conviction in the leader's life. Can a leader really take a stand on some conviction?
restitution (honesty testing)	Some integrity checks force a leader to make right things done wrong in the past, particularly those with on-going ramifications. This is particularly seen in money matters where in the past someone was defrauded. Will a leader be honest, especially about the past?
value check (ultimate value clarification)	Situations frequently force leaders to think through their beliefs about something so that they can identify explicitly a value(s). This value once identified can be evaluated. It can be used more strongly. It may be modified. It may be discarded as not really valid. Can a leader identify the underlying value in a situation?
loyalty (allegiance testing)	God must be first in a life. Frequently, other things become first in a leader's life with perhaps it not even being known by the leader. God can bring to light those things which take His rightful place in our hearts and lives. Who is really first in our lives?
Guidance (alternative testing—a better offer after Holy Spirit led	Frequently a leader is led by God to declare for a certain thing (a ministry, a choice, some option). It is clear that God has led the leader to that choice. After making the choice God may well bring an alternative which looks easier or better

---

[51] These three lists are apparently list idioms in which the initial item on the list is the main assertion and other items illustrate or clarify the primary item. If so, then the major leadership trait is integrity, a moral characteristic implying a consistency between inner and outer life. The items on the list would then illustrate in the Ephesian culture what moral character, integrity, looks like. So then these items in themselves are not necessarily universal characteristics for a leader but are indicative of what moral character and integrity look like in this culture. The obligatory item is inner integrity, moral character. Paul concludes this small section in vs 7 by returning to this important idea to reemphasize it. This is repeated in descriptions of the lesser leader lists described in vs 8-10, 11-13. Note especially vs 8 and 11. See *list idiom*, **Glossary**.

5. Integrity—A Top Leadership Quality   page 45

commitment to some course of action)	simply to test the follow-through on the original decision. Can a leader stick to God's former sure guidance when other challenging guidance comes along?
conflict against ministry vision (guidance/faith testing)	Frequently, a leader will be led into a situation and even have follower support in it. But down the line in the midst of the decision being worked out, particularly when negative ramifications arise, followers or others will oppose the situation. Conflict arises. Note that conflict is a mighty weapon in the hand of God. Usually this integrity check will enforce faith in the leader. Can a leader maintain guidance and believe God will under gird some ministry vision?
word conflict or obedience conflict (complexity testing usually in guidance)	Sometimes a leader will get a word from God or be challenged to obey God in some particular way. Usually this has to do with guidance. Conflict arises as in the previous description. Can a leader trust in his/her ability to hear from God? Or will a leader obey, even if conflict arises?

Table Phm 5-2. The Ways that God Uses Integrity Checks

Identifying Label	Why It Is Used
Follow Through	to see follow-through on a promise or vow
Deepening Burden	to insure burden for a ministry or vision
Edification	to allow confirmation of inner-character strength
Faith Builder	to build faith
Value Clarifying	to establish inner values very important to later leadership which will follow
Lordship	to teach submission
Warnings	to warn others of the seriousness of obeying God

Often the integrity check happens completely unknown to people around the leader. That is because of its inward nature. The secondary causes may be events, people, etc. They may not even know that they are sources. The primary causal source is inward through the conscience. The Holy Spirit shapes the conscience.[52]

There is a three step pattern to an integrity check which is passed positively: (1) the challenge to consistency with inner convictions, (2) the response to the challenge, and (3) the resulting expansion. Sometimes the expansion may be delayed or take place over a period of time but it can definitely be seen to stem from the integrity check. Delayed expansion is seen in Joseph's classic test with Potiphar's wife. Immediate expansion is seen in Daniel's wine test.[53]

There is also a three part pattern to an integrity check which is failed: (1) the challenge to consistency with inner convictions, (2) the response to the challenge, and (3) the remedial testing. God will frequently repeat an integrity check until a leader gets it or will take more drastic action. Instead of remedial testing there may be discipline, or setting aside from ministry, or even death.

Conclusion

Character is crucial to leadership. Integrity is the foundational trait of character in a leader. Let me summarize some observations, principles and values suggested by the importance of integrity in a leader.

a. Ministry flows out of being of which character is a major component and integrity the dominant necessary leadership trait within character.
b. Leaders without character cannot be trusted and will be followed only to the extent that they have coercive power to back up their leadership claims.

---

[52] Conscience refers to the inner sense of right or wrong which is innate in a human being but which also is modified by values imbibed from a culture. This innate sense can also be modified by the Spirit of God. See **Article**, *Paul's Use of Conscience*.
[53] See testing *patterns, positive and negative*, **Glossary**. See **Article**, *Daniel Four Positive Testing Patterns*.

5. Integrity—A Top Leadership Quality

    c. A leader must be conscious of what others think of him/her, character-wise. Integrity is universal and occurs in every culture as a notion. But it will take on cultural manifestations peculiar to a culture that demonstrate to those in the culture what integrity is.[54]

    d. A leader must seek to have a testimony respected by others (within the bounds of God's ministry assignments).[55]

    e. Even though the source of some character trial may be Satanic, a leader should use it to purge impure character traits and rest in God's overriding purposes through the testing.[56]

    f. A leader should recognize that character integrity checks will be used by God as foundational training for increased usefulness.[57]

Do the people you influence see you as deceptive or a person of integrity? Do the people outside your ministry see you as deceptive or a person of integrity? Conscience is the inner governor of character—and especially integrity. Remember Paul's challenging statement.

> **Because I believe in an ultimate accounting before God, I make every effort always to keep my conscience clear before God and man. Ac 24:16**

---

[54] For example, oath-keeping was a high value of integrity in the Hebrew O.T.

[55] Paul repeats this notion over and over in 1Ti when advising Timothy about his consulting ministry with the Ephesian church.

[56] Job shows us that behind the apparent things happening to us there may be an unseen spiritual source causing it (Satanic). But even where bad things happen, God can use them to shape character.

[57] A basic understanding of integrity checks can aid one in recognizing much earlier and giving a godly response to them. Forewarned is forearmed.

Article 6

Relevance of the Article to Paul's Philemon Letter

Paul is in the midst of isolation, a type of deep processing. He is set aside from direct ministry. Note how he is responding to this time in his life—with a sovereign mindset, a prisoner of Jesus Christ, not the Roman Empire.

6. Isolation Processing—Learning Deep Lessons From God

Introduction

Leaders get set aside from ministry. <u>Isolation</u> is the term used to describe this process. Sometimes the leader is directly set aside by God, sometimes by others, sometimes by self. Whatever the case, isolation results in deep processing in the life of a leader. More than 90% of leaders will face one or more important isolation times in their lives. Most do not negotiate these times very well. Knowing about them and what God can accomplish in them can be a great help to a leader who then faces isolation.

Defining and Describing Isolation

What is isolation?

Definition <u>Isolation processing</u> refers to the setting aside of a leader from normal ministry or leadership involvement due to involuntary causes, partially self-caused or voluntary causes for a period of time sufficient enough to cause and/or allow serious evaluation of life and ministry.

Some notable Biblical examples include Job, Joseph, Moses, Jonah, Elijah, Habakkuk, Jesus, Paul. Usually this means the leader is away from his/her natural context usually for an extended time in order to experience God in a new or deeper way. Sometimes isolation can occur in the ministry context itself.

Isolation experiences can be short—like intensive time spent away in solitude to meet God. Or it can last up to several months and occasionally more than a year. Figure Phm 6-1 describes isolation in terms of three major categories.

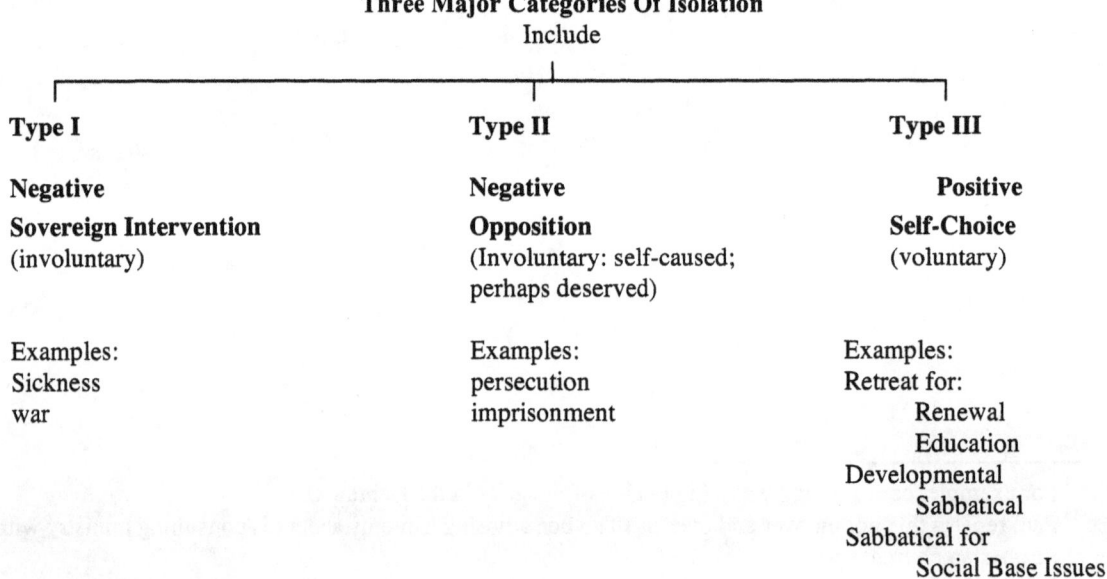

Figure Phm 6-1. Three Types of Isolation Experiences

6. Isolation Processing—Learning Deep Lessons From God

These isolation experiences can be viewed in terms of perceived intervention of God in them. Figure Phm 6-2 gives a continuum correlating the isolation experiences to a leader's understanding of God's place in them.

|───|

Clear—Divine Intervention   Less clear—Providential

TYPE I
- sickness

TYPE II
- personality conflicts
- prison
- persecution
- ministry issues

TYPE III
- self-choice renewal
- organizational issues
- self-choice development
- artificial, short intensive
- self-choice for social base

Figure Phm 6-2. Isolation Sovereignty Continuum

Table Phm 6-1 list some results that have been observed in comparative studies of leaders in isolation.

Table Phm 6-1. Isolation Results

Isolation Type	Results or Uses of Isolation
I. Negative/ Sovereign Intervention	lessons of brokenness; learning about supernatural healing; lessons about prayer; deepening of inner life; an intensified sense of urgency to accomplish; developing of mental facilities; submission to God; dependence upon God.
II. Negative/ Opposition	lessons of brokenness; submission to spiritual authority; value of other perspectives; dependence upon God
III. Positive/ Self-choice	new perspective on self and ministry; rekindling of sense of destiny; guidance; oneself to change; upon wider body of Christ

Overlapping Features in Many Isolation Experiences

Table Phm 6-2 lists some common things that happen to leaders in isolation.

Table Phm 6-2. Common Happenings in Isolation

Isolation Type	Some Happenings
I or II	1. Sense of Rejection
I or II	2. Sense of stripping away—getting down to core issues
I, II or III	3. Eventually a deep need for God
I, II or III	4. Searching for God
I, II, or III	5. Submission to God
I, II, or III	6. Dependence upon God
I, II, or III	7. Rekindling of desire to serve God in a deeper way

Bible Characters and Isolation Lessons From Their Lives

Job, Moses, Elijah, and Paul provide some important isolation lessons. See the Tables which follow listing each of these Bible Characters and observations about isolation.

6. Isolation Processing—Learning Deep Lessons From God

Job

Job faced sickness, loss of life, loss of wealth, loss of friends, and loss of status as an important person. Table Phm 6-3 suggests some things that can be learned from Job's Type I isolation experience.

Table Phm 6-3. Job and Type I Isolation

Step	Explanation
1.	**Begin With The End In Mind** (need a framework/ perspective). In isolation, deep-seated ideas are challenged in such a way as to capture our attention and force us to come to essential values. Maybe it is only in isolation that they could be challenged. But know that isolation will end and God will teach lessons even about deep-seated ideas.
2.	**Analyze From The Known To The Unknown.** Apart from unusual revelation, we can only search out answers in terms of what we know. That is, the first step in the isolation process—search out what is happening in terms of what you do know (e.g. paradigms).
3.	**Recognize That The Unknown Can Serve Two Functions.** When anomalies arise we must recognize that they may not really be anomalies and will be cleared up in the end (in which case it is a matter of faith and waiting), or they are real and will force us into new paradigms.
4.	Expect God's Intervention. **God may give insight if a new paradigm is needed or may require a faith response.**
5.	**Believe In God's On-Going Answer.** The book of Job shows us that God is in charge of our individual processing—no matter how or through whom it may come, even including Satanic origin. We do not have all the answers. He does. We must trust Him in them.

Moses

In Ex 2:11-15, there is an incident in which Moses kills an Egyptian and then flees (He 11:23-28 and Ac 7:23 give an interpretation of this). Then in Ex 3:7 and following, God calls Moses to a major task, the very one he had tried on his own and given up. There is a major difference in the Moses of Ex 2 and the Moses of Ex 3. Nu 12:3 describes it. Something happened. I want to suggest that it was a brokenness[58] experience. And that brokenness experience was part of isolation processing for Moses.

Moses experienced this Type II isolation processing. It included aspects of geographical and cultural isolation. Three characteristics of geographic and cultural isolation include: 1. It is more powerful in its early effects; wears off with time and as assimilation occurs. (This is seen also in the life of Daniel.) 2. In Geographic/ cultural isolation there is a loss of self-esteem. The things you were and value in the old culture are usually not so respected and valued in the new. 3. There is often a loss of momentum and vision.

Table Phm 6-4. Moses and Type II Isolation

Lesson	Explanation/ Generalized
1	**Look for leadership committal processing as a means toward ending isolation.** Often isolation involves and may terminate with God's renewal of call. See *progressive calling*; **Glossary**.
2	**God has to sometimes take a vision away in order to later accomplish that vision in his way.** Keep an open hand to plans, visions, future work.
3	**Humility is often the fruit of isolation processing—an unhealthy egotism is broken.** God can unleash great power through a broken/ humble leader without fear of that leader abusing the power.

---

[58] See *brokenness*, **Glossary**.

Elijah

Elijah had two impactful isolation experiences. The first was a Type I, clearly God directed. The second was a Type II. I do not think Elijah ever fully recovered from the second experience. Table Phm 6-5 gives some observations about the Type I experience. Table Phm 6-6 gives the Type II isolation experience which arose due to persecution.

Table Phm 6-5. Elijah's Type I Isolation Experience, 1Ki 17:1-6—Some Observations

Observation	Explained
1	Isolation was God-directed (vs 2,3)
2	Success brings problems (vs 7 brook dries up--he prayed for no rain)
3	God will provide in isolation (vs 4, 9, 14)
4	God protects in isolation (I Kings 18:10).

Elijah's Type II isolation experience was the fallout from one of the most successful ministry events recorded in the O. T. He has just seen God move mightily in a power encounter[59] with the prophets of Baal on top of Mount Carmel—a true mountain top experience. When he flees from persecution he moves into an isolation experience—again a mountain top experience—this time, Mount Sinai. Note that again as with the first experience, success brings with it problems.

Table Phm 6-6. Elijah's Type II Isolation Experience, 1Ki 19—Persecution—Running For His Life

Observation	Explained

1. The Situation	Vs4 Desert Isolation—
	    1. Hope gone; despair; take my life, (vs 4,5)
	    2. Angel touches him--provision (vs 5,7)
	    3. Horeb--Mountain of God--40 days/ 40 nights); cave
	 What are you doing? God shows up.

2. Notice the Steps	Step 1. The feelings: I alone/ stood up for God/ persecution Step 2. Presence of God—the antidote to the feelings. Step 3. God answers--not you alone (vs11), 7000 who have not bowed the knee
3. The Price To Pay	Power encounters can be costly—they drain away energy—After mountain-top experiences expect attacks from Satan, evil forces; you may well crash hard in the valley. Elijah never again has a major ministry success?
4. Rejection/ God's Affirmation	In isolation there is a sense of personal rejection and a need for divine affirmation. Notice how God does this. **Small Still Voice.** Not the spectacular like you might expect or hope for.
5. Leadership Selection	Elijah imparted power and authority to Elisha—one who was faithful, tenacious, wanted what Elijah had. He carried on Elijah's ministry with more power than Elijah. Elijah's isolation experiences brought spiritual authority. Emerging leaders are drawn to leaders with spiritual authority.

One of the most important things to see from Elijah's isolation experiences is that isolation is frequently accompanied by a sense of personal rejection. It is divine affirmation that we need. God will meet us—maybe not in the way we expect.

---

[59] This is the classic power encounter which defines others. The steps of a *Power Encounter* include:
1. There is a confrontation between God and Evil. 2. The forces are recognized for that—the issues are who is more powerful and thus deserving of allegiance. 3. There is a public demonstration so that both forces can be seen by all as to who is more powerful. 4. God demonstrates publicly His power and defeats the evil forces so that there can be no doubt about to whom allegiance should be given. 5. Aftermath—God is glorified, evil forces are punished; there may be a response toward God. See *power encounter*, **Glossary**.

6. Isolation Processing—Learning Deep Lessons From God

Paul

Paul had numerous isolation experiences. It is from his life that the concept of repeated isolation experiences occurring in a leader's life emerged. Five are worth noting—1) his short days in Damascus with Ananias, Ac 9; 2; 2) His 2 to 3 years in Arabia mentioned in Gal; 3) His short prison experience in Philippi seen in Ac 16:23; 4) His four years in Rome (during which Eph, Col, Phm, Php were written); 5) His short few months in Rome just before his death. Table Phm 6-7 suggests nine observations drawn from a comparative study of Paul's isolation experiences.

Table Phm 6-7. Nine Observations from Paul's Isolation Experiences

Isolation Experience	Description and Observations
Galatian Isolation **1. Reflection**	Paul's Galatian/Arabia—Pre-Ministry isolation was a Type III self-choice isolation. It was a time of Reflection in which he worked out his Christology. Basic Principle: **Reflection is a major goal and means of processing during isolation.** Reflection will happen in isolation. Depending on the kind of isolation there will be questions. A seeking after something—time for thinking. (2Ti is especially filled with reflection; a looking back on a lifetime given to the Gospel.)

2. Prison Isolation; Response Attitude	A. In general, the following principle makes the difference in whether the isolation is profitable or not.
	    A sovereign mindset in processing makes the difference in
	    immediate response and in long lasting results.
	Attitude is everything. Notice Paul's attitude as reflected in: Eph 3:1; 4:1; Col 4:3,9,10; Phm 1; Php 1:12; 4:22. Paul saw a God-ordained purpose behind isolation. What does it mean to have a *sovereign mindset* in processing? It means to recognize that however the isolation may have come about—unjust determination, terrible circumstances, or whatever—you must recognize that God has an ultimate purposes in it: 1) to demonstrate the sufficiency of the supply of the Spirit of Christ, 2) to do specific things fitting the immediate situation, 3) to open up new thinking that could not have been possible, 4) to bring long-range productivity out of it (spiritual authority).

3. Intense Focus	**Critical issues come into focus during isolation processing.** Isolation forces one to focus usually first on why, causes of it, and then later on the purposes of it. And finally with a powerful concentration that allows for problem solving, new revelation to meet situations, and insights that could only come because of the situation.
4. Evaluation— Divine Perspective	**Divine evaluation of character, leadership commitment, and perspective is in focus in isolation processing.** Frequently, what happens is a recognition that God is allowing you to search your life and ministry and evaluate it in light of the situation and often with resulting paradigm shifts that will affect your ministry philosophy and the rest of your life.
5. Deepened Relationship	**A deepened relationship with God is always a major goal of isolation processing.** Philippians, the last of the first set of prison epistles and the most positive upbeat of all of Paul's letter culminates four years of isolation which have been filled with crises. It is filled with the importance of union with Christ. Its message points out what can happen in isolation processing—a grasping of the sufficiency of Christ for life.
6. Basis for Long Range Productivity	**Long lasting productivity is often rooted in isolation processing.** The prison epistles may never have been written had Paul been on the go. But set aside, reflection time produced thinking in regard to his own personal sanctification intimacy with Christians (Php), church problems (Col), the nature of the church (Eph), the solving of a problematic social institution (Phm). But not just products, attitudes and ideas are born in isolation, which may come to fruition down road. 1. Specific things—people touched, saved, advise given, etc. 2. Modeling—an intangible product 3. written achievements—one tangible product of isolation.
7. The importance of praise	**Praise is a major weapon in isolation processing.** In external isolation you probably feel less like praising than almost anything else, yet it is at that juncture that praise is probably the most important faith challenge. See Php jail

6. Isolation Processing—Learning Deep Lessons From God

	experience, Ac 16, and the tone of praise in all the prison epistles—most of the opening prayers carry that note of praise. Praise will release power, new perspective in isolation.
8. Short Isolation	**Life changing and ministry changing revelation may come even in a short isolation experience.** Moses, 40 days of isolation by self-choice (divine drawing); Paul in two different times (Ac 9, Ananias, Ac 16 Philippian jail experience)
9. Intensified Prayer	**Isolation processing often presses a person into intensified prayer burdens and efforts.**

Let me summarize what we can see in Paul's isolation experiences. Such experiences will tell a leader whether or not that leader has a *sovereign mindset*. They will also force reflection and evaluation of one's self in relation to: God, truth, a ministry, the past, the future. Critical issues come into focus. Peripheral issues are seen for what they are. In normal times we worry about a lot of things—many peripheral and non-essential. But in isolation times we get down to basic issues: who we are, what we really know, where we are going, who God really is, what He wants from us, etc. A leader will deepen his/her relationship with God—because that is what really matters—more than our ministry, more than the problems around us. A leader may discover the importance of praise or see an intensified outpouring of prayer, or the roots for long range productivity in our lives.

Knowing these things, so what? How can observing these principles in the life of Paul help us as we life schedule or as we work through a present isolation experience? How can we be proactive? Here are some suggestions:

1. **Reflection**—If you are not a thinker or if you are a thinker but are confused in isolation, because you know that reflection is important, you should get with someone in the body of Christ who has either natural abilities of analytical skills, discernment, or spiritual gifts of exhortation, teaching, word of wisdom, word of knowledge and ask for help on getting an overall perspective on what the intent of God is in the isolation. In terms of mentor types, you need to get with a spiritual guide or mentor counselor.

2. **Response Attitude**—Acknowledge that God is in this isolation. By faith accept this and then move with a learning posture through it. I am going to learn great things from God. Others may be to blame but God is in it.

3. **Intense Focus**—Recognize that critical issues will be pointed out in the isolation processing.

4. **Divine Perspective Evaluation**—Do self-evaluation of your life and ministry. Some suggestions as to how to do this: Be alert to values. Expect new revelation. Know that paradigm shifts often occur in isolation.

5. **Deepened Relationship**—Spend time in intimacy disciplines with God; extended times of silence, solitude, prayer, Bible study, fasting.

Conclusion

Here are some final warnings and assurances about isolation.

1. **Expect it.** About 90% of leaders go through an isolation experience of Type I or II.
2. **Recognize that there will be a sense of rejection in it.** Because of this it is helpful to keep a log of your *divine affirmation* and *ministry affirmation* items (see *affirmation*, **Glossary**). Review them alone with God and feel anew His acceptance.
3. **Determine beforehand to go deep with God.** He will take you into a place of more dependence, perhaps a place of intimacy that you could not have without this kind of processing.
4. **Know that God will indeed meet you in isolation** though at first He may appear remote. Do not try to move out of isolation on your own until God has met you. Otherwise, you may go through a repeated isolation experience.

6. Isolation Processing—Learning Deep Lessons From God

5. **Know the uses of isolation** and seek to see and sense which of these God is working into your life.
6. For a Type III isolation experience **set goals** for personal growth that include dependence, intimacy, and a deeper walk with God.
7. **Talk to other Christians who have gone through deep processing**. They will give you perspective with a proper empathy.

As a leader you will face isolation. Will you meet God in it and see His purposes in it fulfilled? Remember, isolation processing comes to almost all leaders. Expect repeated isolation processing. It is needed throughout a lifetime. Don't forget, attitude is crucial. Perspective can make the difference—knowing what isolation does, that it does end, that it will accomplish many important things. If you sense you are plateauing then self-initiate an extended time of isolation—get help from mentor counselors and mentor spiritual guides.

Article 7

Relevance of the Article to Paul's Philemon Letter

This entire little book is a leadership act. Paul, the leader, is trying to influence Philemon, the follower, to receive back Onesimus, a run away slave. He uses three major leadership styles—that is, influence means—to influence Philemon to respond and receive back Onesimus. Those three leadership styles include: *father-initiator*, *maturity appeal*, and *obligation persuasion*. And he does so in a powerful way, using spiritual authority as his dominant power base.

7. Leadership Act

Leadership Act Defined

Of the seven leadership genre[60] in the Bible, sources from which we can draw leadership insights to inform our own leadership, the three most common are biographical, books as a whole, and leadership acts. There are numerous leadership acts in the O.T. and quite a few in the N.T.

Definition   A <u>leadership act</u> is the specific instance at a given point in time of the leadership influence process between a given influencer (person said to be influencing) and follower(s) (person or persons being influenced) in which the followers are influenced toward some goal.

Examples of leadership acts include: Barnabas in Acts 9:26-30; Barnabas in Acts 11:22-24; Barnabas in Acts 11:25-26; Agabus in Acts 11:27-28; leaders and whole church in Acts 11:29-30; Paul, Barnabas, apostles, Peter, James and elders in Jerusalem, in Acts 15:1-21; almost all of the Pauline epistles.

How To Study A Leadership Act—Seven Steps

A leadership act is a vignette, usually some historical narrative, which contains a leader or leaders, followers, and some situation, which demands leadership. The narrative gives enough information for one to analyze what the leader did and how he/she did it. Usually there are indications of leadership styles used, power bases used, problems being faced, solved or not, etc. Leadership lessons are very readily derived. The three major overarching leadership components—leadership basal elements, leadership influence means, and leadership value bases—provide categories which can be used to screen the data for ideas.

Table Phm 7-1. How To Study a Leadership Act

Step	Procedure
1	Study the passage using normal hermeneutics to get the meaning of the passage in terms of its use in the chapter, section, or book.
2	Describe the macro context and local context in order to understand the situation. See if you can identify the reason why the act is included.
3	Use the 3 Major components of leadership to help stimulate your thinking: (1) leadership basal elements: leader, follower, situation; (2) leadership influence means both individual leadership styles and corporate leadership styles; (3) leadership value bases: underlying cultural or theological values in view). Describe what you see using those as stimulants for discovery. Look

---

[60] See **Article**, *9. Leadership Genre—Seven Types*. Genre refers to a category. Hence seven *Leadership Genre* means seven types of categories of leadership information in the Bible: biographical, leadership acts, books as a whole, macros lessons, indirect contexts, direct contexts, parabolic.

7. Leadership Act

	for God's shaping activities in the life of individual leaders or groups as a whole. See if any of the followership laws are present or absent and if so are significant. Describe the macro context and local context in order to understand the situation. See if you can identify the reason why the act is included.
4	Are there leadership values that are in view? What other lessons are suggested in the act?
5	At this point summarize in the form of principles. Try to raise the level of specific principles for wider application.
6	For each statement of truth, determine where on the leadership truth continuum it is located.
7	Comment on the broader application of your findings.

Most of Paul's letters are in themselves major leadership acts. This is much easier to see in the smaller ones like Phm and Php. Books like Phm and Php serve as more than one leadership genre. For example consider Php: 1. It has *biographical information* on at least six different leaders; 2. Php can be studied as *The Book As A Whole* genre for leadership insights. 3. Philippians is also a *major leadership act* for which you can analyze leader, follower, situation as well as influence means (Pauline leadership styles). 4. It also validates a number of macro lessons, notably, the *prayer macro lesson* that originated in the O.T.

In summary, a leadership act occurs when a given person influences a group in terms of behavioral acts or perception, so that the group acts or thinks differently as a group than before the instance of influence. Such an act can be evaluated in terms of the three major leadership categories: 1) leadership basal elements, 2) leadership influence means and 3) leadership value bases. It should be noted that any given act of leadership may have several persons of the group involved in bringing about the influence. While the process may be complex and difficult to assess, leadership can be seen to happen and be composed essentially of influencer, group, influence means, and resulting change of direction by the group.

End Results of A Study—Example From Joshua's Ministry

The end result of the study of a leadership act is a set of observations, principles, lessons, guidelines, values, or absolutes. For example, the leadership act of Joshua's leading the people to cross the Jordan is full of leadership observations, lessons, and principles. Consider the following:

Table Phm 7-2. Lessons/ Principles Drawn from Joshua 3,4—Crossing the Jordan

Lesson Number	Statement of Lesson
1	Spiritual authority, though conferred by people, is in the ultimate sense given (delegated) by God.
2	In leadership transition of a high level leader, the spiritual authority of the new leader must be established early.
3	In a God-directed leadership transition, the leader can expect a spiritual authority experience which will probably involve a faith challenge or conflict or crisis or isolation experience.
4	Memorials of spiritual benchmarks are important to leadership to serve as reminders of God's deliverance and to engender a faith-filled awe in the leader.
5	Leaders and followers should seek to deliberately set up "stones of remembrance" to commemorate spiritual benchmarks so as to counter tendencies to forget God's mighty power and build expectancies for the future.
6	Great faith challenges will be accompanied by great moments of divine affirmation.
7	A profound sense f God's presence revolutionizes a leader's attitude toward all of his/her leadership.
8	Leaders need a personal inward affirmation from God as well as external affirmation.
9	A Fourfold Pattern of Affirmation for a Major Faith Challenge involves the following four items: (1) A revelation of the Lord. (2) A realization that it is the Lord who will fight for us. (3) Submissive worship of the Lord. (4) M.1 Pattern—rapid response, rapid development.

7. Leadership Act

These observations will range along the leadership truth continuum all the way from suggestions on the left on to guidelines in the middle and perhaps one or two to the far right as absolutes.

Leadership acts provide an excellent source of leadership principles, if you have eyes to see the implications for leadership insights contained within them.

See **Articles** 9. *Leadership Genre—7 Types;* ***Followership—10 Commandments***, *11. Macro Lessons—Defined; 10. Leadership Tree Diagram;* ***Principles of Truth.***

Article 8

Relevance of the Article to Paul's Philemon Letter
The book of Philemon occurs toward the end of Paul's life. This is the sixth leadership era, the church leadership era. The Gospel is spreading. Its influence is reaching out to Asia minor. Its impact upon evil social institutions are being felt, as seen in this little letter. The Gospel's power to change lives is seen in this little epistle, which shows how the church must apply the Gospel to its situation.

8. Leadership Eras in the Bible—Six Identified

Introduction to the Six Leadership Eras
A <u>Bible Centered leader</u> refers to a leader whose leadership is informed by the Bible, who has been personally shaped by Biblical values, has grasped the intent of Scriptural books and their content in such a way as to apply them to current situations and who uses the Bible in ministry so as to impact followers. Notice that first concept again—

whose leadership is informed by the Bible.

Two of the most helpful perspectives for becoming a Bible centered leader **whose leadership is informed by the Bible** include:

(1) recognizing the differences in leadership demands on leaders throughout the Bible, i.e. seeing the different leadership eras, and
(2) Recognizing and knowing how to draw out insights from the seven genre of leadership sources in the Bible.

This article overviews the first of these helpful perspective—seeing the leadership eras in the Bible.

The Six Leadership Eras
Let me start by giving you one of the most helpful perspectives, a first step toward getting leadership eyes, for recognizing leadership findings in the Bible. That first helpful perspective involves breaking down the leadership that takes place in the Bible into leadership eras, which on the whole share common leadership assumptions and expectations for the time period. These assumptions and expectations differ from one leadership era to the next, though there are commonalties that bridge across the eras.

Definition	A <u>leadership era</u> is a period of time, usually several hundred years long, in which the major focus of leadership, the influence means, basic leadership functions, and followership have much in common and which basically change with time periods before or after it.

An outline of the six eras I have iden ified follows.

    I.   **Patriarchal Era (Leadership Roots)—Family Base**

    II.   **Pre-Kingdom Leadership Era—Tribal Base**
            A. The Desert Years
            B. The War Years--Conquering the Land,
            C. The Tribal Years/ Chaotic Years/ Decentralized Years--Conquered by the Land

8. Leadership Eras In The Bible, Six Identified

III. Kingdom Leadership Era—Nation Based
   A. The United Kingdom
   B. The Divided Kingdom
   C. The Single Kingdom--Southern Kingdom Only

IV. Post-Kingdom Leadership Era—Individual/ Remnant Based
   A. Exile--Individual Leadership Out of the Land
   B. Post Exilic--Leadership Back in the Land
   C. Interim--Between Testaments

V. New Testament Pre-Church Leadership—Spiritually Based in the Land
   A. Pre-Messianic
   B. Messianic

VI. New Testament Church Leadership—Decentralized Spiritually Based
   A. Jewish Era
   B. Gentile Era

I have used the following tree diagram[61] to provide an overview of leadership. The three overarching components of leadership include: the leadership basal elements (leader, follower, situation which make up the *What* of leadership); leadership influence means (individual and corporate leadership styles which make up the *How* of leadership); and leadership Value bases (Biblical and cultural values which make up the *Why* of leadership).

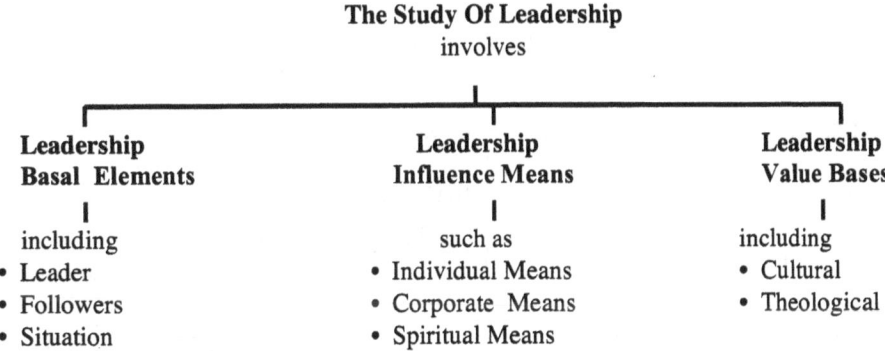

Figure Phm 8-1. Tree Diagram Categorizing the Basics of Leadership

It was this taxonomy which suggested questions that helped me see for the first time the six leadership eras of the Bible. Table Phm 8-1 below gives the basic questions/subjects/categories that helped me identify the different leadership eras. It is these categories that allows comparison of different leadership periods in the Bible.

---

[61] This was derived in a research project, the historical study of leadership in the United States from the mid 18th century to the present—for further study see **A Short History of Leadership Theory**, 1986, by Dr. J. Robert Clinton. Altadena, CA: Barnabas Publishers. See **Further Study Bibliography**.

8. Leadership Eras In The Bible, Six Identified

Table Phm 8-1. Basic Questions To Ask About Leadership Eras

1. **Major Focus**—Here we are looking at the overall purposes of leadership for the period in question. What was God doing or attempting to do through the leader? Sense of destiny? Leadership mandate?
2. **Influence means**—Here we are describing any of the power means available and used by the leaders in their leadership. We can use any of Wrong's categories or any of the leadership style categories I define. Note particularly in the Old Testament the use of force and manipulation as power means.
3. **Basic leadership functions**—We list here the various achievement/ responsibilities expected of the leaders: from God's standpoint, from the leader's own perception of leadership, from the followers. Usually they can all be categorized under the three major leadership functions of task, relational, and inspirational functions. But here we are after the specific functions.
4. **Followers**—Here we are after sphere of influence. Who are the followers? What are their relationship to leaders? Which of the 10 Commandments of followership are valid for these followers? What other things are helpful in describing followers?
5. **Local Leadership**—in the surrounding culture: Biblical leaders will be very much like the leaders in the cultures around them. Leadership styles will flow out of this cultural press. Here we are trying to identify leadership roles in the cultures in contact with our Biblical leaders.
6. **Other**—Miscellaneous catch all: such things as centralization or decentralization or hierarchical systems of leadership; joint (civil, political, military, religious) or separate roles.
Thought Questions—Here try to synthesize the questions you would like answered about leaders and leadership if you could get those answers. We are dealing here with such things as the essence of a leader (being or doing), leadership itself, leadership selection and training, authority (centralized or decentralized), etc.

Using these leadership characteristics I studied leadership across the Bible and inductively generated the Six Leadership Eras as given above. Table Phm 8-2 adds some descriptive elements of the eras.

Table Phm 8-2. Six Leadership Eras in the Bible—Brief Characterizations

Leadership Era	Example(s) of Leader	Definitive Characteristics
1. Foundational (also called patriarchal)	Abraham, Joseph	Family Leadership/ formally male dominated/ expanding into tribes and clans as families grew/ moves along kin ship lines
2. Pre-Kingdom	Moses, Joshua, Judges	Tribal Leadership/ Moving to National/ Military/ Spiritual Authority/ outside the land moving toward a centralized national leadership
3. Kingdom	David, Hezekiah	National Leadership/ Kingdom Structure/ Civil, Military/ Spiritual/ a national leadership—Prophetic call for renewal/ inside the land/ breakup of nation
4. Post-Kingdom	Ezekiel, Daniel, Ezra	Individual leadership/ Modeling/ Spiritual Authority
5. Pre-Church	Jesus/ Disciples	Selection/ Training/ Spiritual Leadership/ Preparation for Decentralization of Spiritual Authority/ Initiation of a Movement/
6. Church	Peter/ Paul/ John	Decentralized leadership/ Cross-cultural Structures led by Leaders with Spiritual Authority which institutionalize the movement and spread it around the world.

8. Leadership Eras In The Bible, Six Identified

When we study a leader or a particular leadership issue in the Scriptures we must always do so in light of the leadership context in which it was taking place. We cannot judge past leadership by our present leadership standards. Conversely, we will find that major leadership lessons learned by these leaders will usually have broad implications for our leadership.

See **Articles**: *9. Leadership Genre—7 Types; 11. Macro Lessons—Defined; 12. Macro Lessons —List of 41 Across Six Leadership Eras.*

Article 9

Relevance of the Article to Paul's Philemon Letter

The book of Philemon illustrates four of the basic leadership genres, two directly—a leadership act and book as a whole (7 leadership topics are discussed)—and two rather indirectly: biographical (shaping activity in three leaders' lives—Paul, Onesimus, and Philemon); macro lessons—especially the complexity macro lesson.

9. Leadership Genre—Seven Types

Introduction to the Seven Leadership Genre

A Bible Centered leader refers to a leader whose leadership is informed by the Bible, who has been personally shaped by Biblical values, has grasped the intent of Scriptural books and their content in such a way as to apply them to current situations and who uses the Bible in ministry so as to impact followers. Notice that first concept again—

whose leadership is informed by the Bible.

Two of the most helpful perspectives for becoming a Bible centered **leader whose leadership is informed by the Bible** include:

(1) recognizing the differences in leadership demands on leaders throughout the Bible, i.e. seeing the different leadership eras, and
(2) Recognizing and knowing how to draw out insights from the seven genre of leadership sources in the Bible.

This article overviews the second of these helpful perspectives—the seven leadership genres and how to get leadership information from them.

The Seven Genre—Derived From Study Across Six Leadership Eras

In a related treatment (see **Article**, *8. Six Leadership Eras in the Bible*) I identified six periods of time, each of which characterized a major leadership era in the Bible. See Table Phm 9-1 below.

Table Phm 9-1. Six Leadership Eras in the Bible

Era	Name	Central Feature
I.	O.T. Patriarchal Era (Leadership Roots)	Family Base
II.	O.T. Pre-Kingdom Leadership Era	Tribal Base
III.	O.T. Kingdom Leadership Era	Nation Based
IV.	O.T. Post-Kingdom Leadership Era	Individual/ Remnant Based
V.	N.T. Pre-Church Leadership	Spiritually Based in the Land
VI.	N.T. Church Leadership	Decentralized Spiritually Based

Further study of each of these leadership eras resulted in the identification of seven leadership genre which served as sources for leadership findings. I then worked out in detail approaches for studying each of these genre.[62] These seven leadership genre are shown in Table Phm 9-2.

---

[62] These detailed approaches are given in my manual, **Leadership Perspectives—How To Study The Bible for Leadership Insights** and my manual **Having a Ministry That Lasts—By Becoming a Bible Centered Leader.**

Table Phm 9-2. Seven Leadership Genre—Sources for Leadership Findings

Type	General Description/ Example	Approach
1. Biographical	Information about leaders; this is the single largest genre giving leadership information in the Bible/ Joseph.	Use biographical analysis based on leadership emergence theory concepts. See **Article**, *Biographical Studies in the Bible— How To Do.*
2. Direct Leadership Contexts	Blocks of Scripture which are giving information directly applicable to leaders/ leadership; relatively few of these in Scripture/ 1 Peter 5:1-4.	Use standard exegetical techniques. Note the passages in 1, 2Ti and Tit which deal with leadership. These three books have more direct contexts dealing with leadership than any other books in the Bible. See my running commentary, overviews and leadership insights sections for these books.
3. Leadership Acts	Mostly narrative vignettes describing a leader influencing followers usually in some crisis situation; /Acts 15	Use three fold leadership tree diagram as basic source for suggesting what areas of leadership to look for. See Figure Phm 10-1 in **Article** *10. Leadership Tree Diagram* for categories helpful for analyzing.
4. Parabolic Passages	Parables focusing on leadership perspectives: e.g. stewardship parables, futuristic parables; quite a few of these in Matthew and Luke./ Luke 19 The Pounds	Use standard parable exegetical techniques but then use leadership perspectives to draw out applicational findings; especially recognize the leadership intent of Jesus in giving these. Most such parables were given with a view to training disciples.
5. Books as a Whole	Each book in the Bible; end result of this is a list of leadership observations or lessons or implications for leadership/ Deuteronomy	Consider each of the Bible books in terms of the leadership era in which they occur and for what they contribute to leadership findings; will have to use whatever other leadership genre source occurs in a given book; also use overall synthesis thinking. I have done this in the Leadership Bible Commentary in the Leadership Insights Section for each of the 8 top leadership books of the Bible. I also have done this for each book of the Bible in another manual, **The Bible and Leadership Values**.
6. Indirect Passages	Passages in the Scripture dealing with Biblical values applicable to all; more so to leaders who must model Biblical values/ Proverbs; Sermon on the Mount	Use standard exegetical procedures for the type of Scripture containing the applicable Biblical ethical findings or values
7. Macro Lessons	Generalized high level leadership observations seen in an era and which have potential for leadership absolutes/ Presence Macro	Use synthesis techniques utilizing various leadership perspectives to stimulate observations. I have made a start on this. See **Articles**, *11. Macro Lessons Defined; 12. List of 41 Macro Lessons.*

A major step in becoming informed about leadership in the Bible is to recognize the various kinds of leadership information sources, the seven genre described above. But the more important step is to start studying these sources for leadership observations, principles, guidelines, macro lessons, and absolutes.

See **Articles**, *11. Macro Lessons Defined; 12. List of 41 Macro Lessons Across Six Leadership Eras; Bible Centered Leader.*

Article 10

Relevance of the Article to Paul's Philemon Letter

All three categories of the leadership tree diagram are vividly represented in this small book of Philemon. It is a leadership act in which the basal elements of leader, follower, and situation are front and center. Three leadership styles illustrate the second category of leadership influence means and the clash between a cultural value of slavery as a legitimate institution and a theological value involving forgiveness are highlighted. The contextualization of the Gospel into this situation shows the importance of this third category dealing with theological and cultural values.

10. Leadership Tree Diagram

The leadership tree diagram was developed from a survey of leadership history from the mid 1800s to the present. From the five leadership eras,[63] basic concepts of this tree diagram were integrated into an overall framework for evaluating leadership in any culture, including the various cultures in the Bible. Figure Phm 10-1 below gives the tree diagram. Table Phm 10-1 shows when each component was identified in terms of leadership history. Then Table Phm 10-2 gives a brief description of each of the components of this tree diagram. This diagram proved especially helpful when analyzing the six Biblical leadership eras.[64] It continues to prove fruitful when analyzing leadership acts and other leadership genre in the Bible.

The Three Categories of A High Level Leadership Framework

Three categories are involved in a high level leadership framework. The first, The *Leadership Basal Elements*, deals primarily with the *What of Leadership*. The second, The *Leadership Influence Means* categorizes the *How of Leadership*. The final element, *Leadership Value Bases*, pinpoints the *Why of Leadership*. These three cross-cultural leadership components can be used to comparatively describe leadership anywhere in the world.

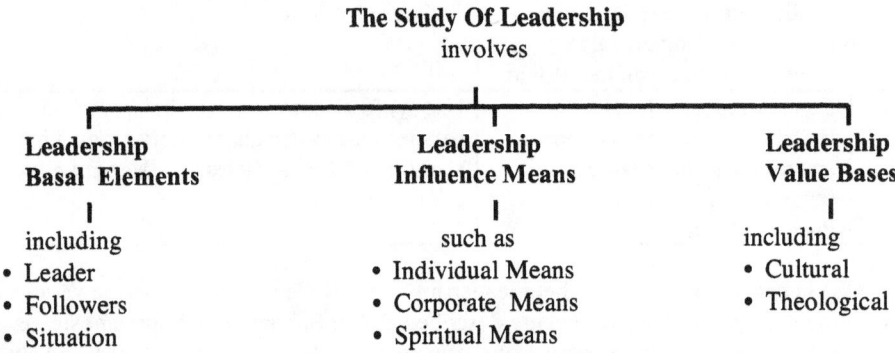

Figure Phm 10-1. Graphic Display of Three High Level Generic Leadership Components

---

[63] Five periods are identified: Phase I. Great Man Era—1841–1904; Phase II. Trait Era—1904–1948; Phase IV. Contingency Era—1967–1980; Phase V. Complexity Era—1980–present. Each of these eras contributed to the basic elements seen in the tree diagram framework.

[64] The six Biblical leadership eras include: I. The Patriarchal Era; II. The Pre-Kingdom Era; The Kingdom Era; The Post-Kingdom Era; The Pre-Church Era; The Church Era.

10. Leadership Tree Diagram

Table Phm 10-1. When Each Component Was In Focus in Leadership Eras

Era	Element in Focus	Explanation
Phase I. Great Man Era—1841–1904	Leaders	Great Man Theory dominated. Great leaders were studied to see what could be learned about leadership. Was leadership innately a genetic thing (leaders are born)? Do they make things happen? Or do the opportunities allow one to rise to the occasion (leaders are made)?
Phase II. Trait Era—1904–1948	Leaders/ Followers	Trait Theory Dominated. Could traits of great leaders be identified at the beginning stages of development of potential leaders.
Phase III. Behavior Era—1948–1967	Individual Influence Means/	Trait theory having been debunked, theorist went on to study what leaders did and how they influenced followers. Leadership style theory emerged.
Phase IV. Contingency Era—1967–1980	Corporate means	Organizational systems begin to be studied and their impact on influence. Cross-cultural studies recognized that in other cultures corporate groups influence as much or more than individuals.
Phase V. Complexity Era—1980–present	Spiritual influence means/ cultural values/ theological values/	No one leadership theory dominates because leadership is now recognized as a very complex thing. There are numerous complex theories being studied. Motivational theory emerged. How do people influence? Christian studies looked at spiritual authority. What are the underlying theological frameworks, or cultural frameworks influence why leaders lead like they lead? Value theory began to emerge. What are the underlying concepts of one's leadership?

Table Phm 10-2. Elements of the Tree Diagram Described

Element	Description
Leadership Basal Elements	The fundamental elements of leadership anywhere are leaders, followers, situations. What leaders, followers, and situations are in different cultures will vary. Expectations will determine much. Situations will determine much. But whatever the manifestation, these three elements can be studied in all cultures.
a. leaders	All cultures recognize the right/authority of some to dominantly influence others. How they recognize, why they recognize, and how they influence others differs markedly but all cultures have leaders. They can be studied and their development analyzed.
b. followers	All cultures recognize that most people will be influenced by leaders. Those being influenced are followers. Various factors determine who followers are. Followers can be studied and the dynamics between followers and leaders can be studied. These will vary markedly in different cultures, but all cultures have dynamics underlying interplay between followers and leaders.
c. situations	Situations affect leaders, followers and the dynamics between them. The major reason trait theory was debunked was that traits of leaders varied with situations. Situations are fluid and dynamic and can even force changes in expectations on leaders and followers.
Leadership Influence Means	In every culture groups are influenced by others. Some cultures are more individualized than others and so individual influence means takes on importance. Some cultures require more conformity to group thinking. Corporate influence means carries more weight in such cultures. Spiritual influencers occur in all cultures. How they influence differs but they exist.
a. individual influence means	Individuals use leadership styles to influence followers. Leadership styles vary greatly between cultures. These can be studied.
b. corporate influence means	How groups influence, whether in formal organizations, or in cultures, can be studied. Coming to the front now is systemic theory which sees interplay between all kinds of organizational elements which exert sometimes hidden influence.

10. Leadership Tree Diagram

c. spiritual influence means	Spiritual leaders can influence by manipulating the spirit world power. Spiritual leaders can exert great influence because of perceived moral standards or competency or giftedness.
Leadership Value Bases	All cultures have underlying values, which undergird their practices. Some are explicit. Others are highly implicit.
a. cultural value bases	Most leaders dominantly are influenced by cultural values of what leaders are to be and do and how they do it.
b. theological value bases	There is a growing concern, especially among Christian leaders, that biblical leadership values ought to inform and influence Christian leaders and leadership.

Conclusion

The strength of this framework for identifying, studying, and assessing leadership is fourfold:

1. It is a framework that developed from synthesizing the best of leadership theoretical studies for the past 150 years. There is a long-term perspective involved.
2. It is an integrated framework manifesting the **what**, **how**, and **why** of leadership.
3. Its categories are generically broad enough to **guide analysis** in any culture **but allow for major differences** in what the manifestations may be.
4. Any theoretical leadership studies done today can be properly evaluated in terms of what they focus on and what they leave out.

Its basic weakness is that it is a static framework. In real life all of these elements are interacting with each other and modifying each other constantly. There is feedback and feedforward between these elements. The framework is changing constantly in terms of what is in focus and what is being defined.

However, the tree diagram depicts leadership issues that must be considered when studying leadership or training leaders.

Article 11

Relevance of the Article to Paul's Philemon Letter
The book of Philemon, in a low-key manner, illustrates several macro lessons: intercession, timing, shaping, and complexity macros. All of these macro lessons are seen throughout all 6 leadership eras.

11. Macro-Lessons—Defined

Macro Lessons inform our leadership with potential leadership values that move toward the absolute. We live in a time when most do not believe there are absolutes. In my study of leadership in the Bible, I have defined a leadership truth continuum, which recognizes the difficulty in deriving absolutes but does allow for them.[65] Figure Phm 11-1 depicts this.

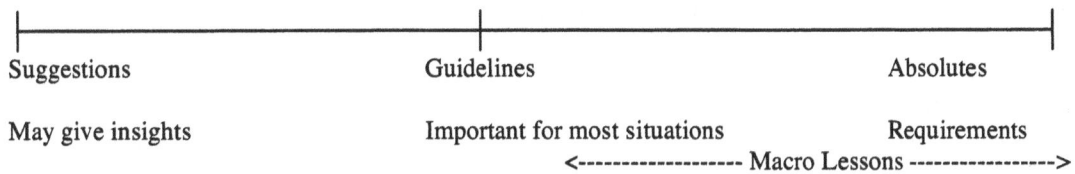

Suggestions	Guidelines	Absolutes
May give insights	Important for most situations	Requirements

<------------------ Macro Lessons ------------------>

Figure Phm 11-1. Leadership Truth Continuum/ Where Macro Lessons Occur

Introduction to Macro lessons
In the *Complexity Era* in which we now live,[66] the thrust of leadership theory has moved, toward the importance of leadership values. The questions being asked today are not as much what is leadership (the leadership basal elements—leader, followers, and situations) and how does it operate (leadership influence means—corporate and individual) as it is *why do we do what we do* (leadership value bases). The first three eras (Great Man, Trait, and Ohio State) answered the question, "What is leadership?" The Contingency and early part of the Complexity Era answered the question, "How do we do it?" Now we are grappling with, "Why do we lead? or What ought we to do?" We are looking for leadership values. A leadership value is an underlying assumption, which affects how a leader behaves in or perceives leadership situations. They are usually statements that have *ought* or *must* or *should* in them. Macro-Lessons are statements of truth about leadership, which have the potential for becoming leadership values. These macro-lessons are observations seen in the various leadership eras in the Bible. Many of these became values for numerous Bible leaders. These macro-lessons move toward the right (requirement, value) of the leadership truth continuum.

What is a macro lesson?

Definition   A <u>macro-lesson</u> is a high level generalization
- of a leadership observation (suggestion, guideline, requirement), stated as a lesson,
- which repeatedly occurs throughout different leadership eras,
- and thus has potential as a leadership absolute.

---

[65] See Clinton, **Leadership Perspectives** for a more detailed explanation of the continuum and for my approach to deriving principles from the scriptures. See **Article**, *Principles of Truth*.
[66] A study of leadership history in the United States from 1850 to the present uncovered 6 Eras (an era being a period of time in which some major leadership theory held sway): 1. Great Man Era (1840s to 1904); 2. Trait Theory (1904-1948); 3. Ohio State Era (1948-1967); Contingency Era (1967-1980); Complexity Era (1980-present). See Clinton, **A Short History of Leadership Theory**. Altadena, Ca.: Barnabas Publishers.

11. Macro Lessons—Defined

Macro lessons even at their weakest provide strong guidelines describing leadership insights. At their strongest they are requirements, or absolutes, that leaders should follow. Leaders ignore them to their detriment.

examples   **Prayer Lesson**: If God has called you to a ministry then He has called you to pray for that ministry. You *must* be responsible to pray for your ministry.
Accountability: Christian leaders *ought* always to minister with a conscious view to ultimate accountability to God for their ministry.
Bible Centered: An effective leader who finishes well *must* have a Bible centered ministry.

Macro Lessons are derived from a comparative study of leadership in the Six Leadership Eras. These Six Leadership Eras and number of macro lessons identified are shown in Table Phm 11-1.

Table Phm 11-1. Leadership Eras and Number of Macro Lessons

Leadership Era	Number of Macro Lessons
1. Patriarchal Era	7
2. Pre-Kingdom Era	10
3. Kingdom Era	5
4. Post-Kingdom Era	5
5. Pre-Church Era	9
6. Church Era	5

I have identified 41 macro lessons, roughly 5 to 10 per leadership era. When a macro-lesson is seen to occur in varied situations and times and cultural settings and in several leadership eras it becomes a candidate for an absolute leadership lesson. When that same generalization becomes personal and is embraced by a leader as a driving force for how that leader sees or operates in ministry, it becomes a leadership value.

The top three Macro Lessons for the four O.T. Leadership Eras are listed in Table Phm 11-2.

Table Phm 11-2. Top Three Macro Lessons in O.T. Leadership Eras

Priority	Leadership Era	Label	Statement
1	Pre-Kingdom	Presence	The essential ingredient of leadership is the powerful presence of God in the leader's life and ministry. (*Therefore a leader must not minister without the powerful presence of God in his/her life.*)
2	Patriarchal	Character	Integrity is the essential character trait of a spiritual leader. (*Therefore, a leader must maintain integrity and respond to God's shaping of it.*)
3	Pre-Kingdom	Intimacy	Leaders develop intimacy with God, which in turn overflows into all their ministry since ministry flows out of being. (*Therefore a leader must seek to develop intimacy with God.*)

The top three Macro Lessons for the two N.T. Leadership Eras are listed in Table Phm 11-3:

11. Macro Lessons—Defined

Table Phm 11-3. Top Three Macro Lessons in N.T. Leadership Eras

Priority	Leadership Era	Label	Statement
1	Church Centered	Word	*God's Word must be the primary source for equipping leaders and must be a vital part of any leader's ministry.*
2	Pre-Church	Harvest	*Leaders must seek to bring people into relationship with God.*
3	Pre-Church	Shepherd	*Leaders must preserve, protect, and develop those who belong to God's people.*

You will notice that some of these macro lessons are already described in value language (should, must, ought) while others are simply statements of observations. I have put in italics my attempt to give the value associated with the observation.

Comparative study across the six leadership eras for macro lessons makes up one of the seven leadership genres, i.e. sources for leadership findings from the Bible.

See **Articles**, *12. Macro Lesson—List of 41 Across Six Leadership Eras*; *9. Leadership Genre—7 Types* (Macro Lessons, Biographical Material, Books as A Whole, Direct Context, Indirect Context, Leadership Acts, Parabolic). See Clinton, **A Short History of Leadership Theory**. Altadena, Ca.: Barnabas Publishers. See also Clinton, **Leadership Perspectives**. Altadena, Ca.: Barnabas Publishers.

Article 12

Relevance of the Article to Paul's Philemon Letter

Note below the *8. Intercession*, *3. Timing*, and *41. Complexity* macros. All three of these macro lessons are illustrated in the book of Philemon. In a lesser way, macro lesson *11. Burden*, is seen in Paul's appeal for Onesimus and his desire for Philemon to grow.

12. Macro-Lessons—List of 41 Across Six Leadership Eras

Macro Lessons inform our leadership with potential leadership values that move toward the absolute. The following are the 41 lessons I have identified as I comparatively studied the six different leadership eras for leadership observations.

No.	Label	Leadership Era	Statement of Macro Lesson
1.	Blessing	Patriarchal	God mediates His blessing to His followers through leaders.
2.	Shaping	Patriarchal	God shapes leader's lives and ministry through critical incidents.
3.	Timing	Patriarchal	God's timing is crucial to accomplishment of God's purposes.
4.	Destiny	Patriarchal	Leaders must have a sense of destiny.
5.	Character	Patriarchal	Integrity is the essential character trait of a spiritual leader.
6.	Faith	Patriarchal	Biblical Leaders must learn to trust in the unseen God, sense His presence, sense His revelation, and follow Him by faith.
7.	Purity	Patriarchal	Leaders must personally learn of and respond to the holiness of God in order to have effective ministry.
8.	Intercession	Pre-Kingdom	Leaders called to a ministry are called to intercede for that ministry.
9.	Presence	Pre-Kingdom	The essential ingredient of leadership is the powerful presence of God in the leader's life and ministry.
10.	Intimacy	Pre-Kingdom	Leaders develop intimacy with God which in turn overflows into all their ministry since ministry flows out of being.
11.	Burden	Pre-Kingdom	Leaders feel a responsibility to God for their ministry.
12.	Hope	Pre-Kingdom	A primary function of all leadership is to inspire followers with hope in God and in what God is doing.
13.	Challenge	Pre-Kingdom	Leaders receive vision from God which sets before them challenges that inspire their leadership.
14.	Spiritual Authority	Pre-Kingdom	Spiritual authority is the dominant power base of a spiritual leader and comes through experiences with God, knowledge of God, godly character and gifted power.
15.	Transition	Pre-Kingdom	Leaders must transition other leaders into their work in order to maintain continuity and effectiveness.
16.	Weakness	Pre-Kingdom	God can work through weak spiritual leaders if they are available to Him.
17.	Continuity	Pre-Kingdom	Leaders must provide for continuity to new leadership in order to preserve their leadership legacy.
18.	Unity	Kingdom	Unity of the people of God is a value that leaders must preserve.
19.	Stability	Kingdom	Preserving a ministry of God with life and vigor over time is as much if not more of a challenge to leadership than creating one.
20.	Spiritual Leadership	Kingdom	Spiritual leadership can make a difference even in the midst of difficult times.
21.	Recrudescence	Kingdom	God will attempt to bring renewal to His people until they no longer respond to Him.

12. Macro Lessons—List of 41 Across Six Leadership Eras

22.	By-pass	Kingdom	God will by-pass leadership and structures that do not respond to Him and will institute new leadership and structures.
23.	Future Perfect	Post-Kingdom	A primary function of all leadership is to walk by faith with a future perfect paradigm so as to inspire followers with certainty of God's accomplishment of ultimate purposes.
24.	Perspective	Post-Kingdom	Leaders must know the value of perspective and interpret present happenings in terms of God's broader purposes.
25.	Modeling	Post-Kingdom	Leaders can most powerfully influence by modeling godly lives, the sufficiency and sovereignty of God at all times, and gifted power.
26.	Ultimate Goal	Post-Kingdom	Leaders must remember that the ultimate goal of their lives and ministry is to manifest the glory of God.
27.	Perseverance	Post-Kingdom	Once known, leaders must persevere with the vision God has given.
28.	Selection	Pre-Church	The key to good leadership is the selection of good potential leaders which should be a priority of all leaders.
29.	Training	Pre-Church	Leaders should deliberately train potential leaders in their ministry by available and appropriate means.
30.	Focus	Pre-Church	Leaders should increasingly move toward a focus in their ministry which moves toward fulfillment of their calling and their ultimate contribution to God's purposes for them.
31.	Spirituality	Pre-Church	Leaders must develop interiority, spirit sensitivity, and fruitfulness in accord with their uniqueness since ministry flows out of being.
32.	Servant	Pre-Church	Leaders must maintain a dynamic tension as they lead by serving and serve by leading.
33.	Steward	Pre-Church	Leaders are endowed by God with natural abilities, acquired skills, spiritual gifts, opportunities, experiences, and privileges which must be developed and used for God.
34.	Harvest	Pre-Church	Leaders must seek to bring people into relationship with God.
35.	Shepherd	Pre-Church	Leaders must preserve, protect, and develop God's people.
36.	Movement	Pre-Church	Leaders recognize that movements are the way to penetrate society though they must be preserved via appropriate ongoing institutions.
37.	Structure	Church	Leaders must vary structures to fit the needs of the times if they are to conserve gains and continue with renewed effort.
38.	Universal	Church	The church structure is inherently universal and can be made to fit various cultural situations if functions and not forms are in view.
39.	Giftedness	Church	Leaders are responsible to help God's people identify, develop, and use their resources for God.
40.	Word Centered	Church	God's Word is the primary source for equipping leaders and must be a vital part of any leaders ministry.
41.	Complexity	All eras	Leadership is complex, problematic, difficult and fraught with risk—which is why leadership is needed.

See Also **Article** *11. Macro Lessons—Defined.*

Article 13

Relevance of the Article to Paul's Philemon Letter
See LEADERSHIP TOPICS 2 MENTOR SPONSOR and 3 RELATIONAL VALUE in Philemon. Paul operates as a sponsor mentor for Onesimus and Timothy and as a teacher mentor/ spiritual director for Philemon.

13. Mentoring—An Informal Training Model

Training Modes
Today's training can be categorized under three modes as shown in Figure Phm 13-1.

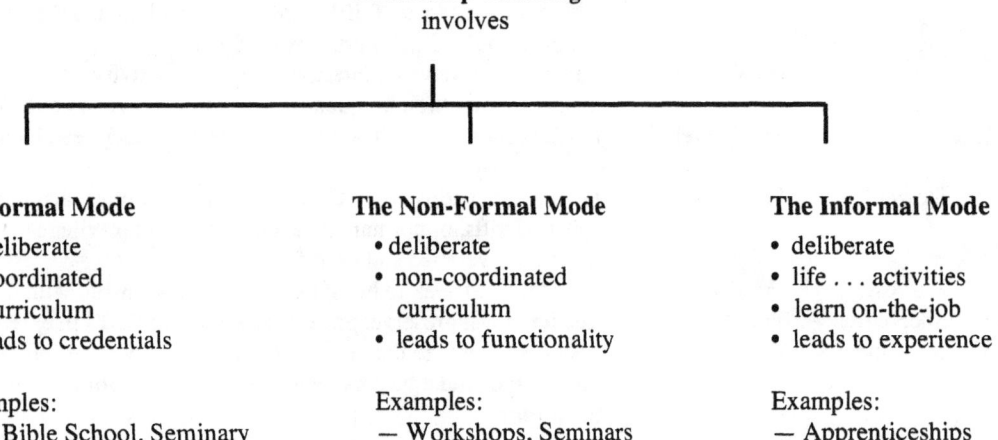

Figure Phm 13-1. Three Training Modes

Mentoring as a training means, while definitely informal in its essence, can be applied to any of the three modes.

Jesus and Paul used the informal training mode as their major training methodology. On-the-job training, modeling, cultural forms of apprenticeships and internships were used. But dominantly it was mentoring which was the primary informal means of training.

Mentoring Defined

Definition   Mentoring is a relational experience in which one person, the mentor, empowers another person, the mentoree, by a transfer of resources.

Empowerment can include such things as new habits, knowledge, skills, desires, values, connections to resources for growth and development of potential. We[67] have identified a number of mentoring functions. Table Phm 13-1 identifies nine mentoring functions we have categorized.

---

[67] My son Dr. Richard W. Clinton, my colleague Paul Stanley and I have all been busily researching and using mentoring in our own personal ministries. See **Connecting** by Stanley and Clinton. See The **Mentor Handbook** by Clinton and Clinton.

Table Phm 13-1. Nine Mentor Functions

Type	Central Thrust
1. Discipler	Basic habits of the Christian life dealing with hearing from God and talking with God; operating in a fellowship of Christians; learning to minister in terms of giftedness; learning to get input from God.
2. Spiritual Guide	Evaluation of spiritual depth and maturity in a life and help in growth in this.
3. Coach	Skills of all kind depending on the expertise of the coach
4. Counselor	Timely and good advice, which sheds perspective on issues and problems and other needs.
5. Teacher	Relevant knowledge that can be used for personal growth or ministry or other such need.
6. Sponsor	Protective guidance and linking to resources so that a leader reaches potential.
7. Contemporary Model	Values impactfully demonstrated in a life that can be transferred and used in one's own life.
8. Historical Model	Values demonstrated in a life and inspiration drawn from that life so as to encourage ongoing development in ones own life and a pressing on to finish well.
9. Divine Contact	Timely Guidance from God via some human source.

Mentoring is a relational experience. Five dynamics are involved: attraction, relationship, responsiveness, accountability, empowerment. The more each of these dynamics are in place the more impactful is the empowerment. Table Phm 13-2 gives the essence of each of the dynamics.

Table Phm 13-2. Five Mentoring Dynamics

Dynamic	Responsibility of	Explanation
attraction	both mentor and mentoree	A mentoree must be attracted to a mentor—that is, see something in the mentor that is desired in his/her own life; A mentor must be attracted to a mentoree and see potential value in working with the mentoree—that is, development of potential for the mentoree is a worth while investment of time and energy.
relationship	both mentor and mentoree	A mentor must build the relationship with a mentoree and vice versa. The stronger the relationship the more likely that the responsiveness and the accountability functions will take place naturally instead of forced.
responsiveness	mentoree	The mentoree must respond to the mentor's suggestions and growth projects. Faithfulness in carrying out assignments is a major trait of responsiveness. The mentor is responsible to help the mentoree grow. The mentoree is responsible to respond/submit to the mentor's plan and methodology for growth.
accountability	mentor	The mentor is responsible to evaluate how the mentoree is doing and to hold the mentoree accountable for following suggestions for growth, for doing what is asked, etc
empowerment	mentor dominantly; mentoree secondarily	Both mentor and mentoree should evaluate and recognize empowerment out of the relationship. The mentor knows and has the best perspective to evaluate empowerment. But the mentoree also should recognize growth in his/her life.

All of these dynamics do not always appear in fullness in the different relationships. They are necessary for the intensive mentoring functions (heavy face-to-face time commitments are usually involved): discipling, spiritual guide, coaching. All do not have to be present in the occasional mentoring functions: counseling, teaching, sponsoring. Empowerment can happen even when all the dynamics are not present. However, the stronger the five dynamics, even in occasional mentoring, the more impactful will be the resulting empowerment. In the passive mentoring functions—contemporary modeling, historical modeling, and divine contact—attraction is present, responsiveness is present and empowerment takes place. But relationship and accountability are essentially missing.

13. Mentoring—An Informal Training Model

Both Jesus and Paul used mentoring. They had individual relationships with trainees. But they also combined individual mentoring relationships with training of groups.

Mentoring relates directly to two of the seven major lessons observed in comparative study of effective leaders.

Effective leaders view leadership selection and development as a priority function in their ministry.

Effective leaders see relational empowerment as both a means and a goal of ministry.

Mentoring will be one of the dominant forces in the training of emerging leaders in the years to come.

See **Articles**: *Leadership Lessons— Seven Major Identified; 19. Paul—Mentor For Many.* See **For Further Study Bibliography**: J. Robert Clinton and Paul D. Stanley, **Connecting—The Mentoring Relationships You Need to Succeed in Life**; J. Robert Clinton and Richard W. Clinton, **The Mentor Handbook—Detailed Guidelines and Helps for Christian Mentors and Mentorees**.

Article 14

Relevance of the Article to Paul's Philemon Letter
The book of Philemon is the powerful illustration of one of the more important functions ministers of the Gospel must do. They must introduce truth to followers in such a way as to bring about behavioral change that demonstrates the impact of Gospel truth in a life and in the culture in which the church finds itself. This means, often, that leaders must take followers through paradigm shifts. Paul beautifully illustrates his approach in moving a leader (Philemon) through a paradigm shift—one that is cognitive, volitional, and experiential.

14. Paradigms and Paradigm Shifts

Introduction—A Surprise
Missionaries, pastors and other students of missiology[68] use the word paradigm and paradigm shifts like they were common words. But imagine my surprise when on a jet from Singapore to Hawaii I heard those words, in casual conversation from the person sitting next to me, a Chinese executive with IBM. I was so startled that I had to ask him where he had been introduced to them. Again I was surprised when he mentioned that IBM was showing Joel Barker's *Discovering the Future* video to all its employers in a training program. Thousands of IBM employees around the world are suddenly adding paradigm and paradigm shift to their vocabulary. We both exchanged comments on the power of that video. So the word *paradigm* and *paradigm shifts* have come a long way since Thomas Kuhn[69] first introduced them to an esoteric audience interested in philosophy and epistemology.[70]

The meaning of paradigms and paradigm shifts has also become less technical that Kuhn's use of the words. And though many of us, who have learned them sort of second hand, can generally use them in a context which roughly supports them we probably don't have a good grasp of the words. And we most certainly have not connected them with God's developmental processes in the shaping of a leader. My comparative study of many leaders has shown that paradigm shifts are a major way that *God breaks through to expand a leader*. And that is the purpose of this article. I want to define, explain, and clarify the use of the terms paradigm and paradigm shift in connection with its use in shaping leaders—For I am convinced that the *paradigm shift* is God's breakthrough processing that opens new leadership vistas.

Let me first suggest some examples of paradigm shifts in the Bible then I will define paradigm and paradigm shifts and suggest five paradigm shifts that are needed if the church is to make an impact in the post-modern world that is upon us now. Table Phm 14-1 lists some Biblical illustrations of paradigm shifts.

Table Phm 14-1. 10 Examples of Biblical Paradigm shifts.

Who	Where In Bible	Paradigm Before	Paradigm After
1. Job	Whole book of Job	Suffering is the result of sin and is deserved. Righteous people should not suffer.	A righteous person can suffer as a part of God's plan for him/her
2. Jonah	Jonah 1-4	God exclusively deals only with Israel in order to bless. God is basically against non-Israelites.	God is not exclusively Israel. He has concerns for all nations—to show His mercy and grace to all who repent.

---

[68] Missiology is the science involved in studying the propagation of the Gospel across cultures.

[69] Kuhn's breakthrough 1974 work, **The Structure of Scientific Revolutions**, was studying paradigms at the higher level of the continuum. He was interested in how a whole scientific community viewed a given science.

[70] Epistemology refers to the science dealing with how we know things.

14. Paradigms and Paradigm Shifts

3. Habakkuk	Habakkuk 1-3	God is unjust and unfaithful in His dealing with groups of people in history. He does not keep His promises.	God is just. He is complex in His dealings with nations. Ultimately His purposes and justice will be seen by all.
4. Elisha's servant	2 Kings 6:8-23; Note vs 16	Sees only natural situation. Fear of the physical warfare to come.	Sees the supernatural; sees the unseen Angelic Band protecting. Now believes in unseen world.
5. Nicodemus	John 3	Kingdom of God is external and has expected political ramifications.	Must have an inner transformation by the Spirit in order to perceive God's Kingdom (God's rule).
6. Apostles	Acts 2	No church. No one is sure of what will happen next.	Coming of Holy Spirit. Church is born. Message of salvation is for others.
7. Whole Church (example of Ananias and Sapphira)	Acts 5	Moral issues are relative; can follow cultural ethics.	Dishonesty is against God whether inward or outwardly known; integrity is a thing of the heart. God wants whole hearted obedience.
8. Saul	Acts 9	Persecuted Christians; saw Christ as a leader of a cult opposing Judaism.	Saw Christ as the resurrected Lord; loved Christians; propagated Christianity.
9. Peter	Acts 10	Gentiles not acceptable to God; Jews should not fellowship with them.	Gentiles accepted by God. All Christians are one.
10. Woman at the well	John 4	Believed Smaritans had religious views comparable with Jews. Lived an unsatisfied life. Religion not satisfying.	Saw Jesus as one sent from God who had access to supernatural revelation. Christ's religious views brought hope.

Probably the most famous paradigm shift is that of the Apostle Paul whose conversion radically turned him around from opposing Christ to serving Christ. Paradigm shifts can bring about major breakthroughs in a life or ministry.

Definition   A <u>paradigm</u> is a controlling perspective (symbolized by r), which allows one to perceive and understand **REALITY** ((symbolized by R).

Definition   A <u>paradigm shift</u> is the change of a controlling perspective and the perceptive result of that change (little **r**) so that one perceives (new little **r'**) and understands **REALITY** in a different way.

Essentially, then as we have described it a paradigm shift occurs by a changed little **r**, one's perception of reality, which in effect allows us to see more of **R** (absolute reality) or at least some different aspect of it.

A change of little **r** could be simple one like a single idea. Or it could be a change of an idea that ramifies throughout a whole group of related ideas. Not all changes of little **r** have the same impact upon our mental models.

14. Paradigms and Paradigm Shifts

Three Categories of Paradigm Shifts

Comparative study of real life paradigm shifts in case studies of leaders has led to the following three categories. These categories include:

1. **Cognitive**—which dominantly deals with the concept of new ideas or frameworks of thinking as the basis for a paradigm shift. These new Ideas (information, categories, etc.) allow for seeing new things. The heart of the shift has to do with a new idea for seeing things, a possibility not considered before. The cognition may also be accompanied by a volitional to use it but the heart of it is the discovery of the validity of the idea. Examples include: a mono-cultural to cross-cultural perspective; getting church growth eyes; getting new leadership style insights; learning a stewardship philosophical leadership model; learning about change dynamics theory; seeing women as fully qualified leaders in ministry.
2. **Volitional**—which dominantly focuses on the fact of committing oneself to something whether understood cognitively or not. There is a committal by an act of a will to use some idea even though it may not be fully understood or experienced. The heart of the shift is a recognition of the importance of letting go and following the new perspective whether or not it is understood. Usually there is a surrender of the will involved and an acknowledgment to God of this. Examples: radical adult conversion; leadership committal; call to ministry
3. **Experiential**—which dominantly focuses on experiences of something and an affective shift which may ramify toward a volitional and eventually a cognitive shift. These have to do with experiencing the effects of something or wanting to experience it. After the experience there may be a growing awareness of its meaning. Usually these have to do with life power or gifted power or personal experiences with the supernatural—that is, unusual experience with the Holy Spirit and supernatural power breakthroughs. Life power (the appropriation of the Holy Spirit to enable victorious living) examples include: entire sanctification—Brengle's experience; baptism of Holy Spirit—Torrey's experience; deeper life experience—McQuilkin's experience; Union life shift—Taylor's experience of the exchanged life; infilling of Holy Spirit—Luke's description of several in Acts. Gifted Power (the appropriation of God's power via the Holy Spirit to use giftedness with effective power) in ministry examples include: a major healing experience; experiences with prophetic; confirmed experiences with word of knowledge or word of wisdom or discernings of spirits; miracles; tongues or interpretation of tongues verified; anointing of Holy Spirit for a ministry; experience of unusual effectiveness with giving, helps, mercy, teaching, evangelism, apostleship, pastoral, or any of the normally considered non-supernatural gifts. Power encounters, spiritual warfare, spiritual authority, prayer power, and unusual intercessory experiences involving divine initiative praying are other miscellaneous power type experiential paradigm shifts. Some experiential paradigm shifts have to do with personhood and include such things as: personality shifts through brokenness or deep processing; isolation and other maturity cluster processes.

Some General Suggestions for Follow-Up

Let me offer four rather simplistic suggestions. They seem almost anticlimactic after offering so much information on paradigm shifts. But they can make a difference.

Suggestion 1. Study Paradigms and Paradigm Shifts Thoroughly

Step 1 for having these ideas impact you is to study them thoroughly so that you understand them and can recognize in real life situations around. Study carefully each of the Biblical examples of paradigm shifts that were given. Study especially the leadership commentary notes in John. John is a *major paradigm shift book*. Study the other paradigm shift books with a view toward identifying paradigm concepts. These include: Job, Jonah, Habakkuk, Acts, and Galatians. Thorough understanding of paradigmatic concepts is a preliminary to actual positive use of them in ministry.

14. Paradigms and Paradigm Shifts

Suggestion 2. Be Open To Them

Recognize that most leaders are usually somewhat inflexible. That's one reason they have convictions and are willing to lead. Also recognize that God uses paradigm shifts to move an inflexible leader. So be open to paradigm shifts to help you become more flexible. Remember, one of your goals is to finish well. One means of doing that is to respond to processing by God, which will break unneeded flexibility and develop your potential.

Suggestion 3. Needed Paradigm Shifts in Our Day

Table Phm 14-2 lists some paradigm shifts I believe will be necessary if we are to minister, to lead, and to see lives changed in the post-modern era facing the church.

Table Phm 14-2. Needed Paradigm Shifts; If Leaders Are to Impact the Post-Modern Era

Paradigm Shift	Explanation
Authentication: Power shift.	Leaders must be able to demonstrate the power of God in ministry in order to break through to post-modern people.
Ministry Base: Shift from doing to being.	Leaders must minister out of being, which involves giftedness, character, intimacy with God, inner values, destiny. Success and achievement must not be the driving force. They will be by-products of the essential issue which is to minister out of being.
Social base: Demonstrate God's enablement for this.	Living victoriously as singles and marrieds must be demonstrated. Our world around us is falling apart in terms of social base issues.
Relational Empowerment: Developmental bias	Leaders must develop emerging leaders with mentoring relationships. Developing others must be a major priority.
Future Perfect Thinking: Leading with hope.	Leaders who lead with a future perfect perspective can impart hope. Hope will desperately be needed in a post-modern culture, which has at best only hopelessness.

Suggestion 4. Expect Them

Paradigm shifts will come unless you are deliberately fixed in your views and perspectives for viewing things. Especially is this true for some of the needed ones I have listed under suggestion 3. We need these if we are to minister to the post-modern generation. Therefore be expecting God to challenge you with them. Be on the look out for them. Desire them. Ask for them.

Remember, God is full of surprises. When we get to heaven we will find out that things were not always the way we thought them to be. Be open for those surprises, which often come wrapped up in paradigm shift wrappings.

See Jn Key Leadership Insights, **Topic 5—Paradigms**, See *powershift, mentoring definitions, future perfect paradigm*, **Glossary**. See **Article,** *Future Perfect Paradigm*.

Article 15

Relevance of the Article to Paul's Philemon Letter

The book of Philemon very clearly illustrates Paul's value of personal ministry—**Leaders should view personal relationships as an important part of ministry.** Nine people are named. And it is clear that Paul is involved with them in a personal way.

15. Paul—And His Companions

Introduction—Paul Concerned About Leaders

Paul developed leaders. He did this through teaching, modeling, and on-the-job training. A comparative study of his relationships with numerous leaders reveals that he exemplifies a number of mentoring roles: discipler, spiritual guide, coach, teacher, contemporary model, sponsor. He operated as a mentor with individuals. He also mentored in a team context.

Several Pauline leadership values[71] under girded this drive to develop leaders.

> **Leaders Must Be Concerned About Leadership Selection And Development.**
>
> **Leaders Should View Personal Relationships As An Important Part Of Ministry.**
>
> **A Christian Leader Ought To Have Several Life Long Mentorees Who He/She Will Help Over A Lifetime To Reach Their Potential In Leadership.**

And the following two major lessons are the foundation for the above three.

> **Effective Leaders View Leadership Selection And Development As A Priority In Ministry.**
>
> **Effective Leaders View Relational Empowerment As Both A Means And A Goal In Ministry.**

This article simply points out that Paul had a personal ministry. Paul developed many leaders, his companions in ministry. It also seeks to exhort us by example.

Paul's Companions

Luke's *we sections* in Ac points out that Paul frequently had a team with him. A number of the people listed below actually traveled on teams with Paul. Others were in ministry with him in various locales. Still other were acquaintances he thought highly of. But all of them had some personal relationship with Paul. Table Phm 15-1 lists the many folks Paul related to personally. Many of them were leaders.

Table Phm 15-1. Paul's Companions—Reflected in His Epistles

Who	Vs	Comments
Achaicus	1Co 16:17, 24	One of three men who brought Paul financial support when he was in Philippi, from the Corinthian church. Also one of three men who were present when the first letter to the church at Corinth was penned. So, he along with the other two probably supplied Paul with lots of information about the church at Corinth.
Ampliatus	Ro 16:8	A close friend in the church at Rome.

---

[71] A <u>leadership value</u> is an underlying assumption, which affects how a leader perceives leadership and practices it. Leadership values contain strong language like should, ought, or must. Must statements are the strongest.

15. Paul—And His Companions

Andronicus	Ro 16:7	An apostle and Christian before Paul. Was in prison probably with Paul. Paul calls him a kinsman but whether this is a brother in Christ or physically is not certain.
Apelles	Ro 16:10	A Christian friend well thought of by Paul in the church at Rome. In his greeting he gives affirmation for this person.
Apollos	Seen 10 times in Ac, 1Co, Tit	A strong Christian worker and well known as a public rhetorician, mighty in the Scriptures. Was mentored by Priscilla and Acquilla. Associated with the church at Corinth. Late in Paul's ministry, when Titus was in Crete, Paul asked Titus to raise funds in Crete to support Apollos.
Apphia	Phm 2	A female Christian, probably the wife of Philemon. Paul loved her dearly and thought highly of her in his greeting in the Phm letter.
Aquila	Ac 18:2, 18, 26; Ro 16:3, 1Co 16:19; 2Ti 4:19.	A Jewish believer married to Priscilla. They were persecuted under Claudius and driven out of Rome. A tentmaker by trade he and his wife associated with Paul (bi-vocational; financial support) and were taught by him in the Christian faith. They were teammates with Paul and made a ministry trip with him. Paul affirmed them to the church at Rome as co-ministers with him and as those who had saved his life—putting their own lives on the line. Priscilla and Aquila apparently had house churches where ever they went. They were in Ephesus when Timothy went there to do apostolic consulting work.
Archippus	Col 4:17; Phm 1,2	A Christian worker well thought of by Paul. He ministered in the church at Colossee and in the church in Philemon's home. Paul calls him a fellow soldier—a beautiful compliment.
Aristarchus	Ac 19:29; 20:4; 27:2	A fellow preacher with Paul. He was persecuted in Ephesus. He traveled on one of Paul's teams from Ephesus to Turkey. Also accompanied Paul to Rome. Suffered in prison with Paul. Mentioned in Phm as a fellow worker.
Aristobulus	Ro 16:10	A Christian friend well thought of by Paul in the church at Rome. In his greeting he gives affirmation for this person.
Artemas	Tit 3:12	On Paul's team when he wintered in Nicopolis, late in Paul's ministry. Probably sent as a messenger to Titus on Crete.
Asyncritus	Ro 16:14	One of several Christians at Rome that Paul greeted warmly. Most likely a small group leader since he greets not only him but the Christians with him. See Ro 16:14 Salute **Asyncritus**, Phlegon, Hermas, Patrobas, Hermes, and the brethren which are with them.
Barnabas	Mentioned 33 times; Many times in Ac; 1Co 9:6, Ga 2:1,9, 13 ; Col 4:10	A mentor sponsor of Paul who brought Paul into the work at Antioch. He led the first missionary team (Paul and his nephew John Mark). Paul became the leader of that team when it moved from Cyprus to Asia minor. Barnabas continued to sponsor Paul with the Jerusalem church. His generosity and giving values impacted Paul. He and Paul had a falling out and split before Paul's second missionary journey. Paul still thought highly of him as seen by his mentioning him in 1Co.
Cephas	1Co 1:12; 3:22; 9:5; 15:5; Gal 1:18; 2:9, 11, 14.	Paul uses this name for Peter several times. Paul recognized and respected Peter as the leader of the Jewish Christian movement. He also clashed with Peter concerning contextualizing the Gospel. Peter respected Paul and recognized that God had revealed truth through him—Scriptural truth.
Claudia	2Ti 4:21	A Christian at Rome. Paul mentions her in his last words to Timothy in 2Ti. She is probably a local house church leader or small group leader since Paul singles our her name and then says also all the Christians. Probably among those Christians giving support to Paul in Rome.
Clement	Php 4:3	A fellow Christian worker with Paul in Phillipi. Paul ask the unnamed pastoral leader at Philippi to aid Clement.
Crescens	2Ti 4:10	Crescens was part of a team around Paul in his second Roman imprisonment. He is mentioned as having left Paul. The context is not clear whether he was on some mission or left for some other reason.

15. Paul—And His Companions

Crispus	Ac 18:8; 1Co 1:14	He was the chief ruler of the Jewish synagogue at Ephesus. Paul led him to Christ. And Paul baptised him. Crispus led his family to the Lord, always a difficult thing with Jewish people.
Demas	Col 4:10; Phm 24; 2Ti 4:10	Demas was part of a team around Paul in his second Roman imprisonment along with Luke and Titus. He is mentioned as having deserted Paul to go to Thessalonica. The context indicates this was not pleasing to Paul. He loved this present world (does that mean he didn't want to be martyred with Paul or that he loved worldliness?)
Epaphroditus	Php 2:25; 4:18	Took a gift from the Php church to Paul while Paul was in prison. He helped Paul while Paul was imprisoned. Nearly died of some sickness. He was a fellow Christian worker with Paul. Paul sponsored him to the Philippians.
Epaphras	Col 1:7; 4:12; Phm 23.	A fellow minister of the Gospel, from the church in Colosse and probably sent out by them. Paul speaks very highly of him calling him a faithful servant of Christ, an intercessor praying for the maturity of the church at Colosse. He was also a fellow prisoner with Paul.
Epenetus	Ro 16:5	Paul speaks highly of this Christian calling him beloved and identifying him as the first Christian in the Achaia (region surrounding Corinth). Probably was in Rome at the time of Paul's writing the Roman epistle.
Erastus	Ac 19:22; Ro 16:23; 2Ti 4:20	He was a missionary with Paul, on one of his traveling teams on his third missionary journey. He was a city treasurer at Corinth so a man of influence. He is mentioned as staying in Corinth when Paul was in prison the second time in Rome. He was one of several people, probably a support team for Paul, who heard Paul dictate the letter to the Romans. One of the team took the dictation.
Eubulus	2Ti 4:21	A Christian at Rome. Paul mentions him in his last words to Timothy in 2Ti. He is probably a local house church leader or small group leader since Paul singles our his name and then says also all the Christians. Probably among those Christians giving support to Paul in Rome.
Eunice	2Ti 1:5	Timothy's mother. A woman of real faith whom Paul highly respected. She gave Timothy a foundation in the O.T. Scriptures and modeled a life of faith and piety for him.
Euodias	Ph 4:2,3	A woman who co-labored in the Lord with Paul at Philippi. She was having problems with another woman, Syntyche, in the church at the time Paul wrote the Php epistle. He spoke highly of her as he entreated her to make up her differences with Syntyche.
Fortunatus	1Co 16:17,24	One of three men who brought Paul financial support when he was in Philippi, from the Corinthian church. Also one of three men who were present when the first letter to the church at Corinth was penned. So, he along with the other two probably supplied Paul with lots of information about the church at Corinth.
Gaius	Ro 16:23; 1Co 1:14	Gaius was led to Christ and baptized by Paul in the city of Corinth. Later Paul stayed in his home, at the time of the writing of the epistle to the Romans. Gaius was part of a small group of people that heard Paul dictate the letter to the Romans.
Hermas	Ro 16:14	A Christian at Rome that Paul greeted warmly. Most likely a small group leader since he greets not only him but the Christians with him.
Hermes	Ro 16:14	A Christian at Rome that Paul greeted warmly. Most likely a small group leader since he greets not only him but the Chrstians with him.
Hermogenes	2Ti 1:15	He is described as one who has turned away from Paul.
Herodion	Ro 16:11	A Christian at Rome that Paul greeted warmly. Paul identified him as a kinsman (spiritual or other, it is not clear).
Jason	Ro 16:21	Maybe a relation of Paul. One of a privileged group who heard Paul dictate the letter to the church in Rome (Timothy, Lucius, Jason, Sosipater, Tertius, Gaius, Erastus and Quartus).

15. Paul—And His Companions

John Mark (Marcus)	Ac 12: 25; 13:5, 13; 15:37, 39; Col 4:10; Phm 24; 2Ti 4:11; 1Pe 5:13	Also called Mark or John. John Mark was a relative of Barnabas (most likely a cousin or nephew). He was on Barnabas and Paul's missionary team which went to Cyprus. He quit the team when it went on to Asia minor. Paul would not have him on his second missionary journey. Paul and Barnabas split over this. Later he went with Barnabas back to Cyprus and Paul took Silas with him on his 2nd missionary journey. Later Paul received him back and sponsored him. Mark also served with Peter and is the author of the Gospel of Mark.
Julia	Ro 16:15	A Christian woman at Rome greeted warmly by Paul. Probably a local church leader since Paul also mentions the saints that are with her.
Junia	Ro 16:7	A female apostle and Christian before Paul. Was in prison probably with Paul. Paul calls her a kinsperson but whether this is a sister in Christ or physically is not certain.
Linus	2Ti 4:21	A Christian at Rome. Paul mentions him in his last words to Timothy in 2Ti. He is probably a local house church leader or small group leader since Paul singles our his name and then says also all the Christians. Probably among those Christians giving support to Paul in Rome.
Lois	2Ti 1:5	Timothy's grand mother. A woman of real faith whom Paul highly respected. She along with Timothy's mother Eunice gave Timothy a foundation in the O.T. Scriptures and modeled a life of faith and piety for him.
Lucius	Ro 16:21	One of a privileged group who heard Paul dictate the letter to the church in Rome (Timothy, Lucius, Jason, Sosipater, Tertius, Gaius, Erastus and Quartus). He could possibly be the prophet who was at Antioch in Ac 13:1 when Paul and Barnabas received their great sense of destiny call to missions.
Luke	2Co 13:14; Col 4:14; 2Ti 4:11; Phm 24	Luke was called the beloved physician. He was on one of Paul's traveling teams, the second missionary journey. He went to Rome with Paul (including the shipwreck). He ministered faithfully to Paul in his imprisonments. He authored the Gospel of Luke and the book of Acts. Both these writings reflect the deep impact that Paul made on Luke.
Mary	Ro 16:6	A Christian at Rome who was noted for her ministry of helps to Paul.
Narcissus	Ro 16:11	A Christian at Rome who Paul greeted warmly. Probably a small group leader or house church leader as Paul also mentions his household (could be only his kin or a housechurch set up).
Nereus	Ro 16:15	A Christian at Rome that Paul greeted warmly. Probably a local church leader since Paul also mentions the saints that are with him.
Nymphas	Col 4:15	Said to have been a wealthy and zealous Christian in Laodicea. Hosted a house church and was probably a small group leader.
Olympas	Ro 16:15	A Christian at Rome that Paul greeted warmly. Probably a local church leader since Paul also mentions the saints that are with them.
Onesimus	Col 4:9, 18; Phm 10, 11;	A runaway slave whom Paul led to the Lord while he was in prison in Rome. After some mentor discipling, Paul sent him back to his master, Philemon, a Christian who had a church in his home. This was a challenge both to Onesimus and Philemon, showing the power of the Gospel to break up a major social institution, slavery. Tradition had it that Onesimus became a very influential church leader in the region.
Onesiphorus	2Ti 1:16; 4:19	This man ministered unashamedly to Paul during his second imprisonment. He vas probably a small group leader or elder in the work at Ephesus.
Patrobas	Ro 16:14	A Christian at Rome that Paul greeted warmly. Most likely a small group leader since he greets not only him but the Christians with him.
Persis	Ro 16:12	A Christian woman at Rome. Paul uses the word beloved in describing her and that she labored much in the Lord's work.
Philemon	Phm 1. See whole book.	A wealthy landowner in the Colosse region. He became a Christian under Paul's two year teaching ministry at Ephesus. Philemon hosted a house church. Paul asked him a special favor—to take back a runaway slave named Onesimus. He gave strong affirmation to Philemon for his Christian testimony.

15. Paul—And His Companions

Philologus	Ro 16:15	A Christian at Rome that Paul greeted warmly. Probably a local church leader since Paul also mentions the saints that are with him.
Phlegon	Ro 16:14	A Christian at Rome that Paul greeted warmly. Most likely a small group leader since he greets not only him but the Christians with him.
Phoebe	Ro 16:1	A fellow leader, female, in the church at Corinth. Paul sponsored her to the church in Rome.
Phygellus	2Ti 1:15	He is described as one who turned away from Paul.
Priscilla	Ac 18:2, 18, 26; Ro 16:3, 1Co 16:19; 2Ti 4:19.	A Jewish woman, a believer married to Acquila. They were persecuted under Claudius and driven out of Rome. A tentmaker by trade he and his wife associated with Paul and were taught by him in the Christian faith. They were teammates with Paul and made a ministry trip with him. Paul affirmed them to the church at Rome as co-ministers with him and as those who had saved his life—putting their own lives on the line. Priscilla and Aquila apparently had house churches where ever they went. Their final ministry was in Ephesus. They were in that church when Timothy went there to do apostolic consulting work. Priscilla was apparently the word gifted person of the pair.
Pudens	2Ti 4:21	A Christian at Rome. Paul mentions him in his last words to Timothy in 2Ti. He is probably a local house church leader or small group leader since Paul singles our his name and then says also all the Christians. Probably among those Christians giving support to Paul in Rome.
Quartus	Ro 16:23	One of a privileged group who heard Paul dictate the letter to the church in Rome (Timothy, Lucius, Jason, Sosipater, Tertius, Gaius, Erastus and Quartus).
Rufus	Ro 16:13	A Christian at Rome. Paul makes a strong destiny statement about him. He also praises Rufus' mother whom he addresses as his own mother—so close was the relationship.
Sosipater	Ro 16:21	One of a privileged group who heard Paul dictate the letter to the church in Rome (Timothy, Lucius, Jason, Sosipater, Tertius, Gaius, Erastus and Quartus).
Sosthenes	1Co 1:1	Co-authored 1Co with Paul. A respected leader in Corinth. He most likely filled Paul in on many issues of the church situation at Corinth.
Stachys	Ro 16:9	A Christian in Rome greatly loved by Paul.
Stephanas	1Co 16: 15, 17, 24	One of three men who brought Paul financial support when he was in Philippi, from the Corinthian church. Also one of three men who were present when the first letter to the church at Corinth was penned. So, he along with the other two probably supplied Paul with lots of information about the church at Corinth. Paul asks the Corinthian church to support this man who has gone into full time ministry.
Silvanus	2Co 1:19; 1Th 1:1; 2Th 1:1	A Roman citizen and fellow missionary. A part of Paul's traveling team. Co-authored two books, 1,2Th. A respected leader by Paul.
Syntyche	Php 4:2,3	A woman who co-labored in the Lord with Paul at Philippi. She was having problems with another woman, Euodias, in the church at the time Paul wrote the Php epistle. He spoke highly of her as he entreated her to make up her differences with Euodias.
Tertius	Ro 16:22	One of a privileged group who heard Paul dictate the Roman epistle (Timothy, Lucius, Jason, Sosipater, Tertius, Gaius, Erastus and Quartus).
Timothy	Occurs 31 times	The most intimate follower of Paul. Traveled with him on many missionary trips. Was sent on ministry trips for Paul. Best known for his apostolic consultation ministry at Ephesus. One of a privileged group who heard Paul dictate the letter to the church in Rome (Timothy, Lucius, Jason, Sosipater, Tertius, Gaius, Erastus and Quartus). Received two special letters while at Ephesus which reveals the mentoring relationship between Paul and Timothy. These two letters are the top two leadership books in the N.T. Church Leadership Era. In 2Ti Paul passes the baton of leadership over to Timothy.

15. Paul—And His Companions

Titus	Occurs 15 times	Next to Timothy, Paul's closest worker. He was given some of the toughest ministry assignments including one at Corinth dealing with finances and authority problems. He also was given an apolstolic assignment in Crete. The book of Tit written to sponsor him is the third most important book on leadership in the N.T. Church Leadership Era.
Trophimus	2Ti 4:20	He was one of a small group of people close to Paul during Paul's second imprisonment. He became sick and was left at Miletum.
Tryphena	Ro 16:12	A Christian woman in Rome who was described as a worker for the Lord.
Tryphosa	Ro 16:12	A Christian woman in Rome who was described as a worker for the Lord
Tychicus	Eph 6:21, 24; Col 4:7, 18; 2Ti 4:12; Tit 3:12	A Christian worker, part of Paul's support team during his second imprisonment. He also was involved in transcribing and carrying the Ephesian and Colossian letters and traveled with Onesimus as he carried the Philemon letter. Tychicus was well thought of by Paul—described as a beloved brother. He was sent on a mission to Ephesus during the time of the writing of 2Ti.
Urbanus	Ro 16:9	A Christian worker in Rome who had helped Paul in the past (financially or ministry wise—unclear).
Zenas	Tit 3:13	A lawyer whom Titus was to bring to Paul.

Some Observations

Several important observations from Paul's co-ministry and relationship with others should be noted.

1. Paul believe in affirmation both public and private. Affirmation is one of the strongest means a leader has in encouraging emerging workers. Frequently, affirmation involves use of Goodwin's Expectation Principle: *Emerging leaders tend to live up to the genuine expectations of leaders they respect.* Paul not only affirms but challenges through the affirmation. See Goodwin, **Bibliography**.
2. Paul personally related to leaders all up and down the levels of leadership: local church members, lay leaders in general, bi-vocational leaders at small group level, local church elders, fellow bi-vocational workers, full time workers of regional influence, leaders of Christian movement in Jerusalem, etc. He was at home with kings, ambassadors, and with common folk.
3. Paul used networking power as a means of strong influence in numerous leadership ways. He could not have accomplished all that he did with out all kind of help from people whom God had given to him in relationships.
4. Most of Paul's companions, whom he knew at one time or another and supported him, stayed faithful to him. Only a very small few are said to have fallen away from him.
5. A number of Paul's companions were women who ministered in local church situations. Paul did not have a problem with women in ministry (at least from a giftedness or theological standpoint; yes, there were cultural problems).

Conclusion

Paul certainly sets a standard for those who would invest personally in the lives of others. He exemplifies one who held this important value.

Leaders Should View Personal Relationships As An Important Part Of Ministry.

Leaders today with their thoughts on bigness and success may well miss this most important aspect of ministry.

See *mentor; mentoree; mentoring; mentor discipler; mentor spiritual guide; mentor coach; mentor teacher; mentor contemporary model; mentor sponsor; mentor divine contact;* **Glossary**. See **Articles**, *19. Paul—Mentor for Many; 17. Paul—Developer Par Excellence; 25. Timothy—A Beloved Son in the Faith.*

Article 16

Relevance of the Article to Paul's Philemon Letter

Paul is in the midst of deep processing—isolation, crisis and life crisis— even as he writes this letter. He is in prison and facing a trial, which could end in his death. And he is continuing to deal with church situations—almost all of them very problematic. See **LEADERSHIP TOPICS 5. ISOLATION PROCESSING AND ITS RESULTS and 7. CRITICAL INCIDENTS.** Deep processing, responded to properly, will result in character shaping toward Christlikeness and as a by-product, spiritual authority.

16. Paul—Deep Processing

Introduction—Quitting the Ministry?

Do you know someone who has quit the full time ministry? Have you ever felt like quitting the full time ministry? Did you know that there is a large dropout from full time ministry? Well if ever a Christian worker had reasons to quit, it was Paul at the time he wrote 2Co. He was in his mid-fifties and had over 20 years of tough ministry experience behind him.

Here is what he faced. Paul's first letter to Corinth was probably written at Ephesus.[72] Shortly after writing it, he was forced to flee because of the hubbub caused by the shrine makers honoring the goddess Diana.[73] Paul went on to Troas to revisit churches in Macedonia. He intended to travel south to Corinth and visit churches in Achaia.[74] He did eventually get there and stayed about three months.[75] It was in the interval between leaving Ephesus and reaching Corinth that he wrote again to the Corinthians. At the time he was going through deep processing. What he was going through was enough to make any Christian worker give up?

What was he facing? No news from Titus.[76] He had sent Titus to Corinth to deal with some of the problems there. He was anxious about what was happening there. He describes this time in Macedonia as a time when he had *no rest within and deeply troubled from without* as well. The church at Corinth appeared to be in revolt against his leadership. The churches in Galatia were falling away to another Gospel. He had narrowly escaped with his life from the uproar in Ephesus. In addition to disappointment and apprehensiveness, Paul had a physical illness which was almost fatal. Paul described it in his own words,

> 8 I want you to know, dear Christian friends, of the very trying experiences[77] which we faced in the province of Asia. I was overwhelmed,[78] beyond my ability[79] to cope with it. I thought[80] I was going to die. 9 I concluded[81] that I would die. 2Co 1:8,9.

But look at what he learned.

---

[72] See 1Co 16:8.

[73] See Ac 19 for the vignette.

[74] See Ac 20:1,2.

[75] See Ac 20:3.

[76] See 2Co 2:13.

[77]*Trying experiences* (SRN 2347) represents the same Greek word used several times ı 2Co 1:3,4 and often translated as tribulation or affliction.

[78]*Overwhelmed* (SRN 5236) is a translation of a word meaning excessively so (**KJV** beyond measure).

[79]*Ability* (SRN 1411) is a translation of the Greek word, power.

[80]*Thought* (SRN 1820) is a very strong word meaning despaired or to be destitute. It probably would not be too strong to say Paul was depressed.

[81]*Concluded* (SRN 610) represents the noun word usually translated as *sentence* or *judgment*. Hamel comments: 2Co. 1:9 ... the meaning is "on asking myself whether I should come out safe from mortal peril, I answered, I must Die" Paul was in deep trouble.

But as a result I learned not to trust myself but to rely on God, who can raise the dead. 10 He delivered me from that tremendous near death experience. He continues to deliver. He will do so in the future too! 11 You play a part in this by praying for us. As a result, because many prayed, many will give thanks to God for his answered prayer—our safety.[82]

This experiential acknowledging of total dependence on God in a deep processing situation is usually a turning point in this shaping activity by God. Paul was at death's door. To all outward appearances his life and work were coming to an end—and not on a good note. His life, his work, and the fate of the potential of the worldwide movement of Christianity in the Gentile world all hung in the balance. Probably never before had he felt himself so helpless, so beaten down and disconcerted, as he was on that journey from Ephesus to Macedonia. He was laid up sick, unto death, and awaited Titus, not even sure he would last long enough to see Titus. And Titus came. And the news was not all good. For whatever Titus shared prompted a further letter to Corinth. Paul's apostolic authority was in question and with it the whole of the future ministry to the Gentiles. So I do not overstate it when I say Paul knew about deep processing.

If Paul ever felt like quitting, and I am sure he did, this Corinthian thing was top of the list for quitting time. If he wasn't gray headed before I am sure he had gray hairs after this thing. Now listen carefully. This was Paul's finest hour. Two other times run a close second: the Philippian epistle—he is isolated and in jail. 2 Timothy—he is in jail and awaiting death, near the end of his life. But this is his finest hour. What you are in deep processing is what you really are!

Definition Deep processing refers to a collection of process items which intensely work on deepening the maturity of a leader. The set includes the following process items: conflict, ministry conflict, crisis, life crisis, leadership backlash and isolation.

Paul knew what deep processing was. He also knew the benefits of it.

Deep Processing—Some Shaping Activities

While God may use a number of things to take a leader deep with himself, several occur so often with leaders that they can be labeled and described. Six common deep processing items are given.

Definition The conflict process item refers to those instances in a leader's life-history in which God uses conflict, whether personal or ministry related to develop the leader in dependence upon God, faith, and inner-life.

Definition The ministry conflict process item refers to those instances in a ministry situation, in which a leader learns lessons via the positive and negative aspects of conflict with regards to: 1. the nature of conflict, 2. possible ways to resolve conflict, 3. possible ways to avoid conflict, 4. ways to creatively use conflict, and 5. perception of God's personal shaping through the conflict.

Definition Crisis process items refer to those special intense situations of pressure in human situations which are used by God to test and teach dependence

---

[82] Paul recognizes an important dynamic. *Transparency and vulnerability, in sharing by a leader, allows others to identify with and pray more fervently and with understanding for God's answers*. By this sharing then, God receives much more praise and honor because many are partnering with Him. Prayer backers make a big difference in the life of a leader who can share openly with them. Many leaders fear sharing vulnerably and openly. They miss out on one of God's resources for them. Paul models here the kind of open sharing that leaders need to do. See **Article**, *Daniel—Leaders and Prayer Backing.*

16. Paul—Deep Processing

Definition — A <u>life crisis process item</u> refers to a crisis situation characterized by life threatening intense pressure in human affairs in which the meaning and purpose of life are searched out with a result that the leader has experienced God in a new way as the source, sustainer, and focus of life

Definition — <u>Isolation processing</u> refers to the setting aside of a leader from normal ministry involvement in its natural context usually for an extended time in order to experience God in a new or deeper way.

Definition — The <u>leadership backlash process</u> item refers to the reactions of followers, other leaders within a group, and/or Christians outside the group, to a course of action taken by a leader because of various ramifications that arise due to the action taken. The situation is used in he leader's life to test perseverance, clarity of vision, and faith.

Paul and Deep Processing

Paul faced all of these kinds of deep processing—these shaping activities of God which make a person of God. How did Paul face these kind of shaping activities and not give up? Let me suggest several under girding values that made the difference. They are contained in the following verses.

1. <u>2Co 4:1</u>
   1 Because God in His mercy has given me this ministry, I am not going to become discouraged and give up.

Let me paraphrase it emphatically.

Therefore since God put me in this ministry I am not going to quit!

2. <u>1Co 9:24-27</u>
   24 Don't you know that those in a race all run, but only one wins the prize? Run in such a way that you will receive the prize. 25 And everyone who competes[83] for the prize exercises real discipline[84] in order to be ready. Now they do it to win a fleeting prize.[85] We do it for an eternal prize. 26 Therefore I, personally, run my course with definite purpose, to win—to finish well. Thus I box making my punches count. 27 So I discipline myself and exercise strict control, lest after preaching to others, I myself should become a loser.[86]

3. <u>2 Co 12:9</u>
   9 His answer was, "My enabling presence is all you need. My power shows forth much stronger in your weakness." So you can see then, why I boast about my weaknesses. Christ's power will work through me. Therefore I will boast all the more gladly about my weaknesses, so that Christ's power may rest on me.

---

[83] The word translated as *competes* (SRN 75) is the word from which we get our word agonize. It means really struggles (to get ready and participate). Present day marathon runners do train this rigorously.

[84] The word translated as *Exercises real discipline* (SRN 1467) means to practice self-control. It described athletes who were preparing for the Olympic Games. Such an athlete abstained from unwholsome food, wine, and sexual indulgence.

[85] *Prize* (SRN 4735) the wreath or garland which was given as a prize to victors in public games.

[86] This whole context, 9:24-27, is promoting one of the important enhancements that helps leaders finish well. Discipline in the life, is one of five enhancement factors that have been identified with effective leaders who have finished well. All kinds of disciplines, especially spiritual disciplines, will be needed and used with purpose in order to continue toward the finish. Paul is in his 50s here, a time when leaders tend to plateau. Disciplines are needed. See **Articles, *Finishing Well—5 Factors Enhancing; Spiritual Disciplines.***

16. Paul—Deep Processing

4. Acts 26:15-20

"Then I asked, `Who are you, Lord?' "`I am Jesus, whom you are persecuting,' the Lord replied. 16 `Now get up and stand on your feet. I have appeared to you to appoint you as a servant and as a witness of what you have seen of me and what I will show you. 17 I will rescue you from your own people and from the Gentiles. I am sending you to them 18 to open their eyes and turn them from darkness to light, and from the power of Satan to God, so that they may receive forgiveness of sins and a place among those who are sanctified by faith in me.' 19 "So then, King Agrippa, **I was faithfully obedient to this heavenly mandate.** 20 First to those in Damascus, then to those in Jerusalem and in all Judea, and to the Gentiles also, I preached that they should repent and turn to God and prove their repentance by their deeds."

Let me suggest four reasons why Paul persevered in ministry. The first two are from the human side. Paul took responsibility. The last two are from the divine side. Paul counted on God taking responsibility too.

1. He had a sense of responsibility.

1 Because God in His mercy has given me this ministry, I am not going to become discouraged and give up.[87] 2Co 4:1

2. He was Disciplined With A Purpose. He wanted to finish well.

Listen to my paraphrase of 1Co 9:24-27. It was the motivational secret underlying one great leader's sustaining his life and ministry.

> I am serious about finishing well in my Christian ministry. I discipline myself for fear that after challenging others into the Christian life I myself might become a casualty. 1Co 9:24-27.

Paul was aware that many did not make it. He was in his 50s; a time when Christian leaders tend to plateau. He didn't want that. So he did something about it. Did it work? More on this later.

3. He counted on Experiencing The Grace Of God.

There are three great leaders during the Church Era of leadership: Peter, John, Paul. All three knew this under girding principle. Their final words confirm it.

> But grow in the **grace** and knowledge of our Lord and Savior Jesus Christ. To him be glory both now and forever! Amen. 2Pe 3:18

> The **grace** of the Lord Jesus be with God's people. Amen. Rev 22:21

> The Lord be with your spirit. **Grace** be with you. 2Ti 4:22

It is interesting how each of them came to the same inescapable conclusion. You will not make it in the Christian life without grace. Now grace as described here is not unmerited favor—not referring to our standing before God. It is referring to an enabling energy of God.

Definition   **Grace** is the inspirational, enabling presence of God in a life, which encourages one to persevere in Victory throughout life's circumstances. (see also *grace*, **Glossary** for expanded definition of this.

---

[87] This is one of Paul's stronger expressions of his personally embracing the stewardship model. His call from God, his anointing by God and his sense of destiny are behind these words. *See Stewardship Model*, **Glossary**. See Articles, *Entrustment—A Leadership Responsibility, Jesus' Five Leadership Models: Shepherd, Harvest, Steward, Servant, Intercessor.*

So Paul was not just talking lightly when he said in 2Co 12:9,

> 9 His answer was, "My enabling presence is all you need. My power shows forth much stronger in your weakness." So you can see then, why I boast about my weaknesses. Christ's power will work through me. Therefore I will boast all the more gladly about my weaknesses, so that Christ's power may rest on me. 2Co 12:9.

You will not make it apart from knowing and counting upon this grace. The second reason Paul profited from deep processing and made it through it was that he knew how to experience the grace of God, that enabling presence of God.

4. He had a strong Sense Of Destiny Integrated Into A Life Purpose.

> So then, King Agrippa, I was faithfully obedient to this heavenly mandate. Ac 26:19.

But the most important reason for not giving up, not dropping out of ministry, not quitting: a strong sense of destiny that imparted a **life purpose**.[88] His life was tightly integrated, that is, extremely focused around a solid life purpose. In a nutshell, Paul had a sense of destiny. And that destiny focused his life and enabled him to make it through deep processing. Notice his triumphant finish.

> 6 As for me, I am ready to be sacrificed. The time for me to depart this life is near. 7 I have run a good race. I have fulfilled my God-given destiny.[89] I still have my faith intact. 8 And now for my prize, a crown of righteousness. The Lord, the righteous judge, will award it to me at that day. And not to me only, but unto all those who eagerly await his return.[90] 2Ti 4:6-8.

A Major Insight—Paul's Inner-Life Attitude

Paul had a particular attitude about deep processing which made all the difference in his life and ministry. I have labeled it a *Sovereign Mindset*.

Definition   A sovereign mindset[91] is an attitude demonstrated by the Apostle Paul in which he tended to see God's working in the events and activities that shaped his life, whether or not they were positive and good or negative and bad. He tended to see God's purposes in these shaping activities and to make the best of them.

---

[88] A life purpose is a burden-like calling, a task or driving force or achievement, which motivates a leader to fulfill something or to see something done. This is the core focal issue and around which a life is integrated over a lifetime. See **Articles**, *Life Purpose, Biblical Examples; Paul—A Sense of Destiny; Destiny Pattern.*

[89] Fulfilled my destiny, literally I have finished or completed (SRN 5758) a perfect action, i.e. already done it with on going results, my course (SRN 1408). Course, used three times in the N.T., refers to life's destiny, the pathway set before one to do. The destiny pattern usually follows a threefold pattern: destiny preparation, destiny revelation, and destiny fulfillment. This idea of already completing it is the use of a certainty idiom, the prophetic past. It is so certain that he speaks of it in the past tense as if it had already happened. See Ac 20:24 where Paul states his desire to finish his course. See also, Ac 13:25 where the same word refers to John the Baptist's having finished his course. See *certainty idiom, prophetic past, sense of destiny, destiny preparation, destiny revelation, destiny fulfillment,* **Glossary**. See **Articles**, *The Destiny Pattern; Paul—A Sense of Destiny.*

[90] Vs 4:6-8 show that Paul finished well. He is the classic case of a N.T. church leader finishing well. All six characteristics of a good finish are seen: (1) vibrant personal relationship with God; (2) have a learning posture; (3) Christ-likeness in character; (4) live by Biblical convictions; (5) leave behind ultimate contributions; (6) fulfill a sense of destiny. One of the major leadership contributions of 2Ti is this challenge to finish well, which Paul models. See *modeling*, **Glossary**. Article, *Finishing Well—Six Characteristics.*

[91] Sovereign Mindset is a Pauline leadership value seen all through 2Co. *Leaders ought to see God's hand in their circumstances as part of His plan for developing them as leaders.* See **Article**, *21.Sovereign Mindset.*

16. Paul—Deep Processing

There were four keys to Paul's getting and maintaining a sovereign mindset:

1. Paul recognized God's hand in life happenings--no matter who or what the immediate cause.
2. Paul submitted to God's deeper purposes in life happenings.
3. Paul learned and used the lessons derived from these life happenings.
4. Paul shared those lessons (and God's provision in them) with others.

Conclusion

Some one has said, "All great leaders walk with a limp!" The allusion is to Jacob's deep experience with God, wrestling with the Angel of God, and thereafter always walking with a limp due to the injury sustained. Now this of course is a hyperbolic description of something important. Stated in less colorful language,

> **God matures leaders He uses via shaping activities that deepen their walk with God and increase their effectiveness for God.**

These activities for the most part are not pleasant. They may involve physical suffering, or persecution, or crises in the life. In short they will force the leader to go deep with God in order to survive in ministry. Or to say it another way, all leaders will go through some deep processing as they serve the Lord. Some leaders will be repeatedly shaped with deep processing. A very few leaders will experience it to an extent not seen in ordinary leaders. Such a leader was Paul. He was greatly used by God. He was greatly shaped by deep processing.

Two common reactions by leaders in deep processing include:

1. **Turn away from God** (Well, if this is the way God is I don't need or want God!).
2. **Turn toward God. Go deep with God** (God will meet me and take me into more intimacy in this processing and I will walk away from it with God's lessons in my life. I will benefit from this!).

Don't wait till you are in deep processing to make up your mind which of these you will do. In deep processing you most likely will not be able to think clearly. Decide now, as an act of the will, that when deep processing comes, you will go deep with God. And don't forget the basic lessons Paul gives in 2Co 1:3-7, a foundational passage for deep processing.

1. God will meet you in deep processing.
2. You are helped in order to help.
3. Deep processing tests your own belief in the sufficiency of Christ.
4. Your own development through deep processing gives hope that your followers can also know the sufficiency of Christ in their deep processing.

You are modeling and never with more impact than when you are in deep processing. It is clear that Paul was modeling with great impact as he wrote the letter to Philemon. He was in deep processing—imprisonment, with possible death awaiting to him. But note throughout his sovereign mindset.

Article 17

Relevance of the Article to Paul's Philemon Letter

Paul even in the midst of deep processing—is concerned about developing others. Note the mentor sponsoring of Timothy and Onesimus. Notice that the whole letter is an attempt to help Philemon mature as a believer. Note also his references to other Christian workers—in itself, an affirmation process that helps develop.

17. Paul —Developer Par Excellence

Paul selected and trained leaders. No matter where he was or what actual ministry he was actively pursuing he was always developing those around him. He demonstrates, forcefully, two of the major leadership lessons observed from comparative studies of effective leaders.[92]

>**Effective leaders view leadership selection and development as a priority in their ministry.**
>
>**Effective leaders see relational empowerment as both a means and a goal of ministry.**

Paul was a developer of leaders.

Two Pauline leadership values explain this bent for Paul. A leadership value is an underlying assumption, which affects how a leader perceives leadership and practices it. Let me state them first as Pauline leadership values and then generalize them for possible application in other leader's lives.

Value 1	**Leadership Development**
Statement of Value	Paul felt he must identify potential leadership and develop it for ministry in the church.
Generalized	Leaders must be concerned about leadership selection and development.
Value 2	**Personal Ministry**
Statement of Value	Paul saw that in his own life he should use personal relationships as a strong means for doing ministry.
Generalized	Leaders should view personal relationships as an important part of ministry.

---

[92] I have identified seven which repeatedly occur in effective leaders: 1. Life Time Perspective—Effective Leaders View Present Ministry In Terms Of A Life Time Perspective. 2. Learning Posture—Effective Leaders Maintain A Learning Posture Throughout Life. 3. Spiritual Authority—Effective Leaders Value Spiritual Authority As A Primary Power Base. 4. Dynamic Ministry Philosophy—Effective Leaders Wh.. Are Productive Over A Lifetime Have A Dynamic Ministry Philosophy Which Is Made Up Of An Unchanging Core And A Changing Periphery Which Expands Due To A Growing Discovery Of Giftedness, Changing Leadership Situations, And Greater Understanding Of The Scriptures. 5. Leadership Selection And Development—Effective Leaders View Leadership Selection And Development As A Priority Function In Their Ministry. 6. Relational Empowerment—Effective Leaders See Relational Empowerment As Both A Means And A Goal Of Ministry. 7. Sense Of Destiny—Effective Leaders Evince A Growing Awareness Of Their Sense Of Destiny. See the **Article,** *Leadership Lessons—Seven Major Identified.*

17. Paul—Developer Par Excellence

These two values are at the heart of being a developer.

Defining a Developer

What is a developer? Let me define it.

Definition A <u>developer</u> is a person with a mentoring bent who readily sees potential in an emerging leader and finds ways to help move that emerging leader on to becoming an effective leader.

Developers are mentors who have a variety of mentoring methods.

Definition <u>Mentoring</u> is a relational experience in which one person, the mentor, empowers another person, the mentoree, by a transfer of resources.

The resources which empower can be habits, skills, perspectives, specific advice, training, connection to other resources, etc.

What does it take to be a developer? It takes the ability to do several key mentoring functions. A developer is a mentor who usually uses three or more of the following mentoring functions effectively in developing people:

<u>Mentor Function</u>	<u>Basic Empowerment</u>
Discipler	basic habits of Christian living
Spiritual Guide	perspective on spiritual growth
Coach	basic skills usually related to doing ministry
Counselor	perspective and advice to meet situational and growth needs
Teacher	basic information that applies to the emerging leader's situation
Model	demonstrates values and skills for possible emulation
Sponsor	watches over the mentorees development and makes sure doors are open for development to potential

Paul operated in all the above mentor functions. This is best seen in his developing ministry with Timothy. Frequently, his development involved a traveling team ministry using on-the-job experience. Leaders whom he worked with and developed include: Priscilla, Acquila, Timothy, Titus, Luke, Silas, Epaphras, Archippus, John Mark, Aristarchus, Philemon, Onesimus and many others.

Developers are concerned about the future of ministry. Paul was. Paul represents the most prominent leader in the Church leadership Period. He is an important model. We need to learn from his life. *Paul The Developer* sets the pace for us, concerning leading with a developmental bias.

No organization or church will last long with effectiveness if it is not developing people. Churches and Christian organizations, without exception, need developers. What should they do? They should identify developers, reward developers, help the developers develop themselves, and help promote mentoring relationships so that these developers not only have access to emerging leaders but are encouraged in behalf of the organization or church to develop people. And keep it simple. No programs. Just relationships.[93]

See Also **Articles**, *Leadership Lessons—Seven Major Identified*; *Pauline Leadership Values*; *13. Mentoring—An Informal Training Model*; *25. Timothy A Beloved Son of the Faith*; *15. Paul—and His Companions*; ***Leading With A Developmental Bias.***

---

[93] Most developers need the freedom to move a mentoring relationship along the most natural lines for developing it. They can work within programs of development, which are broad enough to let them freely identify mentoring needs and pursue them.

Relevance of the Article to Paul's Philemon Letter
Paul prayed for those involved in his ministry. This book certainly illustrates that. See **LEADERSHIP TOPIC 4. PRAYER ENCOURAGEMENT PRINCIPLE.**

18. Paul—Intercessor Leader

A prayer macro lesson identified in every leadership era, and specifically highlighted in Moses, Samuel, Jesus, and Paul's ministries states,

Intercession   Leaders Called To A Ministry Are Called To Intercede For That Ministry.

Paul interweaves this throughout his ministry. Paul mentions praying in every Church epistle except one.[94]

The Leader Intercessor Model
Ministry philosophy refers to a related set of values that underlies a leader's perception and behavior in his/her ministry. The values may be ideas, principles, guidelines or the like, which are implicit (not actually recognized but part of the perceptive set of the leader) or explicit (recognized, identified, articulated). For any given leader a ministry philosophy is unique. It is dynamic and related to three major elements: Biblical dynamics, giftedness, and situation. The intercessor model flows out of the prayer macro lesson and shows the concern of a leader for God's intervention in ministry. It is not clear to who this model applies—all leaders or those leaders who have the gift of faith. It may also well apply to some who are not leaders but who have the gift of faith.

definition   The <u>intercessor model</u> is a philosophical model based on the central thrust of the prayer macro lesson (applies to all leaders as a role) and an additional responsibility for praying for a ministry, which flows out of the faith gift or some aspects of the prophetical gift.

Biblical examples reflecting the prayer macro lesson and intercession occur in every leadership era.[95] Abraham and the macro lesson: Ge 18:16-33; Moses and the macro lesson: Ex 32:7-14; Samuel and the macro lesson: 1 Sa 12:1-25; Daniel and the macros lesson: Dan 9; Jesus and the macro lesson: some 44 different verses indicate Jesus praying throughout his ministry. One especially important prayer passage occurs in Jn 17. Paul and the macro lesson: see this article.

Basic Values Underlying the Intercessor Model
1. A leader who is called to ministry must accept responsibility for prayer for that ministry.
2. A leader should show acceptance of responsibility for a ministry by interceding for that ministry and involving others to intercede.
3. A leader must seek God's leading in prayer, the divine initiative, as to how and what to pray for.
4. A leader should bathe major decision making in prayer.
5. A leader ought to encourage the development of emerging leaders by praying for them and telling them of prayer for them.

---

[94] He mentions pray, prayer, praying, etc. 60 times in his epistles. Only Gal of his epistles to churches has prayer references left out. Paul hits the ground running in Gal to correct a fundamental heresy. Apart from a possible veiled allusion to prayer in Gal 4:19 (travail SRN 5605) Paul does not speak of praying. He is angry with the Galatians and bent on correcting a fundamental heresy. Paul also omits prayer references in his personal letter to Titus.

[95] There are six leadership eras in the Bible: 1. Patriarchal; 2. Pre-Kingdom; 3. Kingdom; 4. Post-Kingdom; 5. Pre-Church; 6. Church.

18. Paul—Intercessor Leader

6. A leader should cultivate an attitude of prayer at all times and ought to break into prayer when prompted to do so.
7. Crises should drive a leader deeper into intercessory ministry.
8. Extended times alone in prayer should be used for intercession, for personal renewal and for revelation from God for guidance, breakthroughs in ministry, and for decision making.

Some Implications Flowing From the Model
1. No ministry will long endure without intercessors behind it.
2. Quantity (the number of and amount of time spent by) of intercessors is not as important as quality of intercession of the ones doing the interceding.
3. Leaders with the gift of faith will do personal intercession with a zeal, passion and fruitfulness beyond that of leaders who do this as a role.
4. Leaders should cultivate relationships with faith-gifted intercessors and recruit them to help in the ministry.
5. Power in ministry comes from giftedness and from prayer. Both are needed.

The Intercessor Model is the most specific of the leadership models. It is the most gift related. Gifts of faith, apostleship, and in general, the revelatory gifts (word of knowledge, word of wisdom, prophecy, word of faith) will usually be associated with leaders operating strongly in this model. Now, all leaders have the duty to intercede for their ministries. But those who are drawn to this model will be gifted to see its impact more than just that which results from praying in general. It is not clear to what extent each leader will be involved in this model. Paul exemplifies this model.

Prayer Concerns of Paul for the Churches
Paul had a burden for the churches that he had founded and was associated with.

> Beside outward circumstances pressing me, there is the inward burden, i.e. the anxiety
> and care, I feel daily for all the churches. 2Co 11:28

He expresses this burden so beautifully in his prayers for the churches. Table Phm 18-1 lists just a few of his references to burden to pray for the various churches.

Table Phm 18-1. Paul's Prayer Concerns for the Churches

Church	Passage	Prayer Thrust
At Rome	Ro 1:8-10 12:12	(1) Thankfulness for this church's strong testimony of faith toward God—its worldwide impact. (2) That God would take him to this church for ministry there.
At Corinth	1Co 1:4	That the Corinthian church respond to his admonitions so that he would not have to come and discipline them in person.
At Ephesus	Eph 1:15-20; 3:1, 14-21	(1) Continuously gives thanks for them. (2) Holy Spirit imparted wisdom. (3) Intimacy with God. (4) Perspective, especially promises, which will give hope. (5) Recognize and appropriate the resurrection-like power available in them. (6) Gentile acceptance into God's kingdom. (7) Inward strength via the Holy Spirit. (8) Realization of the indwelling Christ in their inner selves. (9) Know more fully the love of God.
At Philippi	Php 1:3	(1) Thankfulness for this church—the joy it brings and for its support of Paul and for its co-ministry with him. (2) God's continued work in their midst.
At Colosse	Col 1:3 1:9-14; 2:1	(1) Thankfulness for faith toward God and love for God's people. (2) Fruit of the Spirit, love. (3) knowledge of God's will. (4) Spirit given wisdom. (5) Lead lives pleasing to the Lord. (6) Enabled by God's power to endure. (6) That these believers would be thankful to God.
At Thessalonica	1Th 1:3, 2:13;	(1) Thankfulness to God for them. (2) Put their faith into practice. (3) Thankfulness for response to Gospel. (4) Thankfulness for a growing faith. (5)

18. Paul—Intercessor Leader

	5:23; 2Th 1:3,11-13; 2:13	Thankfulness for greater expression of love. (6) Thankfulness for the way they are bearing up in persecution. (7) That their lives may express God's work. (8) Entire final and full sanctification. (9) That they might be enabled by God's power to complete their walk and honor Jesus. (10) Thankfulness for them in that they responded first to the Gospel.
In Philemon's home	Phm 4-6	(1) Thankfulness for Philemon's love and faith. (2) Realization of union with Christ in everyday life. (3) Thankfulness for joy resulting from Philemon's testimony.

What Can We Learn From Paul's Prayers And His Teaching on Prayer?

Here are a few observations that may help us see more of what an intercessor leader is all about.

1. Paul shows how important thankfulness is in praying. Over and over again he is thankful to God for individuals and for churches (see references in Table Phm 18-1 above).
2. Paul operates daily with a spirit of prayer which bursts into praying. He openly states that he prays continually for people and churches (see 1Th 5:17; see Ro 12:12 and many others).
3. Paul prays specific requests for individuals and tells them what he is praying (2Ti 1:3 et al, see *prayer encouragement principle*, **Glossary**).
4. Paul prays for churches almost always giving thanks for them and almost always praying for their growth and appropriation of resources they have in Christ.
5. Intercessory prayer is hard agonizing work (see Ro 15:30, Col 2:1; 4:12. Note especially SRN 4865 used both in Ro 15:30 and Col 2:1, a word meaning agonize, strive at).
6. Paul shares vulnerably concerning his own situation so that people can pray knowingly and with empathy for him (Ro 15:30,31; 2Co 1:11 and many others).
7. Paul prays for believers to know God's power; that the Holy Spirit might enable them to live strong Christian lives.
8. Paul admonished that believers lift holy hands (that is, come to God with clean consciences and an awareness of what the Gospel has done for them) as they pray.
9. Paul admonishes believers to pray for governmental leaders (1Ti 1:1,2).
10. Paul exhorts believers to pray in the Spirit—meaning led of the Spirit in what and how to pray (Eph 6:18; see also Jude 20). He also speaks of praying in the Spirit meaning praying in tongues (and singing in tongues). Both are talked about. Paul also recognizes a praying in which the Spirit prays through us (Ro 8:26) in utterances that express what we should pray for even when we may not know what it is about or what we ought to pray.
11. Paul, not only prays for his own ministry, but prays for others' ministry (i.e. the Jews, see Ro 10:1).
12. Paul recognizes that believers will need to exercise disciplines involving fasting and praying—though he never commands believers to do this (1Co 7:5).
13. Paul suggests that believers should pray for needed giftedness (1Co 14:1, 13).
14. Paul prays for financial resources for needy churches, for individual Christian workers, and for his own self (2Co 8:14; 9:14 et al).
15. Paul asks prayer for himself for God-given opportunities for ministry and for effective impactful ministry (Col 4:3,4; 2Th 3:1).

Paul was an intercessor leader.

Conclusion

Apostolic leaders (especially Harvest leaders) need intercession for their ministries. Pastors (especially Shepherd leaders) need intercession for their ministries. God can gift them for this and/or provide others in their sphere of influence to carry this out. The prayer macro is still valid today.

Intercession   Leaders Called To A Ministry Are Called To Intercede For That Ministry.

See *modeling*, **Glossary**. See **Article**, *Vulnerability and Prayer Power; Jesus—Five Leadership Models: Shepherd, Harvest, Steward, Servant, Intercessor.*

Article 19

Relevance of the Article to Paul's Philemon Letter
In this short book of Philemon, Timothy and Onesimus receive the benefit of sponsor mentoring by Paul. Philemon receives personal attention about his spiritual growth—teaching mentoring and spiritual guide mentoring. Mentoring was a major way Paul demonstrated his value of personal ministry.

19. Paul—Mentor for Many

Introduction—Prolific Mentor
Paul was an outstanding mentor. He used mentoring as a major means of developing leaders. Mentoring is a relational experience in which one person, called the mentor, empowers another person, called the mentoree, by a transfer of resources. Empowerment can include such things as new habits, knowledge, skills, desires, values, connections to resources for growth and development of potential. We[96] have identified a number of mentoring functions. Usually any given leader will not be an ideal mentor and perform all of the mentoring functions. Instead a given leader will usually be proficient in three or four of the mentor functions. The set of mentoring functions that a leader uses in ministry is called his/her mentor-mix. It is easiest to demonstrate that Paul was an outstanding mentor by illustrating his mentoring relationship with Timothy.

Table Phm 19-1 identifies the nine mentoring functions:

Table Phm 19-1. Nine Mentor Functions

Type	Central Thrust
1. Discipler	Basic Habits of the Christian Life dealing with hearing from God and talking with God; operating in a fellowship of Christians; learning to minister in terms of giftedness; learning to get input from God.
2. Spiritual Guide	Evaluation of spiritual depth and maturity in a life and help in growth in this.
3. Coach	Skills of all kind depending on the expertise of the coach.
4. Counselor	Timely and good advice, which sheds perspective on issues and problems and other needs.
5. Teacher	Relevant knowledge that can be used for personal growth or ministry or other such need.
6. Sponsor	Protective guidance and linking to resources so that a leader reaches potential.
7. Contemporary Model	Values impactfully demonstrated in a life that can be transferred and used in one's own life.
8. Historical Model	Values demonstrated in a life and inspiration drawn from that life so as to encourage on-going development in ones own life and a pressing on to finish well.
9. Divine Contact	Timely Guidance from God via some human source.

Paul over the course of his 30+ years in ministry demonstrated almost all of the nine functions. With Timothy, as seen in the Acts and the two epistles to Timothy, several of the mentoring functions can be seen. Figure Phm 19-1 gives Paul's Mentor-Mix[97] in a pictorial format. This is called a Venn diagram. Each separate oval represents a mentor function. The larger the size of a symbol the more important it is. Overlap of symbols indicates some of both functions taking place. Non-overlap of a symbol with other symbols

---

[96] My son Dr. Richard W. Clinton, my colleague Paul Stanley and I have all been busily researching and using mentoring in our own personal ministries.

[97] Mentor-mix refers to the set of mentoring functions that a leader demonstrates in his/her ministry over time—not necessarily seen at any one given time but over a lifetime.

19. Paul—Mentor for Many

indicates exclusive manifestation of the symbol. Table Phm 19-2 takes these mentor functions and indicates where the mentoring function is indicated in the Scriptures and perhaps some empowerment.

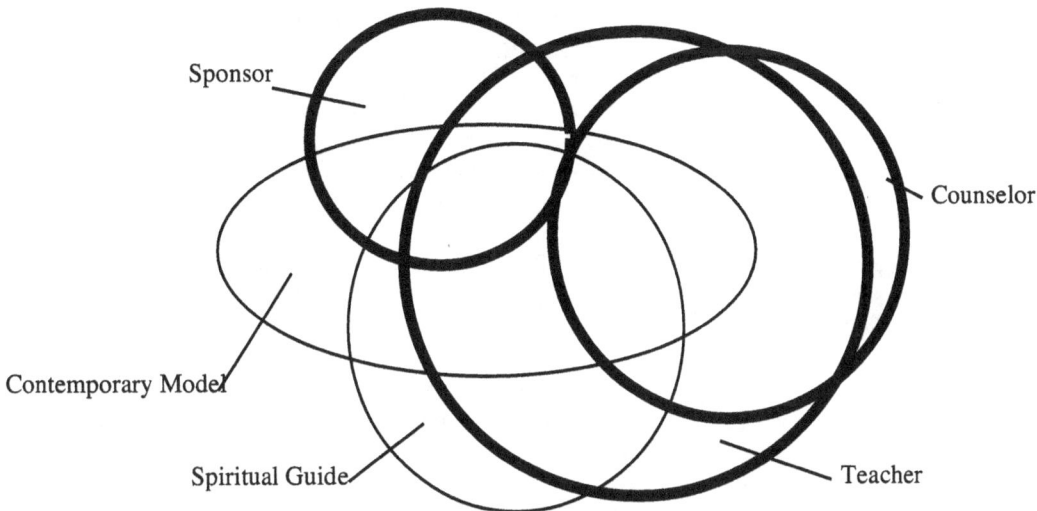

Figure Phm 19-1. Paul's Mentor-Mix with Timothy

From the Venn diagram in Figure Phm 19-1 it can be seen that the three most important mentor functions (indicated by the heavier lines) that Paul did with Timothy were teacher, Counselor, and sponsor. He also models and gives spiritual advice for Timothy's own growth.

Table Phm 19-2. Mentor Functions of Paul With Timothy

Kind	Where Seen	Empowerment
Teacher	Ac 16, 17, 18, 19, 20; 2Ti 3:10 Ro 16:21; 1Co 4:17; 2Co 1:19	Timothy was familiar with all of Paul's teaching from the Scriptures. For example, he heard the teaching on the material that was later incorporated as Romans given at Corinth; he was present for the dictation of the book of Romans. He spent hours on the road with Paul and chatted with him.
Counselor	1,2Ti are laced with words of advice	1Ti ch 1,2 Paul's advice on major problems in the church, 1Ti ch 3 Paul's advice on local leadership selection, 1Ti ch 5 Paul's advice on the problem of widows and discipline of leaders.
Sponsor	1,2Ti	He is listed by Paul as co-author (a sponsoring function) of six epistles (See 2Co 1:1; Php 1:1; Col 1:1; 1Th 1:1; 2Th 1:1, Phm 1:1). The material in 1,2Ti is dominantly written with a view to the church there reading it and knowing that Paul was giving Timothy instructions for that church.
Model	2Ti 3:10-17; Php	Philippians gives Paul's comprehensive treatment of his use of modeling.
Spiritual Guide	1,2Ti	See especially 1Ti 4 Paul's personal advice to Timothy on How to Handle Himself.—especially maintaining the balance of developing self and developing ministry.. See also 2Ti 1;3-10 on developing giftedness.

Five Features of Paul's Mentoring

Table Phm 19-3 below lists five features noticeable in Paul's mentoring or that supplemented his mentoring.

Table Phm 19-3. Five Features About Paul's Mentoring

Feature	Explanation
Personal Value	Paul often talked straight from the heart to those he ministered to. He illustrates one of his strongest leadership values when he does that. And this is even more true in his mentoring relationships. A leadership value is an underlying assumption, which affects how a leader behaves in or perceives leadership situations. Paul felt ministry ought to be very personal. Stated more generally for all leaders, *Leaders should view personal relationships as an important part of ministry both as a means for ministry and as an end in itself of ministry.* In his epistles Paul names almost 80 people by name—most of whom he ministered with or to or in some way they ministered to him. Of the five dynamics of mentoring (attraction, relationship, responsiveness, accountability, empowerment) relationship was Paul's strong suit. And with Timothy relationship is seen more clearly than any of Paul's companions. See **Article**, *25. Timothy, A Beloved Son in the Faith.* Principle: *The development of a personal relationship between a mentor and mentoree will increase the effectiveness of the mentoring.*
Took People With Him; On-the-Job training.	Whenever possible, Paul never went into ministry alone. He almost always took someone with him—frequently, one he had a mentoring relationship with, one who he was developing as a leader. Principle: *Modeling as a major means of influencing or developing emerging leaders best happens in on-the-job training.*
Teams	Whenever possible, Paul took more than one person with him. He used teams of people. And he would send various team members on important errands. See **Article**, *15. Paul and His Companions*. Note especially the *we sections* in Acts 16 etc. See also the number of folks around in Romans 16:20-22 (Timothy, Lucius, Sosipater, Tertius, Gaius, Erastus, Quartus) when he dictated the letter.
Little/Big; Ministry Tasks	Paul used the basic principle of the Luke 16:10 little/ big: *The one faithful in little things will be faithful in bigger things.* Give people little things to do and if they are faithful in them, give them bigger things to do. This was especially true of the ministry tasks given Titus and Timothy. A ministry task is an assignment from God, which primarily tests a person's faithfulness and obedience but often also allows use of ministry gifts in the context of a task which has closure, accountability, and evaluation. See Titus' five ministry tasks (3 in Corinth 1 in Crete and 1 in Dalmatia). As the person grows the ministry task moves more from the testing of the person's faithfulness toward the accomplishment of the task.
Goodwin's Expectation Principle	Goodwin's expectation principle states, *Emerging leaders tend to live up to the genuine expectations of leaders they respect.* A well-respected leader can use this dynamic to challenge younger leaders to grow. The challenge embodied in the expectation must not be too much or the young leader will not be able to accomplish it and will be inoculated against further challenges. The challenge must not be too little or it will not attract. It must be a genuine expectation. Paul uses this with Timothy, Philemon, and Titus several times (see fn 1Ti 6:11; See fn 2Ti 1:5).

The end result of mentoring is the empowerment of the mentorees. Luke, Titus, Timothy, Philemon, Onesimus, Archippus, Priscilla, Phoebe and many others attest to the power of Paul's mentoring. And of all of Paul's mentoring functions, probably the most effective was the modeling. Note in his mentor-mix how modeling subtly interweaves itself throughout every other mentoring function. Paul personally related to numerous leaders to develop them. He left behind a heritage—men and women who could continue to lead and carry out his life purpose and use his values in their lives and ministry.

See **Articles**: *17. Paul—Developer Par Excellence; 15. Paul and His Companions*. For more detailed study see **Bibliography for Further Study**, Stanley and Clinton 1992, **Connecting**. Clinton and Clinton 1993, **The Mentor Handbook.**

Article 20

Relevance of the Article to Paul's Philemon Letter
One of the most important leadership concepts illustrated in the book of Philemon is Paul's use of leadership styles to influence Philemon. Three styles are seen in Philemon. Those three leadership styles include: *father-initiator*, *maturity appeal*, and *obligation persuasion*. This use of Paul's influence in Philemon is the defining illustration for the style, *obligation persuasion*.

20. Pauline Leadership Styles

Introduction—Leadership Style and Relation to Leader Definition
Consider the fundamental definition for leader that permeates this Handbook.

Definition   A leader is a person with God-given capacity and God-given responsibility who is influencing a specific group of people toward God's purposes.

How does one influence? Leadership style is one measure of how a leader influences. Paul again sets an example for leaders in the N.T. Church Leadership Era.

In Php, I point out that Paul uses the maturity appeal (opening salutation) and imitation modeling leadership styles (throughout the book, see especially Php 4:9). In Phm, I show how Paul uses several leadership styles: father-initiator (Phm 19), maturity appeal (Phm 9), and obligation persuasion (Phm 8-21). In 1Co and 2Co I repeatedly make comments on Paul's leadership styles. In 1Co I point out his Father-initiator style (4:14,15), his Apostolic leadership style (9:1,2), his confrontation style (1Co 5:1-5), his indirect conflict leadership style (1Co 5:1-4) and his imitator leadership style (1Co 4:16). In 2Co I point out maturity appeal (6:9,10), obligation persuasion (8:8), Father-initiator (2Co 10:14). Paul is a multi-style leader—a very modern concept in leadership style theory. What is a multi-style leader? Some definitions are needed in order to understand leadership style. Then I will move on to examine Pauline leadership styles.

Definition: The dominant leadership style of a leader is that,
1. highly directive or
2. directive or
3. non-directive or
4. highly non-directive

consistent behavior pattern that underlies specific overt behavior acts of influence pervading the majority of leadership functions in which that leader exerts influence.

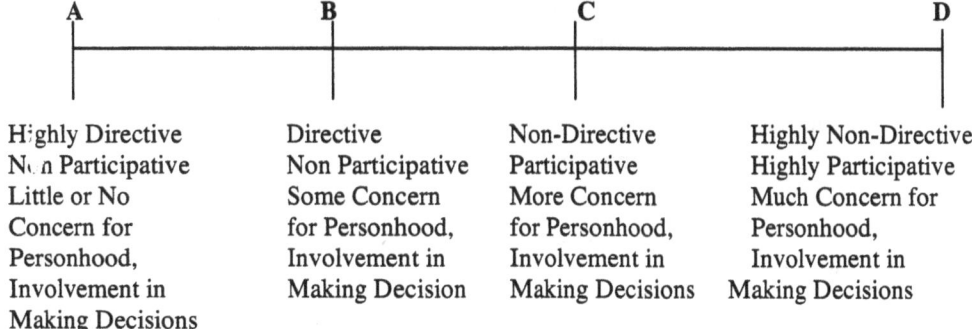

Figure Phm 20-1. Influence Behavior Along a Continuum

20. Pauline Leadership Styles

Leadership style deals with the individual behavioral expression a leader utilizes in influencing followers. This individual expression includes methodology for handling crises, methodology for problem solving, methodology for decision making, methodology for coordinating with superiors, peers and subordinates, methodology for handling leadership development. The individual methodology for a specific leadership act (or series) can often be identified on the Directive—Non-Directive continuum.

My study of Paul's influence identified ten styles. These were given specific labels. Paul was multi-styled[98] in his approach to influencing followers. The styles are not defined exclusively. That is, there is some overlap of concepts between different styles. Let me describe the ten styles I labeled.

Ten Pauline Styles Observed

1. Apostolic Style

Where a person demonstrates with self-authenticating evidence that he/she has delegated authority from God—that is, there is a sense of spiritual authority about the leadership—then that person can use the apostolic leadership style.

Definition: The apostolic leadership style is a method of influence in which the leader

- assumes the role of delegated authority over those for whom he/she is responsible,
- receives revelation from God concerning decisions, and
- commands obedience based on role of delegated authority and revelation concerning God's will.

A synonym for this style is the command/demand style. This style is implied in 1Th 5:12, 13. "And I want you, fellow Christians, to personally know the leaders who work among you, and are over you in the Lord, and warm you. Lovingly honor them for their work's sake." It is implied in 1Ti 5:17: "Church leaders that are exercising good leadership should be evaluated as worthy of double pay—especially the ones who are working hard teaching the word." Another example implying this style is seen in Heb 13:17: "Obey those leaders who are set over you. Submit to their leadership. For they watch for your souls, as those who must give account. And they want to do so with joy and not with grief. Make it worth their while." This style is also seen in 1Th 2:6; even though Paul chooses not to command obedience, he asserts that he could have done so as was his apostolic right. The essence of the apostolic style is the legitimate right from God to make decisions for others and to command or demand their compliance with those decisions.

This style with its top-down command/demand approach is considered the most highly directive leadership style.

2. Confrontation Style

Many leaders try to avoid problems, particularly those involving troublesome people and those carrying heavy emotional ramifications. The basic rationale seems to be, "this is a tough problem; if I try to do anything about it I'm going to incur wrath, maybe have my character maligned, lose some friends and be drained emotionally. Perhaps if I just ignore it, it will go away by itself." For some problems, perhaps this is a good philosophy; time does give opportunity for a clearer perspective, for healing, and for indirect conflict to occur. But for most problems, leaders must confront the problem and parties involved directly. At least this seems to be the approaches exemplified in Jude, John, Peter, and Paul in their Scriptural writings.

Definition: The confrontation leadership style is an approach to problem solving

- which brings the problem out in the open with all parties concerned,
- which analyzes the problem in light of revelational truth,
- and which brings force to bear upon the parties to accept recommended solutions.

---

[98] Doohan, a noted author on Pauline leadership also concludes that Paul is multi-styled. See Helen Doohan, **Leadership in Paul**. Wilmington, Del.: Michael Glazier, Inc., 1984.

This style is usually seen in combination with other styles. Seemingly, the majority of cases emphasize *obligation-persuasion* as the force for accepting the solution, but *apostolic* force is also seen in the Scriptures. The book of Jude is an example. Several of the leadership acts in the book of 1Co utilize this style. Paul also uses this style in the Philippian church. See the problem between Euodia and Synteche. This style, like the apostolic style, is highly directive since the solutions to the problems are often the leader's solutions.

3. Father-Initiator Style

Paul resorts to this leadership style when exerting his influence upon the Corinthian church. He is establishing his authority in order to suggest solutions to some deep problems in the church.

Definition: The <u>father-initiator leadership style</u> is related to the apostolic style, which uses the fact of the leader having founded the work as a lever for getting acceptance of influence by the leader.

In 1Co 4:14, 15 Paul writes, "14 I do not write these things to shame you, but as my beloved children I warn you. 15 For though you might have ten thousand Christian teachers, you only have one father in the faith. For I became your spiritual father when I preached the Gospel to you." Paul uses the father-initiator style in this case." Note in this example the force of the two powerful figures: the absolute for the relative in verse 14 and the hyperbole in verse 15.

The father-initiator style is closely related to the obligation-persuasion style, in that obligation (debt owed due to founding the work) is used as a power base. However it differs from obligation-persuasion in that more than persuasion is used. The decision to obey is not left to the follower. It is related to the apostolic style in that it is apostolic in its force of persuasion.

This style is highly directive/directive style.

4. Obligation-Persuasion Style

One method of influencing followers over which you have no direct organizational control involves persuasion. The leader persuades but leaves the final decision to the follower. A particularly powerful technique of persuasion is obligation-persuasion in which normal appeal techniques are coupled with a sense of obligation on the part of the follower due to past relationship/experience with the leader. Such a leadership style is seen with Paul's treatment of the Onesimus/Philemon problem.

Definition: An <u>obligation-persuasion leadership style</u> refers to an appeal to followers to follow some recommended directives which

- persuades, not commands followers to heed some advice;
- leaves the decision to do so in the hands of the followers, but
- forces the followers to recognize their obligation to the leader due to past service by the leader to the follower;
- strongly implies that the follower owes the leader some debt and should follow the recommended advice as part of paying back the obligation; and finally
- reflects the leader's strong expectation that the follower will conform to the persuasive advice.

The classic example of this is illustrated in the book of Philemon. Paul uses this style in combination with other styles in 1,2Co also.

This is a directive style. The expectation is high, though the actual decision to do so passes to the follower.

5. Father-Guardian Style

This style, much like the nurse style, elicits an empathetic concern of the leader toward protection and care for followers.

Definition: The <u>father-guardian style</u> is a style which is similar to a parent-child relationship and has as its major concern protection and encouragement for followers.

Usually this style is seen when a very mature Christian relates to very immature followers. 1Th 2:10, 11 illustrates this style. "You know it to be true, and so does God, that our behavior toward you believers was pure, right, and without fault. You know that we treated each one of you just as a father treats his own children. We encouraged you, we comforted you, and we kept urging you to live the kind of life that pleases God, who calls you to share in his own Kingdom and glory."

Usually this style is directive, but because of the caring relationship between leader and follower and the follower maturity level it does not seem directive, since influence behavior always seem to have the follower's best interest at heart.

6. Maturity Appeal Style

The book of Proverbs (see especially 1:20-33, a great personification passage teaching this very point; but see also the whole book which derives lessons from life;) indicates that all of life is an experience that can be used by God to give wisdom. And those who have learned wisdom should be listened to by those needing yet to learn. Maturity in the Christian life comes through time and experience and through God-given lessons as well as giftedness (see *word of wisdom gift*, **Glossary**). Leaders often influence and persuade followers by citing their *track record* (learned wisdom) with God.

Definition: A <u>maturity appeal leadership style</u> is a form of leadership influence, which counts upon
- Godly experience, usually gained over a long period of time,
- an empathetic identification based on a common sharing of experience, and
- a recognition of the force of imitation modeling in influencing people in
order to convince people toward a favorable acceptance of the leader's ideas.

Heb 13:7 carries this implication: "Remember your former leaders who spoke God's message to you. Think back on how they lived and died and imitate their faith."

See also 1Pe 5:1-4, 5-7 where Peter demonstrates maturity appeal. "I, an elder myself, appeal to the church elders among you. I saw firsthand Christ's sufferings. I will share in the glory that will be revealed. I appeal to you to be shepherds of the flock that God gave you. Take care of it willingly, as God wants you to, and not unwillingly. Do your work, not for mere pay, but from a real desire to serve. Do not try to rule over those who have been put in your care, but be an example to the flock. And when the chief Shepherd appears, you will receive the glorious crown which will last."

Paul's description of his sufferings as an Apostle (2Co 11:16-33) and experience in receiving revelation (2Co 12:1-10) are exemplary of the maturity appeal style leadership.

This style moves between the categories of directive to non-directive depending on how forcefully the desired result is pushed for.

7. Nurse Style

In 1Th 2:7, Paul uses a figure to describe a leadership style he used among the Thessalonian Christians. The figure is that of a nurse. It is the only use of this particular word in the N.T., though related cognates do occur. The essential idea of the figure is the gentle cherishing attitude of Paul toward the new

Christians in Thessalonica with a particular emphasis on Paul's focus on serving in order to help them grow.

> Definition: The nurse leadership style is a behavior style characterized by gentleness and sacrificial service and loving care, which indicates that a leader has given up "rights" in order not to impede the nurture of those following him/her.

The primary example is given in 1Th 2:7, "But we were gentle among you, even as a nurse cherishes her children." Paul commands an attitude of gentleness to Timothy in 2Ti 2:24–25. "24 The Lord's servant must not quarrel; instead be gentle unto all, skillfully teaching and being patient, 25 gently instructing those opponents. Perhaps God will give them opportunity to repent and see the truth."

The nurse style is similar to the father-guardian style in that both have a strong empathetic care for the followers. It differs in that the father-guardian style assumes a protective role of a parent to child. The nurse role assumes a nurturing focus, which will sacrifice in order to see nurture accomplished.

The nurse style is non-directive.

8. Imitator Style

Paul seemed continually to sense that what he was and what he did served as a powerful model for those he influenced. He expected his followers to become like him in attitudes and actions. It is this personal model of *being* and *doing* as a way to influence followers that forms part of the foundational basis for spiritual authority.

> Definition: The *imitator style* refers to a conscious use of imitation modeling as a means for influencing followers. It reflects a leader's sense of responsibility for what he/she is as a person of God and for what he/she does in ministry with an expectant view that followers must and will and should be encouraged to follow his/her example.

Paul emphasizes this in Php 4:9 which illustrates this leadership style. "9 Those things, which you have both learned, and received, and heard, and seen in me, do—and the God of peace shall be with you. A second Pauline illustration is seen in 2Ti 3:10,11. 10 "But you fully know my teaching, my lifestyle, my purpose in life, my faith, my steadfastness, my love, my endurance. 11 I was persecuted at Antioch, at Iconium, at Lystra; I endured those persecutions. Yet the Lord delivered me out of them." Paul goes on to give the response he expects of Timothy based on this imitation modeling and maturity appeal.

The whole book of Php emphasizes this influential methodology as being one of the most powerful tools a leader can use to influence followers. This style is highly non-directive.

9. Consensus Style

Decisions, which affect people's lives and for which leaders must give account require careful spirit-led consideration. One leadership style approach to decision making involves consensus decision making. This style is often used in coordination situations where ownership is desired. Cultures, which stress group solidarity, such as many of the tribes in Papua New Guinea, see this style used frequently by leaders.

> Definition: Consensus leadership style refers to the approach to leadership influence, which involves the group itself actively participating in decision making and coming to solutions acceptable to the whole group. The leader must be skilled in bringing diverse thoughts together in such a way as to meet the whole group's needs.

In a consensus style there is much give and take in arriving at decision. Unless there is a *check in the spirit,* which prohibits an agreement, the final decision carries the weight of the entire group and thus will *demand* all to follow through on implications and ramifications, which follow. James apparently gives a consensus decision reflecting the entire group's corporate will in the Ac 15 decision. Note this decision was identified as Spirit-led. The Ac 6 decision concerning distribution of good to widows is an example of both of consensus (within the plurality of Apostles) and apostolic (commanded to the followers) leadership styles.

This style is highly non-directive.

10. Indirect Conflict Style

A powerful style for dealing with crises and problem solving involves the concept of dealing with *first causes*, that is, the primary motivating factors behind the problem rather than the problem itself. This style recognizes that spiritual conflict is behind the situation and must be dealt with before any solution will take hold. The parties directly involved may not be aware that the leader is even doing problem solving. A leader who uses this approach must be skilled in prayer, understand spiritual warfare and either have the gift of discerning spirits or access to a person with that gift.

> Definition   The indirect conflict leadership style is an approach to problem solving which requires discernment of spiritual motivation factors behind the problem, usually results in spiritual warfare without direct confrontation with the parties of the problem Spiritual warfare is sensed as a necessary first step before any problem solving can take place.

See the context of Mt 16:21–23 especially verse 23: "Get away from me Satan. You are an obstacle in my way, because these thoughts of yours don't come from God, but from man." This is an example of indirect conflict leadership style. Mk 3:20–30 gives the underlying idea behind this style. See especially verse 27: "No one can break into a strong man's house and take away his belongings unless he first ties up the strong man; then he can plunder his house." See also Eph 6:10–20, especially verse 12: "For we are not fighting against human beings but against the wicked spiritual forces in the heavenly world, the rulers, authorities, and cosmic powers of this dark age."

Conclusions

I think the following are worth noting because they point out what I have been attempting to do in this section dealing with biblical styles, most of which come from Pauline material.

1. I have demonstrated how to use the generic (directive/non-directive continuum) as the overarching umbrella on which to pinpoint specific leadership-style behaviors.
2. I have identified 10 different Pauline leadership styles.
3. These 10 models of specific styles are transferable to many situations, which we as leaders face today.
4. I have indicated that Paul's leadership style was multi-styled.
5. I have pointed out that Paul was a flexible leader who matured in his leadership as he grew older and was able to change to meet change to meet changing situations.

Current leadership style theories differ on whether or not a leader can actually change his/her leadership style. My own observations recognize that some leaders are flexible and can change. Others are not. Perhaps the ideal is a flexible leader who can change. But where this is not possible, then a leader who dominantly uses a certain leadership style should be placed in a situation where that style fits. Directive styles fit best with immature followers who need that direction. As followers mature the leadership styles should move to the right on the directive-non-directive continuum. This allows for follower maturity and for emerging leaders to arise.

Article 21

Relevance of the Article to Paul's Philemon Letter

In the opening salutation, Paul highlights his viewpoint of God's overriding sovereignty in his life. Note the use of the phrase, a prisoner of Jesus Christ. This is a beautiful illustration of Paul's perspective on God's work in His life through all kinds of circumstances—that is, a sovereign mindset.

21. Sovereign Mindset

Introduction—A Relatively New Word

Mindset burst upon our English language scene in the mid-eighties. So it is a relative newcomer to English speakers. Not all English speakers even know it. But its definition is as old as the Bible itself. What is a mindset? A mindset is a fixed mental attitude or disposition—formed by experience, education, prejudice, or the like—that predetermines a person's responses to and interpretations of situations. One of the great Bible leaders, Paul the Apostle, demonstrated a special kind of mindset. I call it a sovereign mindset. A sovereign mindset represents one leadership value[99] that can make the difference for a Christian leader.[100] And I want to suggest that if you do not have this mindset you probably won't make it in ministry—at least not as an effective leader who will finish well.

A leadership value is an underlying assumption a leader holds, which affects how the leader acts or perceives in leadership situations. It is a mindset, an underlying controlling force, which gives meaning to ourselves and explains whey we do things or think things. It can relate to a belief. It can relate to personal ethical conduct. It can relate to personal feelings desired about situations. It can relate to ideas of what brings success or failure in ministry. It can be rooted in personality shaping. It can be rooted in heritage. It can be rooted in the critical shaping activities that describes our personal history of leadership development.

Paul models this leadership value, a sovereign mindset, more than any other New Testament Church leader.[101] Quickly glance through the two passages below to catch the flavor of this important leadership insight. Pay special attention to the boldfaced words.

> 3 Blessed [be] God, even the Father of our Lord Jesus Christ, the Father of mercies, and the God of all comfort; 4 Who comforts us in all our tribulation, **that we may be able to comfort them which are in any trouble**, by the comfort wherewith we ourselves are comforted of God. 5 For as the sufferings of Christ abound in us, so our consolation also abounds by Christ. 6 And whether we **be afflicted, [it is] for your consolation and salvation**, which is effectual in the enduring of the same sufferings which we also suffer: or whether we be comforted, [it is] for your consolation and salvation. 7 ¶ And our hope

---

[99] See also the **Article**, *Pauline Leadership Values*, which touches on 19 important leadership values derived from the book of 2Co. Values are desperately needed today in our world of tolerance for anything except absolutes. This article describes one important Christian leadership value.

[100] It can for a secular leader too. A Christian leader believes that God is involved in the events of life and therefore looks to learn what God has for him/her in the happenings of life. A secular leader who does not believe that God is ⟨ ⁚ is involved in life's events can still also profit greatly from the happenings in life if that leader has a learning posture and believes that life's experiences can be used to teach lessons. The learning posture needed is simply, *All of life is preparing us for all of the rest of life.* We can be better leaders if we learn from life's experiences and let that learning inform our leadership. See also the **Article**, *Leadership Lessons, Seven Major Identified,* one of which deals with learning posture, "Effective leaders maintain a learning posture all of their lives."

[101] Paul is a major model for a Christian leader in the N.T. Leadership Era. We have more biographical information on Paul than any other Church leader. He himself recognizes the importance of modeling. See Php 4:9 and other cross-references.

21. Sovereign Mindset

of you [is] steadfast, knowing, that as you are partakers of the sufferings, so [shall you be] also of the consolation. 2 Corinthians 1:3-7

8 For we would not, brethren, have you ignorant of our trouble which came to us in Asia, that we were pressed out of measure, above strength, inasmuch that we despaired even of life: 9 But we had the sentence of death in ourselves, **that we should not rely on ourselves, but in God which raises the dead: 10 Who delivered us from so great a death**, and does deliver: in whom we trust that he will yet deliver [us]; 11 You also helping together by prayer for us, that for the gift [bestowed] upon us by the means of many persons thanks may be given by many on our behalf. 2 Corinthians 1:8-11

Once you know what a sovereign mindset is, you can easily see it in these two previous quotes. But this sovereign mindset just leaps out from the pages in the following quotes.

For this cause I Paul, the **prisoner of Jesus Christ** for you Gentiles, Eph 3:1

I therefore, the **prisoner of the Lord**, implore you to walk worthy of your Christian calling. Eph 4:1

So that my **bonds in Christ** are manifest in all the palace, and in all other [places]. Php1:13

Don't be ashamed of the testimony of our Lord, nor of me **his prisoner**: but share also in the afflictions of the gospel according to the power of God; 2Ti 1:8

Paul, a **prisoner of Jesus Christ**, and Timothy [our] brother, unto Philemon our dearly beloved, and fellow laborer, Phm 1:1

Yet for love's sake I rather implore you, being such an one as Paul the aged, and now also a **prisoner of Jesus Christ**. Phm 1:9

Paul don't you have that wrong? Aren't you a prisoner of the Roman empire? Why do you say a prisoner of Jesus Christ. What a strange way to make your point! Its all in how you see it. Yes, Paul was a prisoner of the Roman Empire. But no matter what they intended, Paul knew God would use it for God's purposes. For you see, You Paul operated under a sovereign mindset?

Definition　　A <u>sovereign mindset</u> is a way of viewing life's activities so as to see and respond to God's purposes in them.

Remember, a mindset is a 1. A fixed mental attitude or disposition that predetermines a person's responses to and interpretations of situations. Paul had a fixed mental attitude toward the things that happened to him. He saw God in them. Or as he says in 2Ti 3:11, "...out of them all God worked."

God was sovereignly and providentially working through all of life's circumstances to shape Paul, guide him, and make him the great leader he became. Four keys to Paul's sovereign mindset include:

1. Paul recognized God's hand in life happenings—no matter who or what the immediate cause.
2. Paul submitted to God's deeper purposes in life happenings.
3. Paul learned and used the lessons derived from these life happenings.
4. Paul shared those lessons (and God's provision in them) with others.

His deep experiences with God were at the heart of the spiritual authority[102] he had with followers.

Let me come back to the two passages I first cited as indicating a sovereign mindset. I want to draw out some leadership observations that directly apply to Christian leaders.

From 2Co 1:3-7:

---

[102] See also the **Article**, *22. Spiritual Authority*, which describes a major power base for a Christian leader.

21. Sovereign Mindset

1. God will meet us in deep processing.
2. We are helped in order to help.
3. Deep processing tests our own value in the sufficiency of Christ.
4. Our own development through processing gives us hope that our followers can also know the sufficiency of Christ in their deep processing.

From 2Co 1:8-11

1. We really trust in God when we come to the end of our own resources.
2. Deep processing is meant to be shared.
3. Deep processing shared brings partnership in prayer.
4. God receives much more praise when our situation is solved.

A leader with a sovereign mindset recognizes that at the heart of all God's shaping activities is the idea that processing is never just for himself/herself alone. Leaders are shaped by critical incidents and shaping activities for our development, yes! But our processing is also for our followers. It is this confidence in God's meeting us in deep processing that gives us confidence in His sufficiency. And a by-product of that confidence is spiritual authority, the dominant power base of a Christian leader.

Stated as a leadership value, the sovereign mindset mindset strikingly challenges us.

Value **Leaders Ought To See God's Hand In Their Circumstances As Part Of His Plan For Developing Them As Leaders.**

Paul had a sovereign mindset. He kept it till the end. It was one of the secrets of his finishing well. This leadership value is fundamental to a Christian view of the development of a leader.

See **Articles**, *Pauline Leadership Values; Leadership Lessons—Seven Major Identified; Value Driven Leadership.*

Article 22

Relevance of the Article to Paul's Philemon Letter
In the opening salutation Paul carefully avoids using apostolic language. He does not want to command Philemon to accept his advice. He wants Philemon to follow it from the heart. Paul must depend on spiritual authority alone in this delicate task of getting Philemon to accept back Onesimus, the run away slave. If Philemon is to go through the paradigm shift to understand and follow through on Paul's request, he must do it voluntarily and from the heart. Paul relies on spiritual authority alone.

22. Spiritual Authority—Six Characteristics

Introduction—Authority Needed
A Biblical leader is a person with God-given capacities and with God-given responsibility who is influencing specific groups of God's people toward God's purposes for them. To influence, a leader must have some power base. I am indebted to Dennis Wrong[103] for helping me identify a taxonomy of concepts dealing with power. Wrong has influence as the highest level on his taxonomy, power next, and authority third. Influence can be unintended or intended. In terms of leadership we are interested in intended influence. Intended influence can be subdivided into four power forms, the second level: Force, Manipulation, Authority, and Persuasion. All of these are important for Christian leaders with the final two being the most important—authority and persuasion—since spiritual authority is related to both. Authority, the third level, can further be sub-divided into coercive, inducive, legitimate, competent, personal. A leader will need to use various combinations of these power forms to influence people. However,

Effective leaders value spiritual authority as a primary power base.

This is one of seven major leadership lessons that I have identified from comparative study of effective leaders. This article defines spiritual authority and gives some guidelines about its use.

Spiritual Authority—What Is It?
Spiritual authority is the ideal power base for a leader to use with mature believers who respect God's authority in a leader. A simplified definition focusing on the notion of maturity of believers is:

Definition <u>Spiritual authority</u> is the
- right to influence,
- conferred upon a leader by followers,
- because of their perception of spirituality in that leader.

An expanded definition focusing on how a leader gets and uses it is:

Definition <u>Spiritual Authority</u> is that
- characteristic of a God-anointed leader,
- developed upon an experiential power base (giftedness, character, deep experiences with God),

that enables him/her to influence followers through
- persuasion,
- force of modeling, and
- moral expertise.

---

[103] See Dennis H. Wrong, **Power—Its Forms, Bases, and Uses**. 1979. San Francisco, CA: Harper and Row.

Spiritual authority comes to a leader in three major ways. As leaders go through deep experiences with God they experience the sufficiency of God to meet them in those situations. They come to know God. This experiential knowledge of God and the deep experiences with God are part of the experiential acquisition of spiritual authority. A second way that spiritual authority comes is through a life which models godliness. When the Spirit of God is transforming a life into the image of Christ those characteristics of love, joy, peace, long suffering, gentleness, goodness, faith, meekness, temperance carry great weight in giving credibility that the leader is consistent inward and outward. A third way that spiritual authority comes is through gifted power. When a leader can demonstrate gifted power in ministry—that is, a clear testimony to divine intervention in the ministry via his/her gifts—there will be spiritual authority. Now while all three of these ways of getting spiritual authority should be a part of a leader, it is frequently the case that one or more of the elements dominates. From the definitions and description of how spiritual authority comes you can readily see that a leader using spiritual authority does not force his/her will on followers.

What Are Some Guidelines—To Maximize Use and Minimize Abuse

The following descriptive characteristics about spiritual authority sets some limits, describe ideals, warn against abuse and in general gives helpful guidelines for leaders who desire spiritual authority as a primary means of influence.

Six Characteristics And Limits Of Spiritual Authority

These six descriptions were derived from my own observations of leaders and from adaptations made from several writers on power such as Watchman Nee, R. Baine Harris, and Richard T. De George. Nee was a Chinese Christian leader. The other two are secular authorities on power and authority in leadership.

Table Phm 22-1. Six Characteristics of Spiritual Authority

Characterization	Statement
1. Ultimate Source	Spiritual authority has its ultimate source in Christ. It is representative religious authority. It is His authority and presence in us, which legitimates our authority. Accountability to this final authority is essential.
2. Power Base	Spiritual authority rests upon an experiential power base. A leader's personal experiences with God and the accumulated wisdom and development that comes through them lie at the heart of the reason why followers allow influence in their lives. It is a resource, which is at once on-going and yet related to the past. Its genuineness as to the reality of experience with God is confirmed in the believer by the presence and ministry of the Holy Spirit who authenticates that experiential power base.
3. Power Forms	Spiritual authority influences by virtue of persuasion. Word gifts are dominant in this persuasion. Influence is by virtue of legitimate authority. Positional leadership carries with it recognition of qualities of leadership which are at least initially recognized by followers. Such authority must be buttressed by other authority forms such as competent authority, and personal authority.
4. Ultimate Good	The aim of influence using spiritual authority is the ultimate good of the followers. This follows the basic Pauline leadership principle seen in 2Co 10:8.
5. Evaluation	Spiritual authority is best judged longitudinally over time in terms of development of maturity in believers. Use of coercive and manipulative forms of authority will usually reproduce like elements in followers. Spiritual authority will produce mature followers who will make responsible moral choices because they have learned to do so.
6. Non-Defensive	A leader using spiritual authority recognizes submission to God who is the ultimate authority. Authority is representative. God is therefore the responsible agent for defending spiritual authority. A person moving in spiritual authority does not have to insist on obedience. Obedience is the moral responsibility of the follower. Disobedience, that is, rebellion to spiritual authority, means that a follower is not subject to God Himself. He/she will answer to God for that. The leader can rest upon God's vindication if it is necessary.

22. Spiritual Authority—Six Characteristics

Remember,

Effective leaders value spiritual authority as a primary power base.[104]

See *power forms* (various definitions), **Glossary**. See **Articles**, *4. Influence, Power, and Authority; Leadership Lessons—Seven Major Identified*.

---

[104] They also know that it will take varied forms of power including coercive, inducive, positional, personal, competence and others to influence immature believers toward maturity. But the ideal is always there to use spiritual authority with mature believers.

Article 23

Relevance of the Article to Paul's Philemon Letter

The book of Philemon is a beautiful illustration of the starting point plus process model. God is taking a major step forward in dealing with the slavery issue—a strongly imbedded social institution in the Roman empire. He chooses to do this by hitting it at its moral core. It is wrong. Christian love is a major value that will undermine a believer's understanding of slavery.

23. Starting Point Plus Process Model

Introduction—Social Issues

The book of Philemon suggested some principles under the label social issue. In that book, the whole social institution of slavery was being undermined by Christian values. The two principles about social change that were listed include:

a. One means for overcoming a social evil is to undermine it at value level. Many Christian values speak to social issues.
b. Major social change will take a long time to implement. One of the reasons for this is the way God works to bring about change in a culture. The starting point plus model seeks to identify God's methodology for changing cultures and cultural practices.

The Starting Point Plus Process model, outlines 4 major assertions suggesting how God brings about change in cultures and cultural practices. The basic motif is that *God begins where people are and progressively reveals Himself and applicable truth to move them toward supracultural ideals.*

Four Major Assertions

1. Assuming a valid faith-allegiance response,[105] God allows for a range of understanding of Himself and His Will for people, for He starts where people are rather than demanding that they immediately conform to His ideals.
2. This range of understanding of God can assume a variety of potential starting points anywhere from sub-ideal toward ideal perception of God and His ways.
3. God then initiates a process, which involves a revelational progression from a sub-ideal starting point toward the ideal.
4. This process of beginning with a range of sub-ideal starting points of perception and behavior and moving by revelational progression from the sub-ideal toward the ideal can be applied to any doctrine of Scripture and any Scriptural treatment of behavioral patterns.

---

[105] By a faith-allegiance response is meant a valid decision to place God as top priority in a life—a trusting response for God's salvation and work in a life.

Marriage Example

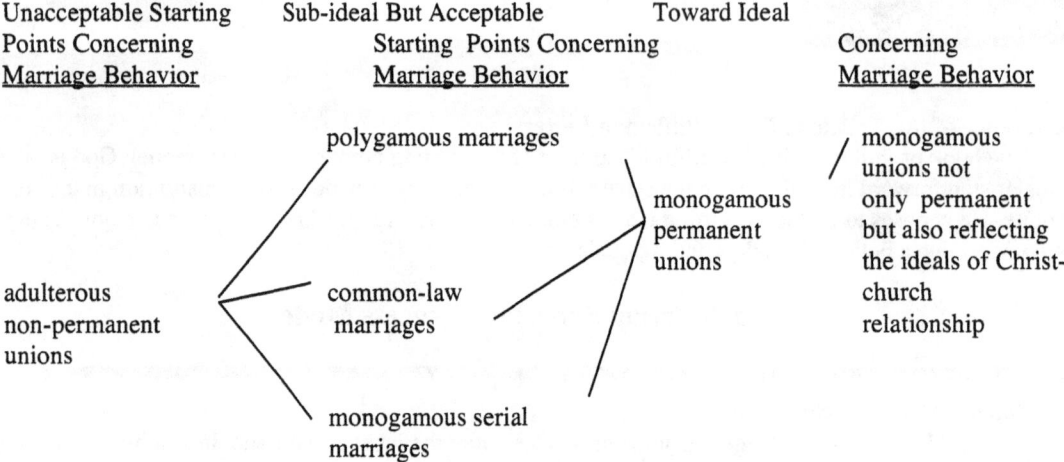

Figure Phm 23-1. Starting Point Plus Process Model-Marriage

As can be seen above, God works in a cultural situation to move toward the ideal on the right. Assuming that a group within a culture has come to Christ and are giving allegiance to Him above all else, God will begin to work. But assume they are at the far left. God will reject the starting point and immediately move that group toward a sub-ideal position. God will move them over time further right toward the sub-ideal and eventually toward the ideal. This is actually the Biblical record of how God worked on marriage in the Old and New Testament. God does not expect immediate attainment toward an ideal but movement toward it. It took hundreds of years to move toward the ideal of monogamous unions not only permanent but reflecting the ideals of Christ-church relationship.

Slavery—A Typical Example

This same *starting point plus process model* can be applied to many kinds of issues and doctrines in which a given culture or society fall short of Biblical ideals. For example, consider the slavery issue. This is a sub-ideal position with regard to the view of a human being made in God's image. So God begins by accepting the viewpoint of slavery but works to improve the conditions under which it takes place. Then He works to eliminate it in its varied forms (actual slavery; pseudo-slavery like Mexican immigrant workers illegally in the United States, child slaves sold into sexual prostitution in Asia, etc.). Then He works to eliminate ethnic prejudice, a subtle form of corporate slavery. And so on, until He obtains the ideal of interdependency between various ethnic groups with respect for all individuals and groups as made in the image of God.

Women in Leadership—Another Example

Or consider gender and leadership (see **Article**, *Gender and Leadership*). I believe that *the starting point plus process model* is seen at work again as God moves from sub-ideal positions on females in some cultures where they are only slightly better than chattel all the way across to the ideal where men and women are equal in standing before God and others (at least due to gender alone) and where men or women are leaders depending on calling and gifting.

Conclusion

We must not expect immediate perfection on some truth in the Scriptures by groups new to this truth, especially when it has taken years to bring the church to this position. And what is true with corporate groups like churches and parachurches is true of individuals. We should expect to reject positions that are less than sub-ideal. But we should be willing to patiently work to move people from sub-ideal to ideal.

Acknowledgment

This model was first identified by one of my colleagues, Dr. Charles H. Kraft in his book on ethnotheology, entitled **Christianity in Culture**. The above description of his model is my adapted version of Kraft's model, taken from my doctoral dissertation.

See **Article**, *Gender and Leadership*.

Article 24

Relevance of the Article to Paul's Philemon Letter
Paul's time line is given in this article. Note when the book of Philemon was written.

24. Time Lines—Defined for Biblical Leaders

A major leadership genre is the biographical source. Below is given 12 steps to use for studying this source. Notice step two in Table Phm 24-1 below.

Table Phm 24-1. 12 Steps For Doing Biographical Study

Step	General Guideline
1	Identify All The Passages That Refer To The Leader.
2	Seek To Order The Vignettes Or Other Type Passages In A Time Sequence
3	Construct A Time-Line If You Can. At Least Tentatively Identify The Major Development Phases In The Leader's Life.
4	Look For Shaping Events And Activities (technically called process items, or critical incidents).
5	Identify Pivotal Points From The Major Process Items Or Critical Incidents
6	Seek To Determine Any Lessons You Can From A Study Of Process Items Or Pivotal Points.
7	Identify Any Response Patterns Or Any Unique Patterns As You Analyze The Life Across A Time-Line.
8	Study Any Individual Leadership Acts In The Life.
9	Use The Three Overall Leadership Categories To Help Suggest Leadership Issues To Look For (leadership basal elements, leadership influence means, leadership value bases).
10	Use The List Of Major Functions (task functions, relationship functions, and inspirational functions) to Help Suggest Insights. Which were done, which not.
11	Observe Any New Testament Passages Or Commentary On The Leader. Especially Be On The Lookout For Bent Of Life Evaluation.
12	Use The Presentation Format For Findings On Bible Leaders To Organize Your Results.

This article briefly describes step two. A time-line is the end result of applying step 2. Time-lines provide an integrating framework upon which to measure development in the life, to organize findings, and to pinpoint when shaping activities occur in a life.

Important Definitions for Time-Lines

Definition — The <u>time-line</u> is the linear display along a horizontal axis, which is broken up into development phases.

Definition — A <u>unique time-line</u> refers to a time-line describing a given leader's lifetime, which will have unique development phases bearing labels expressing that uniqueness.

Definition — A <u>development phase</u> is a marked off length on a time-line representing a significant portion of time in a leader's life history in which notable development takes place. Example Below has 4 development phases indicated by Roman Letters I, II, III, IV.

Definition — A <u>sub-phase</u> is a marked off length on a time-line within a development phase, which points out intermediate times of development during the development phase. In the Example below Development phase III. has 3 sub-phases indicated by A, B, and C.

24. Time Lines—Defined for Biblical Leaders

All leaders can describe a time-line that is unique to them. A unique time-line is broken up into divisions called development phases, which terminate with boundary events. Development phases can themselves be subdivided into smaller units called sub-phases which have smaller boundary terminations.

Below is given the Apostle Paul's time-line with several findings about his life displayed. Paul's life, ministry, and development. I have also numerous other findings about Paul's life, ministry and development located on his time-line. Such things as; pivotal points, mentoring, development of life purpose, development of major role, isolation processing, other process items such as—paradigm shift, leadership committal, double confirmation, divine contact, conflict, crises, ministry conflict, word, obedience, integrity check. Time-lines are very useful to give perspective and force one to see across a whole lifetime of development.

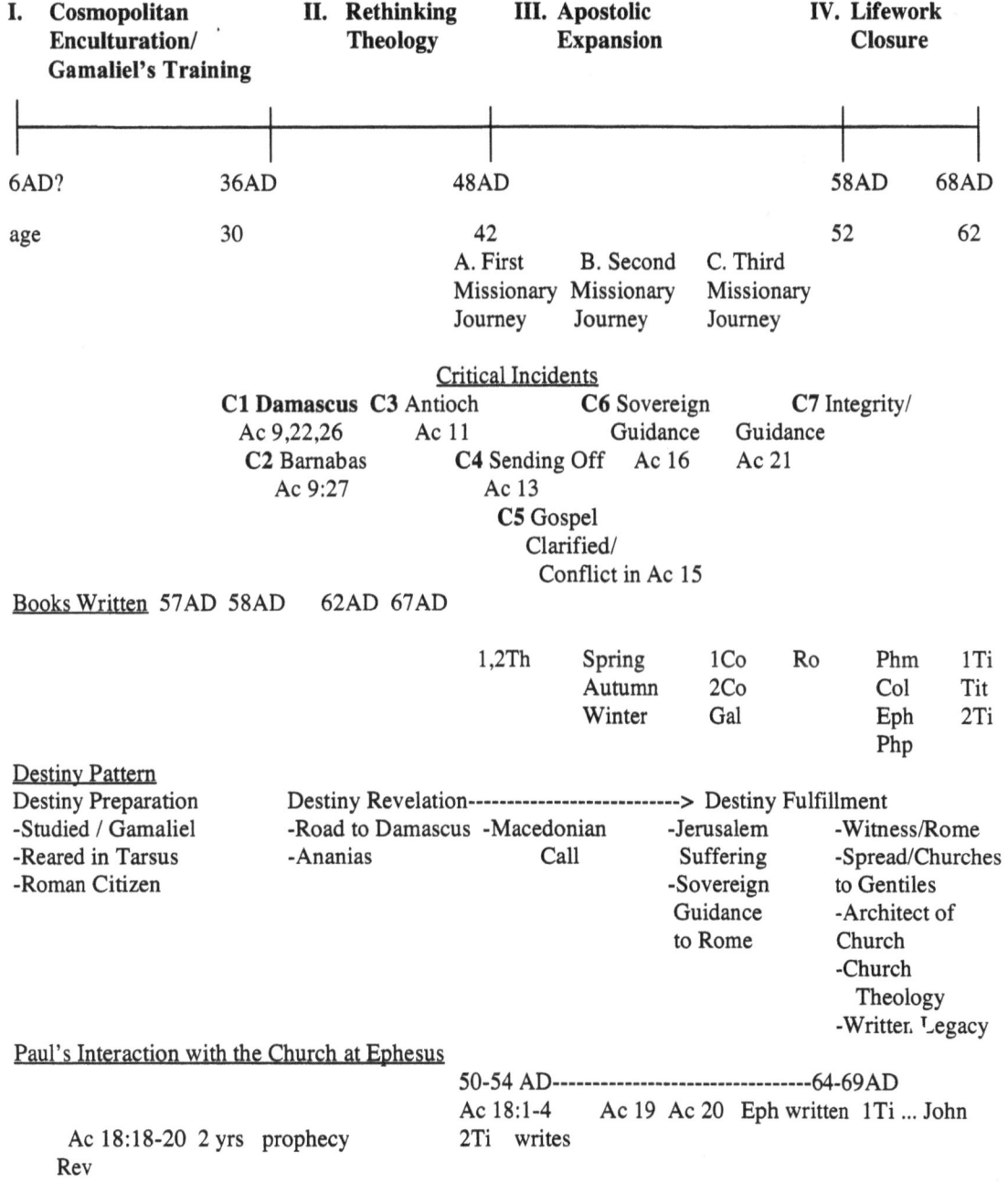

Figure Phm 24-1. The Apostle Paul's Time-Line

24. Time Lines—Defined for Biblical Leaders

For **Further study**: See paper, *Getting Perspective by Using Your Time-Line* listed in the **For Further Study Bibliography**. See also **Article,** *9. Leadership Genre—7 Types*; **See Section Time Lines of Biblical Leaders.**

Article 25

Relevance of the Article to Paul's Philemon Letter

Three Christian brothers are called sons by Paul. Two of them are named in this book—Timothy and Philemon. While it is clear that Timothy was the closest of the three. Both Titus and Onesimus are also accorded this special privilege of intimacy with Paul. Knowing of this special relationship would affect how Philemon thought about Paul's request for Onesimus. The description below, with some slight modification, applies also to Onesimus. See **LEADERSHIP TOPIC 3. RELATIONAL VALUE.**

25. Timothy—A Beloved Son in the Faith

Introduction

Was Paul in sync with the following major leadership lesson identified in comparative study of many leaders?

Effective leaders view relationships in ministry as both a means and an end.

This is one of seven major lessons that I have derived from comparative study of effective leaders. Probably in no leader in the Bible, other than Jesus, is this seen any plainer, than in the life and ministry of Paul the Apostle. Paul was a strong task-oriented leader. But he knew the value of relationships. In his epistles he lists almost 80 people by name whom he had personal relationships with. Paul believed that he ought to personally relate to those around him in ministry. It was good in itself. It was good to accomplish ministry too. Paul indicates this notion of a strong relationship when he uses the phrases: *my own son in the faith, my beloved son, as a son with the father, son, dearly beloved son, my son, own son after the common faith, my son.* For three—Timothy, Titus, and Onesimus—it meant strong intimate relationships. Table Phm 25-1 lists the instances and uses of these strong, special, intimate relationships by Paul.

Table Phm 25-1. Paul and Intimate Relationships

Reference	Phrase	Who	Use
1Co 4:17	who is my beloved son	Timothy	Sponsoring Timothy to the Corinthians so they will receive him with respect as Paul's representative.
Php 2:22	as a son with the father	Timothy	Sponsoring Timothy to the Philippians so they will receive him with respect as Paul's representative.
1Ti 1:2	[my] own son in the faith	Timothy	Greeting of encouragement to Timothy personally.
1Ti 1:18	son	Timothy	Exhortation to Timothy to boldly act as a leader in a tough situation remembering the prophecies and operating with a clean conscience.
2Ti 1:2	[my] dearly beloved son	Timothy	Greeting of encouragement. The most intimate of all the phrases.
2Ti 2:1	my son	Timothy	An exhortation to go on, drawing on the enabling grace found in union with Christ
Tit 1:4	[mine] own son after the common faith	Titus	A word of encouragement; a word sponsoring Titus before the Cretian believers.
Phm 1:10	my son	Onesimus	Sponsoring of Onesimus to Philemon. Shows how strongly Paul believed in him.

Let me suggest an exercise for you. Go back and read each of the references listed in Table Phm 25-1. Read the surrounding context as well. And imagine you are Timothy hearing those words or Titus or Onesimus. How would you feel to hear such words? Paul knew the motivational importance of affirmation.

25. Timothy—A Beloved Son in the Faith

And a personal strong intimate relationship expressed openly to the person not only affirms but motivates them.

Table Phm 25-1 shows that Timothy was Paul's closest associate. He was a beloved and true son in the faith. Leaders need to pass on their heritage. They need to leave behind ultimate contributions. One sure way of doing this is to have relationships with those to whom they minister and with whom they minister. Values are passed on. Ministry methodology, though adapted lives on. Vision is caught and lives on.

Effective leaders view relationship as both a means and an end in ministry.

Paul did. Who are your true sons and daughters? Who will carry on your values, ministry philosophy, and vision?

Glossary—Leadership Definitions

The following leadership related definitions occur throughout several Biblical leadership commentaries. I include them all, though only the * marked entries occur in Philemon. They are listed here alphabetically for convenience in referencing. SRN stands for Strong's Reference Number. These numbers can be used to look up the definitions of these words in the Strong's Exhaustive Concordance containing Hebrew and Greek dictionaries. These numbers are now also used by many other (electronic) Bible study aids.

Item	Definition
abiding	a term used in Jn 15 which refers to an on-going intimate relationship between a believer and Jesus in which the believer is identified with the life of Jesus. This is John's equivalent of union life as given by Paul.
absolute for relative	A comparative idiom of the form not A but B given absolutely. But it is really a relative comparison which really means B is much more important than A and used to emphasize how important B really is. Example 1Pe 3:3,4.
accelerated pattern	a pattern describing the early developmental foundational phase of a leader; that leader has an early rapid development sometimes flowing from generational models, a family heritage of leadership; the leader responds positively very early in life to doing ministry (often co-ministering with parents).
accountability	a term used to describe the fact that a leader will answer to God for his/her ministry. Paul has a major leadership value concerning this. See Ultimate Accountability.
affect	a learning domain, that is, a term describing learning which primarily moves the feelings and emotions.
*affirmation, (divine or ministry)	a personal inner need that leaders have for approval from God (sometimes via others) for personhood (divine affirmation) and for ministry (ministry affirmation).
anthropomorphism	a special idiom. Human language and illustrations are used to talk about God and His ways so that humans can grasp things about God in terms of things they do know. They are not literally true about God but point analogously to spiritual things which are true.
a-periodic scheduling	refers to a mentoring technique which stresses repeated meetings between mentor and mentoree but not on a fixed time schedule. Meetings occur when mentorees are ready—that is, they have responded to the developmental tasks given to them and are ready for feedback on it, perhaps affirmation as well, and new assignments.
apocalyptic literature	a special prophetic genre of literature. Ralph Alexander's definition of apocalyptic is technically helpful. <u>Apocalyptic literature</u> is symbolic visionary prophetic literature, composed during oppressive conditions, consisting of visions whose events are recorded exactly as they were seen by the author and explained through a divine interpreter, and whose

Glossary

	theological content is primarily eschatological. According to this technical definition the following Old Testament passages are classified apocalyptic: Eze 37:1-14; Eze 40-48; Daniel's visions in ch 2, 7, 8 and 10-12; Zec 1:7-6:8. Alexander's research was on the Old Testament so I have no list of New Testament apocalyptic literature.
apostolic style	one of ten Pauline leadership styles—the most highly directive style. The <u>apostolic leadership style</u> is a method of influence in which the leader assumes the role of delegated authority over those for whom he/she is responsible, receives revelation from God concerning decisions, and commands obedience based on the role of delegated authority and revelation concerning God's will. The essence of the apostolic style is the legitimate right from God to make decisions for others and to command or demand their compliance with those decisions.
apostleship	one of the 19 spiritual gifts. The <u>gift of apostleship</u> refers to a special leadership capacity to move with authority from God to create new ministry structures (churches and parachurch groups) to meet needs and to develop and appoint leadership in these structures. **Its central thrust is Creating New Ministry.**
apostrophe	a figure of speech. Apostrophe is a special case of personification in which the speaker addresses the thing personified as if it were alive and listening. e.g. 1Co 15:55 O death, where is your sting? O grave, where is your victory.
apprenticeship	refers to a leadership training model, dominantly done in the informal training mode. It represents a model in which an expert in something, technically called the master, teaches a learner to master that same subject or skill. There is usually some set time over which the learning will occur. The learner is called an apprentice.
artist	a label given to the ultimate contribution of a Christian leader who has creative breakthroughs in life and ministry and introduces innovation. e.g. John the Apostle, C. S. Lewis.
a-service	a training term which refers to when training is given—describes the fact that training does not relate directly to when ministry happens.
*authority insights	from leadership emergence theory. One of 51 process items that God uses to shape a leader. <u>Authority insights</u> describe those instances in ministry in which a leader learns important lessons, via positive or negative experiences, with regards to: submission to authority, authority structures, authenticity of power bases underlying authority, authority conflict, how to exercise authority.
beingness	a term describing the inner life of a person and referring to intimacy with God, character, personality, giftedness, destiny, values drawn from experience, gender influence perspectives. The axiom, ministry flows out of being means that one's ministry should be a vital outflow from these inner beingness factors.
benchmarks, spiritual	this refers to something that happens in the life of the leader which serves as positive proof of God's activity in that life. It is something that a leader can look back upon and be encouraged to continue when confused or in a discouraging situation. Because it is foundational, sure and certain, and had the distinct imprint of God's Hand on the life. See also destiny processing.

Glossary

Bible Centered leader	a leader (1) whose leadership is being informed by the Bible and (2) who personally has been shaped by Biblical values, (3) who has grasped the intent of Scriptural books and their content in such a way as to apply them to current situations and (4) who uses the Bible in ministry so as to impact followers.
bishop	a leadership term (SRN 1985) used in Philippians 1:1, 1 Tim 3:2, Titus 1:7 and 1 Pet 2:25. Occurs as the word overseer in Acts 20:28 and which probably best describes its function. As used in Paul's life time a person responsible for the spiritual welfare of others in a local church situation. Probably synonymous with the term elder.
broadened kinship, idiom	Sometimes the terms son of, daughter of, mother of, father of, brother of, sister of, or begat, which in English imply a close relationship, have a much wider connotation in the Bible. Brother or sister could include various male or female relatives such as cousins; mother and father could include relatives such as grandparents or great-great-grandparents, in the direct family line. Begat may simply mean was directly in the family line of ancestors.
*brokenness	a state of mind in which a person recognizes that he/she is helpless in a situation or life process unless God alone works. It is a state of mind in which a person acknowledges a deep dependence upon God and is open for God to break through in new ways, thoughts, directions, and revelation of Himself that was not the case before the brokenness experience. Example: Jacob in Genesis 32 faced a life-threatening situation in which he was forced to desperately depend upon God.
browse	a technical term taken from continuum reading which refers to the reading of a book in which whole contexts of the book are read such as chapters, units within chapters but not the whole book. See continuum reading. See bibliography, **Reading On The Run**.
burden	a technical term in leadership emergence theory referring to the sense of responsibility a leader has toward some ministry for accomplishing God's purposes for that ministry and/or a sense of giving account for that ministry to God. See also downward burden, upward burden.
*capture	a technical term used when talking about figures of speech being interpreted. A figure or idiom is said to be captured when one can display the intended emphatic meaning of it in non-figurative simple words. e.g. not ashamed of the Gospel = captured: completely confident of the Gospel.
central truth	when referring to parables, mini-parables, parabolic illustrations or the like, one uses the notion of central truth which is the main truth which the entire parabolic teaching is intending to convey. It is a statement which exhibits the meaning intended by the parabolic material which is using comparisons to teach this central truth.

Glossary

change dynamics principle, getting it on the agenda	*Getting it on the agenda* is a basic motivational technique used by a change person. It means to get an idea before a people without them yet knowing it will be important later on in the change process. Frequently, in bringing about change it is better to get an idea out there, subconsciously, where it can start to take root, than to bring it up directly and have it voted down. Once voted down, an idea will be very difficult to later get action on.
change participants	when change is being introduced into some situation, one can analyze the people in the situation in terms of how they will respond to change as they participate in the change process. Usually they can be grouped into three types: favorable, neutral, unfavorable. In John's Gospel we see particularly in the religious leaders two basic type of unfavorable change participants—maintainers and resistors.
change person	a label given to the ultimate contribution of a Christian leader who rights wrongs and injustices in society and in church and mission organizations. e.g. Amos, Micah, John the Baptist.
*chiasmus	a figure of speech in which two pairs of items are listed in a text. The first item really refers to the fourth item and the second really refers to the third. e.g. Philemon 5. Literally, your love and faith toward the Lord Jesus and toward all saints = your faith, which you have in the Lord Jesus, and love for all the saints.
Church Era	shortened form of Church Leadership Era. The leadership era associated with Peter, Paul, and John and to the present. Ushered in at Pentecost. It is a time of spiritual leadership exercised around the world in many cultures.
coercive authority	one of five power forms, identified by Dennis Wrong, which a leader may use to influence followers. In essence the power holder threatens to punish the follower.
cognitive	a learning domain, that is, a term describing learning which primarily focuses on the transmittal and understanding of knowledge and ideas.
competent authority	one of five power forms, identified by Dennis Wrong, which a leader may use to influence followers. In essence the leader has influence with followers because they perceive the leader has having expertise and worthy to be followed.
conative	a learning domain, that is, a term describing learning which primarily focuses on the influencing a person to commit to the things being learned; it wants to bring about volitional compliance—a willingness to use what is being learned. Jesus stresses this emphasis in Jn 7:17 and Jn 13-17.
*conflict	from leadership emergence theory. One of 51 process items that God uses to shape a leader. The <u>conflict proce</u> item refers to those instances in a leader's life-history in which God uses conflict, whether personal or ministry related to develop the leader in dependence upon God, faith, and inner-life.
confrontation style	one of ten Pauline leadership styles—a highly directive style. The <u>confrontation leadership style</u> is an approach to problem solving which brings the problem out in the open with all parties concerned, which

Glossary

	analyzes the problem in light of revelational truth, and which brings authority to bear upon the parties to accept recommended solutions.
conscience	the inner sense of right or wrong which is innate in a human being but which also is modified by values imbibed from a culture. This innate sense can also be modified by the Spirit of God.
consensus	one of 10 Pauline leadership styles. A highly non-directive style. The <u>consensus leadership style</u> refers to the approach to leadership influence which involves the group itself actively participating in decision making and coming to solutions acceptable to the whole group. The leader must be skilled in bringing diverse thoughts together in such a way as to meet the whole group's needs. See Acts 15 for use of this.
contextualization	the process of taking something meaningful in one context and making it relevant to a new context. e.g. the Christian movement which began in a Jewish context had to be reinterpreted by Paul to a non-Jewish context, the Gentiles.
continuum reading	an approach to reading which recognizes: 1) that a book does not have to be read word for word in its entirety in order for a person to profit from it; 2) that different books should be read in different ways. This approach recognizes that books can be read at different levels with each level to the right on the continuum becoming more detailed. The levels include scan, ransack, browse, pre-read, read, and study. It also recognizes that few books will be read to the right of the continuum and many will be read to the left. Leaders with a learning posture must master this approach or have some equally functional equivalent. See manual, **Reading on the Run,** listed in **For Further Study—Bibliography section** for detailed introduction to these concepts.
core books	Bible centered leaders usually have a set of Bible books that have impacted their lives and which they repeatedly use in their ministry to impact others. Such books are called core books.
crash time	time after intensive ministry in which a leader deliberately rests. This involves lots of sleep and recovery of physical strength, maybe exercise, no deliberate ministry, and lots of non-ministry things such as reading and other recreational things, in order to regain physical strength, mental agility, spiritual stamina. Failure to get crash time and to schedule intensive ministries back to back will eventually lead to some form of burnout.
*crisis	from leadership emergence theory. One of 51 process items that God uses to shape a leader. <u>Crisis process items</u> refer to those special intense situations of pressure in human situations which are used by God to test and teach dependence.
*critical incident	a leadership emergence term referring to a specific shaping event in which a major value is taught which permeates on-going ministry from that time or major direction results which guides a leader onto accomplishment of his/her destiny. Or the event could be a combination of a major value and guidance. See Phm. See Jn 21 for Peter.
Day of Christ	or also Day of the Lord, or That Day. A phrase used by Paul to indicate among other things that leaders will be held accountable in the future at this special time for their leadership influence. Paul had a strong value, *Leaders*

Glossary

will ultimately give an account for their ministries. In 2Co 5:10 Paul extends this accountability to all, not just leaders. See Php 1:6, 10; 2:16 and others in 1, 2Th. See also Heb 13:17 for another strong indication of this accountability a leader will face.

deacon
: a leadership term (SRN 1249) translated: as deacon three times—Php 1:1, 1 Ti 3:8, 3:12; as minister 20 times; as servant 8 times. Paul uses this to describe his own self and Phoebe. It is not clear how this role relates to that of bishop and elder. It is distinguished as a separate leadership role and probably of less influence from bishop in 1 Ti 3.

Death/Life Paradox
: a Pauline leadership value seen in 2Co. *The firstfruits of Jesus resurrection life ought to be experienced in the death producing circumstances of life and ought to serve as a hallmark of spiritual life for followers.*

*deep processing
: refers to a collection of process items which intensely work on deepening the maturity of a leader. The set includes the following process items: conflict, ministry conflict, crisis, life crisis, leadership backlash and isolation.

delayed pattern
: a pattern flowing from the foundational developmental phase; describes the developmental pattern of generational Christian leaders (emerging leaders who have a family heritage of Christian leadership) who initially rebel against ministry very early in life but who eventually experience a deep leadership committal process item and though entering the ministry phase late experience rapid acceleration in their development.

destiny item Type I
: a destiny experience which is an awe-inspiring experience in which God is sensed directly as acting or speaking in the life. Example: Moses at the burning bush.

destiny item Type II
: a indirect destiny experience in which some aspect of destiny is linked to some person other than the leader and is done indirectly for the leader who simply must receive its implications. Example: Hannah's promise to give Samuel to God.

destiny item Type III
: the build up of a sense of destiny in a life because of the accumulation of providential circumstances which indicate God's arrangement for the life. See Apostle Paul's birth and early life situation.

destiny item Type IV
: the build up of a sense of destiny in a life because of the sensed blessing of God on the life, repeatedly. Seen by others and recognized by them as the Hand of God on the life. See Joseph.

destiny pattern
: a leadership pattern. The development of a sense of destiny usually follows a three fold pattern of destiny preparation, destiny revelation, and destiny fulfillment. That is, over a period of time God shapes a leader with experiences which prepare, reveal, and finally brings about completion of destiny.

destiny processing
: refers to the shaping activities of God in which a leader becomes increasingly aware of God's Hand on his/her life and the purposes for which God has intended for his/her leadership. This processing causes a sense of partnership with God toward God's purposes for the life and hence brings meaning to the life. See also Type I, II, III, IV destiny items.

Glossary

developer	a concept seen in Paul's life. A developer is a person with a mentoring bent who readily sees potential in an emerging leader and finds ways to help move that emerging leader on to becoming an effective leader.
developmental solution	refers to the process in a regime turnover in which the new regime seeks a developmental solution for old regime leaders, that is, it does its best to develop the old regime leaders so that they can fit in the new regime or moves them on to roles which best fit who they are.
direct ministry	as opposed to indirect ministry. Direct ministry refers to use of spiritual gifts, i.e. word gifts, to influence a face-to-face basic target group in terms of the word gifts themselves—a tactical function.
discernings of spirits	one of the 19 spiritual gifts belonging to the power cluster. The discernings of spirits gift refers to the ability given by God to perceive issues in terms of spiritual truth, to know the fundamental source of the issues and to give judgment concerning those issues; this includes the recognition of the spiritual forces operating in the issue. **Its Central Thrust Is A Sensitivity To Truth.**
disciplines, spiritual	one of five enhancement factors seen in the lives of effective leaders. Spiritual disciplines are activities of mind and body purposefully undertaken to bring personality and total being into effective cooperation with the Spirit of God so as to reflect Kingdom life. Three categories are frequently used to describe spiritual disciplines: abstinence disciplines like solitude, silence, fasting, frugality, chastity, secrecy, sacrifice; engagement disciplines like study, worship, celebration, service, prayer, fellowship, confession, submission; other miscellaneous disciplines like voluntary exile, keeping watch, sabbath keeping, practices among the poor, journaling, listening.
discourse marker	a technical term from linguistic theory which refers to a particular phrase which breaks up a discourse into major sections. The phrase can be summary-like; repeated in other places or in some way enough different from the general flow of context to show that it is concluding something. Examples: Dan 1:21, 6:28.
disputed practice	a practice for which a Christian has freedom to do, from a Biblical and conscience standpoint, but for which other Christians feel is wrong for whatever reasons, a matter of conscience for them. Essentially it deals with the notion of Christian liberty. Some would see the practice as legitimate for a Christian, others would not. Paul gives guidelines on how to approach disputed practices in 1Co 8-10 and Ro 14.
divine affirmation	a concept from leadership emergence theory. The shaping activity of God whereby God makes known to a leader his approval of that leader. This is a major motivating factor to keep one serving the Lord.
Divine Appointment	a Pauline leadership value seen in 2Co. *Leaders ought to be sure that God appointed them to ministry situations.*
*divine contact	from leadership emergence theory. One of 51 process items that God uses to shape a leader. A divine contact is a person whom God brings in contact with a leader at a crucial moment in a development phase in order to accomplish one or more of the following to: affirm leadership potential,

Glossary

	encourage leadership potential, give guidance on a special issue, give insights which may indirectly lead to guidance, challenge the leader God-ward, open a door to a ministry opportunity, other insights helping the emerging leader to make guidance decisions.
*double confirmation	from leadership emergence theory. One of 51 process items that God uses to shape a leader. <u>Double confirmation</u> refers to the unusual guidance in which God makes clear His will by giving the guidance directly to a leader and then reinforcing it by some other person totally independent and unaware of the leader's guidance.
downward burden	that aspect of burden which senses the call of God on a life for a ministry; a deep sense of having to do the ministry because God is directing and involved in it for that leader.
effective methodology	a focused life concept; one of 4 focal issues; An <u>effective methodology</u> is some ministry insight which a leader uses to effectively deliver some important ministry which will contribute to life purpose and achievement of ultimate contributions.
elder	a leadership term (SRN 4245) used by Paul 6 times in Scripture of which 4 refer to local church leadership in Ephesus. It is unclear as to how this leadership role, elder, differs from bishop or deacon. In the book of Titus the word bishop and elder is used synonymously. In Timothy elders are described as ruling and teaching in the local congregation.
entrustment, leadership	the concept of a lifetime of leadership ministry viewed as a gift from God which is entrusted to the leader to manage as a stewardship. Paul is strong on this concept both in 1 Timothy and 2 Timothy. Viewing leadership this way, requires a strong sense of destiny. It also heightens the responsibility a leader feels for carrying out that ministry so as to give an account of it on *That Day*.
enhancement factors	comparative study of effective leaders who finished well has identified five things that enhance their perseverance and ability to finish well. These include: 1. Seeing present day ministry in terms of a life time perspective and in terms of God's perspective for the ages; 2. Experiencing repeated renewals throughout their ministry—some sought, others serendipitous; 3. Maintenance of disciplines in the life, especially spiritual disciplines; 4. Having a learning posture throughout their whole ministry; 5. Having mentors from time-to-time, who enable them in various ways.
eunuch	an emasculated male. Men serving in the palace of powerful rulers were often made eunuchs. Daniel and Nehemiah were most likely eunuchs.
evangelism	one of the 19 spiritual gifts belonging to the Word Cluster and the Love Cluster. The <u>gift of evangelism</u> in general refers to the capacity to challenge people through various communicative methods (persuasion) to receive the Gospel of salvation in Christ so as to see them respond by taking initial steps in Christian discipleship. **Its central thrust is Introducing Others To The Gospel.**
*exhortation	one of the 19 spiritual gifts. It is a spiritual gift belonging to the word cluster. The <u>gift of Exhortation</u> is the capacity to urge people to action in terms of applying Biblical truths, or to encourage people generally with

Glossary

	Biblical truths, or to comfort people through the application of Biblical truth to their needs. **Its central thrust is To Apply Biblical Truth.**
experiential	an integrative learning domain which involves cognitive, affect, and conative domains so that the things being learned are put into the life and used—they are understood (cognitive), appreciated or valued (affect) and have affected the desires to use (conative). Jesus consistently taught so as to move people toward experiential learning.
faith	(also called word of faith). one of the 19 spiritual gifts. It is in the Word Cluster and power cluster. The gift of faith refers to the unusual capacity of a person to recognize in a given situation that God intends to do something and to trust God for it until He brings it to pass. Sometimes the recognition is in the form of a word to challenge others about a future thing God will do. **Its central thrust is A Trusting Response To A Challenge From God.**
faith check	from leadership emergence theory. One of 51 process items that God uses to shape a leader. A faith check is a process item God uses to shape a leader so that the leader can learn to trust God, by faith, to intervene in his/her life or ministry.
*faith challenge	from leadership emergence theory. One of 51 process items that God uses to shape a leader. A faith challenge refers to those instances in ministry where a leader is challenged to take steps of faith in regards to ministry and sees God meet those steps of faith with divine affirmation and ministry affirmation and often with guidance into on going ministry leading to a focused life.
father-guardian	one of 10 Pauline leadership Styles. A directive style. The father-guardian style is a style which is similar to a parent-child relationship and has as its major concern protection and encouragement for followers. 1Th 2:10,11 illustrates this style which is usually seen when a very mature Christian leader relates to very immature followers. Usually this style is directive, but because of the caring relationship between leader and follower and the follower maturity level it does not seem directive, since influence behavior always seems to have the follower's best interest at heart.
*father-initiator	one of 10 Pauline leadership Styles. A highly directive style. The father-initiator leadership style is related to the apostolic style which uses the fact of the leader having founded the work as a lever for getting acceptance of influence by the leader. Seen in Philemon and in 1 Corinthians 4:14,15.
*figure	the unusual use of a word or words differing from the normal use in order to draw special attention to some point of interest. The more important figures (100s used in Bible) include: metaphor, simile, metonymy, synecdoche, hyperbole, irony, personification, apostrophe, negative emphatics (litotes and tapenosis), rhetorical question. See individual definitions for each of these. See **For Further Study Bibliography**, **Figures and Idioms** by Dr. J. Robert Clinton.
Financial Equality Principle	a Pauline leadership value seen in 2Co. *Christian leadership must teach that Christian giving is a reciprocal balancing between needs and surplus.*

Glossary

Financial Integrity	a Pauline leadership value seen in 2Co. *A Christian leader must handle finances with absolute integrity.*
firstfruits	a term indicating a display of something which guarantees something in future. Used of Jesus as being the first to be resurrected and a guarantee of the resurrection of other believers. Also used of transforming work in a life. We shall be like him, the firstfruits. Life out of death producing circumstances for us are the results of Jesus' life out of death.
*flesh act	from leadership emergence theory. One of 51 process items that God uses to shape a leader. A flesh act refers to those instances in a leader's life where guidance is presumed and decisions are made either hastily or without proper discernment of God's choice. Such decisions usually involve the working out of guidance by the leader using some human manipulation or other means and which brings ramifications which later negatively affect ministry and life. See Genesis 16 for an example in Abraham's life. See Joshua's treaty with Gibeonites in Jos 9. See Isa 39:4 for Hezekiah's action with Babylonian envoys.
focal element	the dominate component of a giftedness set—either natural abilities, acquired skills, or spiritual gifts. About 50% of leaders have spiritual gifts as dominant. Another 35% have natural abilities as dominant. About 15% have acquired skills as dominant.
focused life	A focused life is a life dedicated to exclusively carrying out God's unique purposes through it, by identifying the focal issues, that is, the major role, life purpose, unique methodology, or ultimate contribution, which allows an increasing prioritizing of life's activities around the focal issues, and results in a satisfying life of being and doing.
formal training	one of three modes of training; recognized training, usually programmatic, and accepted socially as the means for preparing someone for something. Training which generally has a set curriculum and leads to some credential or formal recognition of completion.
founder	a label given to the ultimate contribution of a Christian leader who starts a new organization to meet a need or capture the essence of some movement or the like. e.g. Peter, James and John and others of Jesus disciples (Eph 2:20).
*future perfect	The future perfect paradigm refers to a way of viewing a future reality as if it were already present which in turn, inspires one's leadership, challenges followers to the vision, affects decision making, and causes one to persevere in faith, which finally results in the future reality coming into being. For leaders who move in revelatory gifts, especially futuristic prophecy and apostolic types, especially with the gift of faith, who must get vision and motivate followers toward it, this is a very necessary paradigm.
generational Christian leaders	refers to emerging leaders who have a family heritage of Christian leadership; often indirect destiny influence comes from the heritage.
*giftedness discovery	from leadership emergence theory. One of 51 process items that God uses to shape a leader. Giftedness discovery refers to instances in which a leader becomes aware of natural abilities, or acquired skills, or spiritual gifts so as

Glossary

	to use them well in ministry. This is a significant advance along the giftedness development pattern.
giftedness set	a term describing natural abilities, acquired skills, and spiritual gifts which a leader has as resources to use in ministry. Sometimes shortened to giftedness.
*gifted power	refers to the empowerment of the Holy Spirit when using giftedness; 1Pe 4:11 gives the basic admonition for this to the use of word gifts. It is naturally extended to other areas of giftedness.
gift-mix	refers to the collection of spiritual gifts that a leader demonstrates repeatedly in ministry over time.
gifts of healings	one of 19 spiritual gifts occurring primarily in the Power Cluster and secondarily in the Love Cluster. <u>Gifts of healings</u> refer to the supernatural releasing of healing power for curing all types of illnesses. **Its Central Thrust is Releasing God's Power To Heal.**
gift projection	the tendency of certain leaders and/or groups to promote certain gifts and require them of all. Strong gifted leaders tend to do this about their own strong gifts (e.g. teachers over emphasize teaching; evangelists over emphasize evangelism; prophets over emphasize prophecy; healers over emphasize healing; word of knowledge people over emphasize word of knowledge). The list of rhetorical questions in 1Co 12:29,30 addresses this issue.
giving	one of 19 spiritual gifts occurring primarily in the Love Cluster. The <u>gift of giving</u> refers to the capacity to give liberally to meet the needs of others and yet to do so with a purity of motive which senses that the giving is a simple sharing of what God has given. **Its Central Thrust Is A Sensitivity To God To Channel His Resources To Others.**
Goodwin's Expectation Principle	Bennie Goodwin in a small booklet on leadership published by InterVarsity Press (see **Bibliography**) identified a social dynamic principle which is helpful in developing leaders. In my own words, *Emerging leaders tend to live up to the genuine expectations of leaders they respect.* The challenge embodied in the expectation must not be too much or the young leader will not be able to accomplish it and will be inoculated against further challenges. The challenge must not be too little or it will not attract. It must be a genuine expectation. Paul uses this with Timothy several times (see fn 1Ti 6:11; 2Ti 1:5).
governments	one of 19 spiritual gifts occurring primarily in the *Love Cluster*. The <u>gifts of governments</u> involves a capacity to manage details of service functions so as to support and free other leaders to prioritize their efforts. **Its Central Thrust Is Supportive Organizational Abilities.**
*grace	carries essentially the sense of freedom; when used in a context describing salvation from God it implies that God freely gave us salvation without our earning or deserving it; when used to exhort continuing in the Christian life it carries the sense of the enabling presence of God in a life so as to free (enable) one to persevere victoriously. Paul uses it especially this way in his last epistles 1Ti, 2Ti, Tit and Phm. Peter does too 2Pe 3:18. And John also, Rev 22:21. It is interesting to observe that the three great church leaders in their closing words stress the importance of grace and its value in

Glossary

	continuing in the Christian life. It is also used by Paul as a metonymy (Corinthians and Romans) standing for spiritual gifts given freely by God.
*guidance	from leadership emergence theory. One of 51 process items that God uses to shape a leader. <u>Guidance</u> is the general category which refers to the many ways in which God reveals information that informs a leader about decisions to be made.
hapax legomena	A word occurring only one time in the original text of the Bible. Its meaning must be determined from the surrounding context or from other documents other than the Bible which were extant at the time of the writing of the Bible book containing the word.
harvest model	one of five philosophical leadership models introduced by Jesus and one which focuses on a leader's responsibility to extend the Kingdom by reaching out to those not in it and challenging them to enter it. See **Article**, *Five Philosophical Leadership Models in the Gospels.*
helps	one of 19 spiritual gifts occurring primarily in the Love Cluster. The <u>gifts of helps</u> refers to the capacity to unselfishly meet the needs of others through very practical means. **Its Central Thrust Is The Attitude And Ability To Aid Others In Practical Ways.**
heresy	refers to deviation from a standard, whether in belief (orthodoxy) or practice (orthopraxy). e.g. See 1Ti where both are present in the Ephesian church (as prophesied in Ac 20:30).
heritage pattern	refers to the early development of a leader in the foundational phase; a foundational pattern which describes the background situation out of which a leader grew up and which describes at least a nominal understanding of God and his ways. Timothy is a positive example of one who had a good heritage. He was grounded in the Scriptures and saw faith modeled by his mom, Eunice, and his grandmother, Lois.
hook	a term used in spiritual warfare and referring to some flaw or internal character weakness in the inner life of a person such as greed, lying, sexual promiscuity or the like, lack of integrity, which provides a starting point for Satan to exert pressure and eventually leading to Satan's control of the person. Jesus refers to this kind of thing in Jn 13:2 pointing out that Satan had no hook within him.
hyperbole	a figure of speech which uses conscious exaggeration (an overstatement of truth) in order to emphasize or strikingly excite interest in the truth. e.g. 2 Sam 1:23 swifter than eagles,...stronger than lions.
identificational forgiveness	an apostolic function. An apostolic gifted person can pronounce forgiveness in the authority of Christ for a follower under that leadership which is binding. See Mt 16:19 and Paul's use of this power in 2Co 2:10,11.
identification repentance	a leadership function. A leader can identify with the sins of followers in the past and genuinely repent for them in such a way as to break the on-going power those sins may be influencing. See Daniel's example in chapter 9.
*idiom	the use of words to imply something other than their literal meanings. People in the culture know the idiomatic meaning of the words. Example, I smell a rat. Some idioms are patterned in which case you can reverse the

Glossary

	pattern to get the meaning. Others must simply be learned in the culture from contextual usage of them.
imitator	one of 10 Pauline leadership Styles. A highly non-directive style. The <u>imitator style</u> refers to a conscious use of imitation modeling as a means for influencing followers. It reflects a leader's sense of responsibility for what he/she is as a person of God and for what he/she does in ministry with an expectant view that followers must and will and should be encouraged to follow his/her example. 2 Timothy 3:10,11 illustrates this style.
indigenized church	A church which has its own leadership from its own people and which is organized to survive independently of outside leadership from other cultures and operates with appropriate forms, rites, and ministry fitting to its own culture. According to Allen it will be self-supporting, self-governing, and self-propagating. Others, however, see a combination of these three items along a continuum moving from dependency to interdependency where differing levels are appropriate for different times in the life of the church. Timothy in 1 Timothy is coming as an outside consultant to an indigenized church having its own leadership.
indirect conflict	one of 10 Pauline leadership Styles. A highly non-directive style. The <u>indirect conflict leadership style</u> is an approach to problem solving which requires discernment of spiritual motivation factors behind the problem, usually results in spiritual warfare without direct confrontation with the parties of the problem. Spiritual warfare is sensed as a necessary first step before any problem solving can take place. Matthew 16:21-23 illustrates this style.
indirect ministry	as opposed to indirect ministry. Whereas, direct ministry refers to use of spiritual gifts, i.e. word gifts, to influence a face-to-face target group in terms of the word gifts themselves, indirect ministry means influencing those who are doing direct ministry—a strategic function.
induced authority	one of five power forms, identified by Dennis Wrong, which a leader may use to influence followers. In essence the leader promises rewards to followers in order to entice them to follow.
informal training	one of three modes of training; usually refers to learning taking place on-the-job or via mentoring or apprenticeships or self-initiated learning. Jesus was trained primarily this way. See Jn 7:15.
in-service	a training term which refers to when training is given—describes the fact that training is given to the trainee while the trainee is doing ministry and the training relates to what the trainee is doing. Jesus and Paul both trained using this timing.
inspirational leadership	a description of one of three major high level generic leadership functions that a leader of an organization is responsible for producing. It describes the motivational force for developing the relational base and for achieving the task. The ability to get and motivate toward vision, the ability to see God's presence in a work, and to believe and challenge toward hope—God's future working in the organization—are all part of inspirational leadership. Whereas some leaders are by personality either task oriented or relationally oriented in their leadership, inspirational leadership appear both in task and relationally oriented leaders. All three functions are necessary for healthy ministry.

Glossary

integrity	the top leadership character quality. It is the consistency of inward beliefs and convictions with outward practice. It is an honesty and wholeness of personality in which one operates with a clear conscience in dealings with self and others.
*integrity check	from leadership emergence theory. One of 51 process items that God uses to shape a leader. The integrity check refers to the special kind of process test which God uses to evaluate heart –intent, consistency between inner convictions and outward actions, and which God uses as a foundation from which to expand the leader's capacity to influence. The word check is used in the sense of test—meaning a check or check-up. See also testing patterns.
Integrity and Openness	a Pauline leadership value seen in 2Co. *Leaders should not be deceptive in their dealings with followers but should instead be open, honest, forthright, and frank with them.* See **Article**, *Integrity—A Top Leadership Quality*.
internship	a training model in which a trainee gets on-the-job training under the watchful eye of a supervisor. Theoretically, the trainee is practicing things already learned and getting advice during the experience. This model is sometimes used in conjunction with the formal training mode and also with the informal training mode.
interpretation of tongues	one of the 19 spiritual gifts. It belongs to the power cluster. The gift of interpretation of tongues refers to the ability to spontaneously respond to a giving of an authoritative message in tongues by interpreting this word and clearly communicating the message given. **Its Central Thrust Is Interpreting A Message Given In Tongues.**
Interrupted in-service	a training term which refers to when training is given—describes the fact that training is given to the trainee while the trainee is doing ministry but the trainee is isolated from ministry responsibility for the period of time that the training involves. Probably one the most effective means/timing for training.
intimacy	synonym: vertical intimacy. Intimacy with God refers to a close, private, and personal relationship with God in which there is mutual affection, a sharing of interests, and a sense of growing familiarity with God based upon an accumulation of experience with God. Such a relationship is indicated by intimate times like: times in which God's presence is sensed, times of revelation of truth—when God shows something or shares it, times of affirmation by God, times of fulfillment of God's purposes in our lives (destiny fulfillment), moments of faith, in which we sense God is doing business with us and we accept it, crises—in which God delivers, times of committal, repentance, renewal (fresh starts).
intimacy, horizontal	Intimacy, which ultimately is a gift of God, is an on-going process of reciprocal sharing between two people in which there is transparency in which each feels safe to be open, vulnerability flowing from some kinds of transparency which is respected and not taken advantage of, empathy—a caring affirming reflection on what is shared together, and acceptance of the other without necessarily an agenda for change, and which results in a feeling of belonging and significance in both parties. Nine categories around which horizontal intimacy can be build include: work intimacy, recreational intimacy, intellectual intimacy, emotional intimacy, proper physical intimacy outside of marriage, conflict intimacy, crises intimacy,

Glossary

	physical intimacy in marriage, spiritual intimacy. See resources for further study, Hershey.
intimacy instance	a term referring to a given moment in which a believer's intimacy with Jesus is seen through some symptomatic outward indication such as obeying his truth, having joy, loving other believers, answered prayer upon Jesus' authority. These symptoms show that a believer is "abiding." See John 15.
invincibility principle	protection of a leader by God till He is finished with that leader; this principle was derived because of the observed confidence that Jesus and Paul asserted based on their relationship with God and their understanding of their destiny and an awareness of timing in their lives such that they sensed that God would protect them until their accomplishment of their destiny was completed. See Jn 7:30; see Paul's shipwreck in Ac 27.
irony	a figure of speech, the use of words by a speaker in which his/her intended meaning is the opposite (or in disharmony with) the literal use of the words. e.g. Jas 5:5 you have heaped treasures for the last days. capture: Your life here on earth has been full of pleasure.
*isolation	from leadership emergence theory. One of 51 process items that God uses to shape a leader. <u>Isolation processing</u> refers to the setting aside of a leader from normal ministry involvement in its natural context usually for an extended time in order to experience God in a new or deeper way.
Jews, the	a phrase, *the Jews*, used in John's Gospel to identify a set of Jewish religious leaders who were opposed to Jesus' ministry.
Kingdom Era	a shortened form of The Kingdom Leadership Era. the leadership era ushered in by Samuel when he anointed Saul and associated with the kings of Israel and Judah. This era was ended by the Babylonian captivity.
Kingdom of God	an idiom expressing analogously the concept of God's rule on earth and among His people. Used by Gospel writers (euphemistically by Matthew as Kingdom of Heaven) and Paul.
last days	a term used by Paul to describe the end times before the coming of Christ.
leader	in terms of Biblical leadership a leader is a person with God-given capacity, God-given responsibility who is influencing a specific group of people towards God's purposes for it.
*leadership backlash	from leadership emergence theory. One of 51 process items that God uses to shape a leader. The <u>leadership backlash process</u> item refers to the reactions of followers, other leaders within a group, and/or Christians outside the group, to a course of action taken by a leader because of various ramifications that arise due to the action taken. The situation is used in he leader's life to test perseverance, clarity of vision, and faith.
leadership basal elements	leaders, followers, and situations are the major components of <u>leadership basal elements</u>.
*leadership challenge	a leadership emergence theory term referring to the shaping process God uses to give a leader an on-going renewal experience about leadership and to direct that leader to some new leadership task.

Glossary

*leadership committal	a special shaping activity of God observed in leadership emergence theory which is usually a spiritual benchmark and produces a sense of destiny in a leader. It is the call to leadership by God and the wholehearted response by the leader to accept and abide by that call. Paul's Damascus road experience, the destiny revelation given by Ananias, and Paul's response to it as a life calling provide the New Testament classic example of leadership committal.
leadership development	the term referring to the process whereby a given leader develops over a lifetime toward that potential God has placed in him/her. This can include non-deliberate processes of life as well as informal, non-formal, and formal training which focuses deliberately on development.
*leadership era	A period of time in Biblical history which describes a certain kind of leadership differing from the other eras preceding and following it. Six leadership eras are identified in Scripture. See Patriarchal Leadership Era, Pre-Kingdom Era, Kingdom Era, Post-Kingdom Era, Pre-Church Era, Post Church Era.
leadership functions	Leadership functions is a technical term which refers to the three major categories of formal leadership responsibility: task behavior (defining structure and goals), relationship behavior (providing the emotional support and ambiance), and inspirational behavior (providing motivational effort).
leadership labels	See elder, minister, bishop, deacon, servant.
leadership release	Leadership release is the process whereby an existing leader deliberately encourages and allows an emerging leader to accept responsibility for and control of leadership positions, functions, roles, and tasks.
leadership selection	the life-long process of divine initiative and human recognition whereby a leader emerges. The process is punctuated with critical incidents, as viewed from a two-fold intermeshing perspective—the divine and the human. God selects a leader as indicated by various kind of shaping activities and human leadership affirms that selection, recognizing the shaping activities of God and working with God in that processing.
leadership stewardship	see entrustment, leadership viewed as a stewardship from God.
*leadership style	the individual tendency of a leader to influence followers in a highly directive manner, directive manner, non-directive manner, or highly non-directive manner. It is that consistent behavior pattern that underlies specific overt behavior acts of influence pervading the majority of leadership functions in which that leader exerts influence. The style is the means that the leader uses in influencing followers toward purposes. I identify 10 Pauline leadership styles. See Clinton **Coming To Conclusions on Leadership Styles.**
leadership training	the deliberate use of means either formally, non-formally, or informally to develop a leader.
leadership transition	Leadership transition is the process whereby existing leaders prepare and release emerging leaders into the responsibility and practice of leadership positions, functions, roles, and tasks.

Glossary

*leadership value	an underlying assumption which affects how a leader behaves in or perceives leadership situations. Usually when explicitly identified and written the statement will contain strong forceful words like should, ought, or must to indicate the strength of the value. e.g. A specific Pauline leadership value—*Paul felt he should view personal relationships as an important part of ministry, both as a means for ministry and as an end in itself of ministry.* Or generalized to all leaders—*Leaders should view personal relationships as an important part of ministry, both as a means for ministry and as an end in itself of ministry.* Stronger would be the word ought and even stronger the word must.
learning posture	an attitude of willingness to learn even though what may be learned may differ and expand or even contradict what has been previously learned. Such an attitude reflects what has been noted as a major leadership lesson: *Effective leaders maintain a learning posture all of their lifetimes.*
left hand of God	in contradistinction to the phrase the right hand of God which refers to an evident manifestation of God's power in a situation, usually through His people or His leaders, this phrase, the left hand of God, refers to God's use of people, nations, events not necessarily recognizing Him or what He is doing for His own purposes. (e.g. Cyrus). See also Jn 11:49-51.
legitimate authority	one of five power forms, identified by Dennis Wrong, which a leader may use to influence followers. In essence the leader has a position recognized by followers as one to which they owe loyalty, submission and obedience due to the position and their relationship to it.
life crisis	from leadership emergence theory. One of 51 process items that God uses to shape a leader. A <u>life crisis process item</u> refers to a crisis situations characterized by life threatening intense pressure in human affairs in which the meaning and purpose of life are searched out with a result that the leader has experienced God in a new way as the source, sustainer, and focus of life.
life purpose	a focused life concept; one of 4 focal issues; A <u>life purpose</u> is a burden-like calling, a task or driving force or achievement, which motivates a leader to fulfill something or to see something done. This is the core focal issue and around which a life is integrated over a lifetime.
list idiom	an idiomatic use of a list of items. The initial item on the list is the main assertion and other items illustrate or clarify the primary item.
litotes/tapenosis	a negative emphatic figure of speech. It is used quite a bit by Luke and also by Paul. Something is diminished in order to emphatically stress just its opposite. e.g. not ashamed of the Gospel in Romans 1:16 means emphatically—completely confident in the Gospel. While technically different I group litotes and tapenosis together as a class of negative emphatics. They essentially emphasize the opposite of what is denied.
love gifts	a category of spiritual gifts which are used to demonstrate the effects of God's transformation of lives and His care for people. Love gifts demonstrate the beauty of the unseen God's work in lives in such a way as to attract others to want this same kind of relationship. These include: pastoring, evangelism, gifts of healings, governments, helps, giving, mercy, (word of knowledge, word of wisdom sometimes).

Glossary

Loyalty Testing	a Pauline leadership value seen in 2Co. *Leaders must know the level of followership loyalty in order to wisely exercise leadership influence.* See **Article**, *Followership—Ten Commandments*.
Luke 16:10 Principle	an application principle drawn from Luke 16:10. An emerging leader who is faithful in small tasks will be faithful later in larger tasks.
*macro-lesson	is a high level generalization of a leadership observation (suggestion, guideline, requirement), stated as a lesson, which repeatedly occurs throughout different leadership eras, and thus has potential as a leadership absolute. Macro lessons even at their weakest provide at least strong guidelines describing leadership insights. At their strongest they are requirements, that is absolutes, that leaders should follow. Leaders ignore them to their detriment. Example: *Prayer Lesson: If God has called you to a ministry then He has called you to pray for that ministry.*
major role	a focused life concept; one of 4 focal issues; A <u>major role</u> is the job platform which basically describes what a leader does and which allows recognition by others and which uniquely fits who a leader is and lets that leader effectively accomplish life purpose(s). It is broken up into two components: base (more formal) and functional (more informal). See **Article** *A Focused Life*.
*maturity appeal	one of 10 Pauline leadership styles. A non-directive to directive type of style. The <u>maturity appeal leadership style</u> is the form of leadership influence which counts upon godly experience, usually gained over a long period of time, an empathetic identification based on a common sharing of experience, and recognition of the force of imitation modeling in influencing people in order to convince people toward a favorable acceptance of the leader's ideas. Used in Phm. See also 1Pe 5:1-4 where Peter uses this style.
*mentor	in a mentoring relationship the person helping the mentoree. This is also a label given to the ultimate contribution of a Christian leader whose has a major focus in ministry of personal ministry to individuals as opposed to public ministry. e.g. Jesus, Paul the Apostle. Mentoring is also one of the five enhancement factors enabling effective leaders to finish well.
mentor-mix	the set of mentoring roles that a leader functions in. e.g. spirituality mentor, counselor, contemporary model.
*mentoree	in a mentoring relationship the person being helped by a mentor.
*mentoring	a relational experience in which one person, the mentor, empowers another person, the mentoree, by sharing God-given resources. See the 9 mentor roles: mentor discipler, mentor spiritual guide, mentor coach, mentor counselor, mentor teacher, mentor sponsor, mentor contemporary model, mentor historical model, mentor divine contact. e.g. The apostle Paul demonstrated many of these roles in his relationships with team members and others in his ministry. See Stanley and Clinton **Connecting** for a popular treatment of mentoring. See Clinton and Clinton **The Mentor Handbook** for a detailed treatment of mentoring.
*mentor coach	one of nine mentor roles. Coaching is a process of imparting encouragement and skills to succeed in a task via relational training.

Glossary

*mentor discipler	one of nine mentor roles. A mentor discipler is one who spends much time, usually one-on-one, with an individual mentoree in order to build into that mentoree the basic habits of the Christian life. It is a relational experience in which a more experienced follower of Christ shares with a less experienced follower of Christ the commitment, understanding, and basic skills necessary to know and obey Jesus Christ as Lord.
*mentor divine contact	one of nine mentor roles. A person whose timely intervention is perceived of as from God to give special guidance at an important time in a life. This person may or may not be aware of the intervention and may or may not have any further mentoring connection to the mentoree.
*mentor model (contemporary)	one of nine mentor roles. A mentor contemporary model is a person who models values, methodologies, and other leadership characteristics in such a way as to inspire others to emulate them.
*mentor model (historical)	one of nine mentor roles. A mentor historical model is a person whose life (autobiographical or biographical input) modeled values, methodologies, and other leadership characteristics in such a way as to inspire others to emulate them.
*mentor spiritual guide	one of nine mentor roles. A spiritual guide is a godly, mature follower of Christ who shares knowledge, skills, and basic philosophy on what it means to increasingly realize Christlikeness in all areas of life. The primary contributions of a Spiritual guide include accountability, decisions, and insights concerning questions, commitments, and direction affecting spirituality (inner-life motivations) and maturity (integrating truth with life).
*mentor sponsor	one of nine mentor roles. A mentor sponsor is one who helps promote the ministry (career) of another by using his/her resources, credibility, position, etc. to further the development and acceptance of the mentoree.
*mentor teacher	one of nine mentor roles. A mentor teacher is one who imparts knowledge and understanding of a particular subject at a time when a mentoree needs it.
mercy	one of 19 spiritual gifts occurring primarily in the Love Cluster. The <u>gift of mercy</u> refers to the capacity to both feel sympathy for those in need (especially the suffering) and to manifest this sympathy in some practical helpful way with a cheerful spirit so as to encourage and help those in need. **Its Central Thrust Is The Empathetic Care For Those Who Are Hurting.**
metaphor	a figure of speech which involves an implied comparison in which two unlike items (a real item and a picture item) are equated to point out one point of resemblance. e.g. The Lord is my shepherd. These can be simple (all elements present) or complex (verbal metaphor, some element may be missing and has to be supplied). 2Ti 1:6 stir up the gift is complex, a verbal metaphor. Gift is compared to a flame which has gotten low. Timothy is urged to develop and use with power that gift.
*metonymy	a figure of speech in which one word is substituted for another word to which it is related. This is to emphasize both the word and call attention to the relationship between the two words. e.g. Philemon 6 communicate your

Glossary

	faith = communicate what you believe and on which you have strong convictions.
minister	a leadership term (SRN 1249) synonymous with deacon, actually translating the same Greek word. Paul uses it to describe himself and several of his companions. It is unclear when Paul uses it to describe himself and others of the leadership role implied.
ministerial formation	the shaping activity in a leader's life which is directed toward instilling leadership skills, leadership experience, and developing giftedness for ministry.
ministry affirmation	a concept from leadership emergence theory. The shaping activity of God whereby God makes known to a leader his approval of that leader's ministry efforts. This is a major motivating factor to keep one serving the Lord.
ministry conflict	from leadership emergence theory. One of 51 process items that God uses to shape a leader. The ministry conflict process item refers to those instances in a ministry situation, in which a leader learns lessons via the positive and negative aspects of conflict with regards to: 1. the nature of conflict, 2. possible ways to resolve conflict, 3. possible ways to avoid conflict, 4. ways to creatively use conflict, and 5. perception of God's personal shaping through the conflict.
ministry entry patterns	a leadership emergence theory pattern which describes how leaders move from non-involvement in ministry to involvement in ministry. Of importance in the process is the recognition of God's challenges to ministry and of self-initiative in attempting to do something about the challenges.
ministry philosophy	a phrase describing the leadership values which are implicit or explicit and which under gird a leader's perception of ministry and decision making and practice of ministry.
*ministry task	one of 51 process items that God uses to shape a leader. A ministry task is an assignment from God which primarily tests a person's faithfulness and obedience but often also allows use of ministry gifts in the context of a task which has closure, accountability, and evaluation. e.g. Barnabas trip to Antioch; Titus had 5 ministry tasks.
miracles	also called working of powers. One of the 19 spiritual gifts. It belongs to the Power Cluster. The <u>workings of powers</u> (gift of miracles), refers to the releasing of God's supernatural power so that the miraculous intervention of God is perceived and God receives recognition for the supernatural intervention. **Its Central Thrust Is The Releasing Of God's Power To Give Authenticity.**
*modeling	a means a leader can use to influence followers; it involves openly demonstrating in one's life the attitudes and actions desired in others. It counts on the followers admiring and wanting what the leader has in their own lives.
Moses, zealous principle	a leadership principle which states that *a leader should not be jealous of another leader's accomplishments but should be zealous for God's work being done no matter who does it.* First seen in Moses' ministry

Glossary

(Numbers 11:26-30); also seen in Jesus' ministry (Mark 11:26-30) and Paul's ministry (Philippians 1:18).

Motivational Force	a Pauline leadership value seen in 2Co. *Leaders should use obligation to Christ (in light of his death for believers) to motivate believers to service for Christ.*
movement	a groundswell of people committed to a person or ideals and characterized by five important commitments:[106] 1. commitment to personal involvement; 2. commitment to persuade others to join; 3. commitment to the beliefs and ideals of the movement; 4. commitment to participate in a flexible, non-bureaucratic cell-group organization; 5. commitment to endure opposition and misunderstanding.
negative emphatic	a figure of speech which negates some concept in order to draw special attention to its opposite (see litotes). e.g. Romans 1:16.
*negative preparation	from leadership emergence theory. One of 51 process items that God uses to shape a leader. <u>Negative preparation</u> refers to the special guidance process involving God's use of events, people, conflict, persecution, or experiences, all focusing on the negative, so as to free up a person from the situation in order to enter the next phase of development with a new abandonment and revitalized interest.
*networking power	a leadership emergence theory term. One of 51 processing items used by God to shape a leader's ministry. It describes how God can connect a leader to resources of all kinds which can come from contacts with people. People provide a bridge, connecting a given leader with other persons or needed resources.
New Covenant	a Pauline phrase used in 1Co 11:25 and 2Co 3:6 to represent a relationship with God in Christ—salvation through faith in Christ and given by the Grace of God. This is opposed to salvation via works and obedience to the law system.
non-formal training	one of three training modes; it usually refers to non-programmatic training leading to more immediate application of the training; today this is represented in workshops, seminars, and conferences. In Jesus day, his large public teachings did some of this kind of training. See Jn 7:15.
non-vested gifts	a concept from leadership emergence theory. When the body meets the Spirit of God may manifest gifts through individuals which are not seen repeatedly over their lifetime. These are situational uses (see 1Co 12:7-13 contrast with Ro 12:3ff which are vested) of spiritual gifts, sometimes called *come and go* gifts. John Wimber called this phenomena *the dancing hand of God*.
normative value	a leadership value which tends toward an absolute and should be required for any leader.
nurse	one of 10 Pauline leadership styles. A non-directive style. The <u>nurse leadership style</u> is a behavior style characterized by gentleness and

---

[106] These five commitments are taken from Gerlach and Hines research. Gerlach, L.P. and Hine, V.H., **People, Power, Change: Movements of Social Transformation**. New York: Bobbs-Merrill Co. (1970).

Glossary

	sacrificial service and loving care which indicates that a leader has given up "rights" in order not to impede the nurture of those following him/her. 1Th 2:7 illustrates this style.
*obedience check	from leadership emergence theory. One of 51 process items that God uses to shape a leader. An Obedience checks refer to that special category of process items in which God tests personal response to revealed truth in the life of a person.
*obligation persuasion	one of 10 Pauline leadership styles. A non-directive style. The obligation persuasion style uses an appeal to a follower toward some recommended directive and which persuades, not commands that the follower heed the advice; but it leaves the decision up to the follower though the follower has some obligation to the leader and will thus feel the pressure to voluntary accept the directive.
Old Covenant	a Pauline phrase used in 2Co 3:14 and Ro 9:4 and indirectly in Gal to represent the law system of salvation as seen in the Old Testament Scriptures. It represents God's promises to Israel. This is opposed to salvation via faith in Christ given freely by God.
overlap	Overlap is that unique time in a leadership transition when the emerging leader and existing leader share responsibility and accountability for tasks, roles, and functions. Seen beautifully in the Moses to Joshua leadership transition.
parable	a true-to-life story, pictorial illustration, or other figurative comparison which teaches a central truth by means of one or more comparisons. This was one of Jesus' favorite means of doing non-formal training.
paradigm	a controlling perspective in the mind which allows one to perceive and understand REALITY.
*paradigm shift	a change of a controlling perspective so that one perceives and understands REALITY in a different way than previously.
pastoring	one of the 19 spiritual gifts. It belongs to the Word Cluster and the Love Cluster. The pastoral gift is the capacity to exercise concern and care for members of a group so as to encourage them in their growth in Christ which involves modeling maturity, protecting them from error and disseminating truth. **Its central thrust is Caring For The Growth Of Followers.**
Patriarchal Era	shortened form of Patriarchal Leadership Era. The leadership era covering the period of time associated with Abraham, Isaac, Jacob, Joseph, Job and lasting till Moses' leadership. This was mainly family oriented leadership beginning to shift over to tribal leadership in its closing stages.
pattern	pattern is the term used in leadership emergence theory to describe a repetitive cycle of happenings (observed in comparative analysis of case studies on leaders) and may involve periods of time, stages of something happening, combinations of process items, or combinations of other identifiable leadership concepts, all of which serve to give perspective. 23 identifiable patterns have been described.
perceived reality	in paradigmatic theory this refers to the interpretive understanding of REALITY (ontological existence of things) existing in a person's mind and

Glossary

	constrained by screening grids such as: physical, focus, reflections, paradigms or other frameworks for interpreting—existing in the mind.
perspective	a term referring to one of five enhancement factors for effective leaders who finish well. Effective leaders view present ministry in terms of a life time perspective. Further, they see their lifetime in terms of God's bigger perspective in the redemptive drama.
personal authority	one of five power forms, identified by Dennis Wrong, which a leader may use to influence followers. In essence the leader has charisma, personality, and leader traits recognized by the culture so the followers are drawn to the leader and voluntary want to follow the leader.
Personal Ministry	a Pauline leadership value seen in 2Co. *Leaders should view personal relationships as an important part of ministry.*
personification	a figure of speech which uses words to speak of animals, ideas, abstractions, and inanimate objects as if they had human form, character, or intelligence in order to vividly portray truth. e.g. Luke 7:35 Wisdom is justified of all her children.
Pharisees	a group of religious leaders, who for the most part opposed Jesus' ministry. They were fundamentalists who legalistically observed the law of Moses and its interpretations by various Rabbis.
pilot project	a phrase used to describe a minimum leadership strategy for implementing change in a situation. A <u>pilot project</u> is a low key attempt to do something without calling any attention to it so that after it has worked it can be used as a model for further more widespread change.
pioneer	a label given to the ultimate contribution of a Christian leader who starts apostolic ministries. e.g. Paul.
*pivotal point	A <u>pivotal point</u> is a critical time in a leader's life in which processing going on will be responded to in such a way that one of three typical things may happen: The response to this processing can: 1. curtail further use of the leader by God or at least curtail expansion of the leader's potential. 2. limit the eventual use of the leader for ultimate purposes that otherwise could have been accomplished, 3. enhance or open up the leader for expansion or contribution to the ultimate purposes in God's kingdom, that is, it may be a springboard to future expanded use by God of the leader.
plateauing	a condition in the development of a leader in which that leader has ceased to grow in one or more important areas of his/her life. The growth may be blocked due to some disobedience to something God has shown, a general condition of loss of drive or energy due to an extended time of pressured ministry, or in general a lack of learning posture.
Post-Kingdom Era	shortened form of Post-Kingdom Leadership Era. The leadership era associated with Daniel, Ezekiel and others who exerted influence after the fall of Jerusalem and the deporting of Israel. This was dominantly a leadership by modeling under trying conditions.
power base	a term referring to the means which enable a leader's influence. Force, manipulation, authority, and persuasion enfold various power means.

Glossary

*power encounter	A phrase first defined by a missiological anthropologist, A. R. Tippett, which identifies a situation in which the power of God is tested over against some other god's power. Several elements that should be present in classical power encounters: a) A crisis between people representing god and other people must be differentiated clearly. b) There must be recognition that the issue is one of power confrontation in the supernatural realm. c) There must be public recognition of the pre-encounter terms (If...Then...). d) There is an actual crisis/ confrontation event (the more public usually the better will be the aftermath). e) There must be confirmation that God has done the delivering as the power encounter resolves. f) Celebration to bring closure and insure continuation of God's purpose in the power event. Examples: Jephthah, Jdg 11:12-32. Da 3.
*power forms	refers to Dennis Wrong's taxonomy of Influence, Power, and Authority. Power forms include (see **Article 4.** *Influence Power and Authority*) : Force, Manipulation, Authority, Persuasion. Each is defined in **Article 4.**
power gifts	a category of spiritual gifts which authenticate the reality of God by demonstrating God's intervention in today's world. These include: tongues, interpretation of tongues, discernings of spirits, kinds of healings, kinds of power (miracles), prophecy, faith, word of wisdom, word of knowledge.
power ministry	refers to use of the power gifts to demonstrate God's intervention and often to validate or vindicate a leader's spiritual authority in a situation.
*power shift	a term describing the paradigm shift in which a leader moves from not believing in God's supernatural intervention in ministry to believing it and using it. See Jn 6:1-15; 16-21.
*prayer encouragement principle	The deliberate sharing by a leader with followers of specific prayer requests being prayed for them, in the will of God, in order to encourage them.
*prayer ministry principle	A macro lesson first seen in Abraham's intercession for Sodom, then in Moses intercession for Israel up on the mountain, and most fully amplified by Samuel's ministry (1Sa 12:23,24). It is stated as, *Leaders called to a ministry are called to intercede for that ministry.*
*prayer model	one of five philosophical leadership models introduced by Jesus and one which focuses on a leader's responsibility to intercede for ministry. See **Article**, *Five Philosophical Leadership Models in the Gospels.* Sometimes called *Intercessory Model.*
prayer power	from leadership emergence theory. One of 51 process items that God uses to shape a leader. <u>Prayer power</u> refers to the specific instance in which God uses the situation to answer prayer and demonstrate the authenticity of the leader's spiritual authority.
preferred value	a helpful leadership value which some leaders choose to follow but which is not necessarily applicable for all leaders.
Pre-Church Era	shortened form of Pre-Church Leadership Era. The leadership era associated with Jesus leadership. It was a transitional time moving from national leadership to spiritual leadership.

Glossary

Pre-Kingdom Era
: shortened form of Pre-Kingdom Leadership Era. The leadership era associated with Moses, Joshua, and the Judges and lasting until Samuel anointed Saul and began the Kingdom Era. This leadership involved an amalgamation of tribes into a commonwealth. It was moving toward a centralized national leadership but was derailed during the judges time.

pre-read
: a technical term drawn from continuum reading; this level of reading assumes that scan, ransack, and browse reading have preceded it. A pre-read browses every chapter and seeks to integrate the book via overall structure and theme. See continuum reading.

pre-service
: a training term which refers to when training is given—describes the fact that training is given to the trainee before the trainee is doing ministry and the training hopefully will be relate to what the trainee might do later on when in ministry.

prison epistle
: Ephesians, Philippians, Colossians, Philemon and 2 Timothy are called the prison epistles since Paul penned them while being in prison. The first four were probably written in 62 A.D., Paul age 56, in Paul's first imprisonment. The last one, 2 Timothy, when Paul was about age 61 and just shortly before his martyrdom. Out of those isolation experiences we see a depth of leadership advice and wisdom born out of the experience of a leader who is mature and is fulfilling his destiny.

process item
: a technical name in leadership emergence theory describing actual occurrences in a given leader's life including providential events, people, circumstances, special divine interventions, inner-life lessons and other like items which God uses to develop that leader by shaping leadership character, leadership skills, and leadership values. These shaping things indicate leadership capacity and/or potential; they expand this potential; they confirm appointment to roles or responsibilities using that leadership capacity; they direct that leader along to God's appointed ministry level for realized potential. Some 51 different shaping activities (process items) have been identified in leadership emergence theory. Synonym: shaping activities of God.

*progressive calling
: the recognition that most leaders will receive on-going leadership challenges from God throughout their lifetimes and not just some initial call; such challenges will bring renewal, divine affirmation, ministry affirmation and will continue to give strategic guidance to a leader's ministry.

progressive revelation
: A concept noted in the Old Testament and New that God is a God who continues to communicate and over time clarifies earlier revelation, expanding on it, filling in more details, helping later leaders see the relevance of it, etc. See especially prophetic ministry. Example: Daniel's prophecies in ch 2, 7, 8, 9, 10-12. There is progress in both content and methodology as observed in various genre in Old and New Testaments.

Prominence of Christ in Ministry
: a Pauline leadership value seen in 2Co. *A leader must not seek to bring attention to himself/herself through ministry but must seek to exalt Christ as Lord.*

promise
: or more specifically, a promise from God is an assertion from God, specific or general or a truth in harmony with God's character, which is perceived in one's heart or mind concerning what He will do or not do for one, and

Glossary

which is sealed in that one's inner most being by a quickening action of the Holy Spirit, and on which that one then counts. See Jn 14 where six such promises are used to inspire the disciples in a crisis moment.

promoter	a label given to the ultimate contribution of a Christian leader who effectively distributes new ideas and/or other ministry related things so as to inspire others to use them. e.g. Jesus, Paul.
prophecy	one of the 19 spiritual gifts. It is in the *Word Cluster* and *power cluster*. A person operating with the <u>gift of prophecy</u> has the capacity to deliver truth (in a public way) either of a predictive nature or as a situational word from God in order to correct by exhorting, edifying or consoling believers and to convince non-believers of God's truth. **Its central thrust is To Provide Correction Or Perspective On A Situation.**
public rhetorician	a label given to the ultimate contribution of a Christian leader who has as a major focus in ministry a productive public ministry with large groups, as opposed to a personal ministry with individuals and small groups. e.g. Jesus, Apollos, Peter.
radical committal pattern	refers to the early development of a leader in the foundational development phase who comes from a non-Christian background or at best a very nominal Christian background in which the leader is more or less processed into whatever values the environment supports; then that leader makes a radical adult decision for Christ which involves significant paradigm shifts in terms of those early values and life-goals.
ransack	a technical term drawn from continuum reading. Ransacking is the second lightest level of reading. A book can be open ransacked or closed ransacked. Ransacking means going through the book looking for anything new (open ransacking) on a given subject or looking only for a special item (closed ransacking).
read	a technical term drawn from continuum reading. Reading is the second heaviest level of reading. Reading assumes that all the previous levels—scan, ransack, browse, pre-read—have been done. Reading requires not only evaluation of the book at structure and theme level but analysis of its import.
reading buddy	a model for lateral peer mentoring which involves two people committing themselves to learning by reading. In an alternate fashion each person chooses the reading material and setting of assignments. Each holds the other accountable.
reality	in paradigm shift language, the perception of REALITY a person has in the mind.
REALITY	in paradigm shift language, the ontological existence of what is whether or not it is perceived (reality) in the mind.
reciprocal commands	the label referring to the one-another commands in the epistles which describe some of the strong relationships and behaviors that should be part of the church community. e.g. love one another; forebear one another.

Glossary

recruitment	refers to the deliberate efforts to challenge potential leaders and to engage them in on-going ministry so that they will develop as leaders and move toward accomplishment God's destiny for them.
regime turnover	Regime turnover refers to the process and practices involved in transitioning an old staff recruited under a former regime until it fits the new leadership's idea of what its people should be and do.
relational oriented leadership	a description of one of three major high level generic leadership functions that a leader of an organization is responsible for producing. It describes the creation of community, of ambiance, development of people, building of a base from which the task can be accomplished. Some leaders by personality and processing are relationally oriented and tend to prioritize everything in terms of getting the relational perspective; this means frequently not getting the task done. All three functions are necessary for healthy ministry.
relationship insights	from leadership emergence theory. One of 51 process items that God uses to shape a leader. Relationship insights refers to those instances in ministry in which a leader learns lessons via positive or negative experiences with regard to relating to other Christians or non-Christians in the light of ministry decisions or other influence means: such lessons are learned so as to significantly affect future leadership.
renewal	one of five enhancement factors helping effective leaders to finish well. Such leaders will experience repeated renewals throughout their ministry. Renewal is a specially meaningful encounter with God in which He communicates with *freshness* various kinds of things needed by a leader such as insights about Himself, affirmation--both personal and ministry, inspiration to continue, breakthrough concepts which inspire one to try them in ministry, a sense of His personal presence and/or power, an unusual sense of intimacy--can be tied to some symbolic thing (like a place, physical object, etc)., perspective on time, now and/or the future so that ones faith is increased to see God in what is happening and will happen, so as to give the leader another anchor upon which to build a sense of a new start, a beginning again, and a desire to rededicate and continue on in following God. Type I renewals refer to renewal serendipitously engendered externally by God and Type II renewals refer to renewals which come because the leader is seeking them, usually through exercise of spiritual disciplines.
researcher	a label given to the ultimate contribution of a Christian leader who studies various aspects of Christianity, analyzes it, and develops new ideation or furthers thinking about it. e.g. Luke.
rhetorical question	a figure of speech in which a question is not used to obtain information but is used to indirectly communicate an affirmative or negative statement, the importance of some thought by focusing attention on it, and/or one's own feeling or attitudes about something. 1 Tim 3:5 For if anyone knows not how to rule his own house, how shall that one take care of the church of God. Captured: A person who can not lead his/her own family can't lead people in a church.
ruling	one of the 19 spiritual gifts. It is in the word cluster. A person operating with a ruling gift demonstrates the capacity to exercise influence over a group so as to lead it toward a goal or purpose with a particular emphasis on

Glossary

	the capacity to make decisions and keep the group operating together. **Its central thrust is Influencing Others Toward Vision.**
role enablement	a pattern observed in leadership emergence theory concerning giftedness. A leader in a situation which warrants it may be given a spiritual gift needed for that situation. After completing or leaving that situation the leader in a new place or ministry may not see the gift in the new situation. That is, it was a temporary enablement for a specific role which needed it. See vested gifts. Probably the case with Timothy (2Ti 4:5).
saint	a label given to the ultimate contribution of a Christian leader who models a Godly life in such a way as to demonstrate Christ-likeness, the fruit of the Spirit, union life and which draws others to want to emulate it. e.g. Paul the Apostle.
scan	a technical term from continuum reading. This is the lightest type of reading and involves a short time spent in a book in order to categorize the book and determine the level at which it should be read on the continuum.
sense of destiny	an inner conviction arising from an experience or a series of experiences in which there is a growing sense of awareness that God has His hand on a leader in a special way for special purposes. See destiny pattern.
sentness	a term capturing the divine backing of Jesus' intervention in the world to represent and reveal God to our world. It carries the notion of anointing and appointment by God for a mission, but in Jesus' case—more since it was the incarnation of God in human form. The closest functional equivalent for leaders today is divine appointment.
servant (leader)	A special leadership term which Paul uses to describe himself and Timothy (SRN 1401). It is used of one who gives himself up to another's will, those whose service is used by Christ in extending and advancing his cause among people. It emphasizes leadership wise the vertical aspect of servant leadership. A leader first of all serves Christ. Secondly, he/she serves those being influenced or led.
Servant Leadership	a Pauline leadership value seen in 2Co. *A leader ought to see leadership as focused on serving followers in Jesus' behalf.*
servant model	one of five philosophical leadership models introduced by Jesus and one which focuses on a leader's inward attitude to see ministry as service to God and service to those being ministered to. See **Article**, *Five Philosophical Leadership Models in the Gospels.*
shepherd model	one of five philosophical leadership models introduced by Jesus and one which focuses on a leader's responsibility to relate to, protect, care for and develop those being ministered to. See **Article**, *Five Philosophical Leadership Models in the Gospels.*
simile	a figure of speech which involves a stated comparison of two unlike items (one called the real item and the other the picture item) in order to display one graphic point of comparison. The words like or so or as or than are used to indicate the stated comparison between the real and picture items. e.g. 1 Pet 2:24 All flesh is as grass.

Glossary

slain in the spirit	a description of one who has lost strength and usually is flat on one's face or back and who is consciously aware of God's supernatural working or revelation being given. It is an awesome experience in which the direct hand of God is sensed. See Daniel 10 especially. Usually such an experience communicates divine affirmation.
*sovereign mindset	an attitude demonstrated by the Apostle Paul in which he tended to see God's working in the events and activities that shaped his life, whether or not they were positive and good or negative and bad. He tended to see God's purposes in these shaping activities and to make the best of them.
*Sovereign Mindset	a Pauline leadership value seen in 2Co. *Leaders ought to see God's hand in their circumstances as part of His plan for developing them as leaders.* See **Article**, *Sovereign Mindset*.
sphere of influence	refers to the totality of people being influenced and for whom a leader will give an account to God. The totally of people influenced subdivides into three domains called direct influence, indirect influence, and organizational influence. Three measures rate sphere of influence: 1. Extensiveness—which refers to quantity; 2. Comprehensiveness—which refers to the scope of things being influenced in the followers' lives; 3. Intensiveness—the depth to which influence extends to each item within the comprehensive influences. Extensiveness is the easiest to measure and hence is most often used or implied when talking about a leader's sphere of influence.
*spiritual authority	from the standpoint of the follower, Spiritual authority is the right to influence, conferred upon a leader by followers, because of their perception of spirituality in that leader. From the leader's perspective Spiritual Authority is that characteristic of a God-anointed leader, developed upon an experiential power base (giftedness, character, deep experiences with God), that enables him/her to influence followers through persuasion, force of modeling, and moral expertise.
Spiritual Authority—Its ends	a Pauline leadership value seen in 2Co. *Spiritual authority ought to be used to mature followers.* See **Articles**, *Spiritual Authority—defined, Six Characteristics.; Followership—Ten Commandments*.
spiritual authority insights	from leadership emergence theory. One of 51 process items that God uses to shape a leader. Spiritual authority insights refers to any discovery a leader learns about his/her own spiritual authority—its existence or its use.
spiritual benchmarks	see benchmarks, spiritual—for a description of foundational events which are touchstones or watermarks for a lifetime of ministry.
spiritual formation	the shaping activity in a leader's life which is directed toward instilling godly character and developing inner life.
*spiritual gift	a God-given unique capacity which is given to each believer for the purpose of releasing a Holy Spirit empowered ministry either in a situation or to be repeated during the Church Leadership Era. I identify 19 such gifts from a comparative analysis of the 8 major and 16 minor passages about gifts in Scripture. I categorize these 19 in terms of major purposes for the church as Word gifts, Power gifts, and Love gifts. The 19 include: teaching, exhortation, pastoring, evangelism, apostleship, prophecy, ruling, word of wisdom, word of knowledge, faith, miracles, gifts of healings, governments,

Glossary

helps, giving, mercy, tongues, interpretation of tongues, discernings of spirits. All leaders have at least one word gift. See word gifts. See Clinton and Clinton **Unlocking Your Giftedness** for detailed explanation of leadership and spiritual gifts.

Spiritual warfare	refers to the unseen opposition in the spirit world made up of Satan and his demons and their attempts to defeat God's forces, including believers. It also involves the response by believers to these attempts.
stabilizer	a label given to the ultimate contribution of a Christian leader who can help a fledgling organization develop or can help an older organization move toward efficiency and effectiveness. e.g. Timothy, Titus.
strategic formation	the shaping activity in a leader's life which is directed toward having that leader reach full potential and achieve a God-given destiny.
stewardship model	one of five philosophical leadership models introduced by Jesus and one which focuses on a leader's responsibility to recognize, develop, and use resources given to that leader. See **Article**, *Five Philosophical Leadership Models in the Gospels*.
Study	a technical term drawn from continuum reading. Study is the highest level of reading and involves all previous levels of reading (scan, ransack, browse, pre-read, read). This level not only evaluates the book internally for structure, theme, import and relevance but compares it to other equivalent works in the field. Very few books are read at this level.
stylistic practitioner	a label given to the ultimate contribution of a Christian leader who models a unique ministry style that others want to emulate. e.g. Peter, Paul.
superlative idiom	the Hebrew superlative is often shown by the repetition of a word. e.g. Hebrew of the Hebrews. See Php 2:27, 3:5; 1Ti 1:18; 6:12, and others.
Symbol	a symbol is a visible object, quality of an object, or acted out object lesson which is used to teach a truth by a striking resemblance to the truth for which it stands. There can be visionary objects (7 Golden Lampstands), material objects (bread and wine in the Lord's Supper), and external miraculous (burning bush in Ex 3).
synecdoche	a figure of speech closely related to a metonymy. It is a figure of speech in which one word is substituted for another to which it is related as a part to the whole or whole to the part. e.g. Mt 8:8 come under my roof (roof for house).
tag question	a grammatical construction (signaled by a Greek particle) which proposes a question and expects a negative answer—you didn't catch anything, did you? See fn Jn 21:5-7.
tandem training	Tandem training describes the training technique during overlap used by an existing leader with an emerging leader whom he is transitioning into leadership.
task oriented leadership	a description of one of three major high level generic leadership functions that a leader of an organization is responsible for producing. It describes the thing to be accomplished by the organization, its raison d'être, reason for being. Some leaders by personality and processing are highly task oriented

Glossary

and tend to prioritize everything in terms of getting the task done; this means frequently using people. All three functions are necessary for healthy ministry.

teachable moment — a life situation which is conducive to learning and which can be used by a mentor/developer to develop an emerging leader. The life situation itself prompts learning and catches the attention of the learners. Jesus used this technique many times. e.g. see Mt 21:19,20.

teaching — one of the 19 spiritual gifts. It belongs to the Word Cluster. A person who has the gift of teaching is one who has the ability to instruct, explain, or expose Biblical truth in such a way as to cause believers to understand the Biblical truth. **Its central thrust is To Clarify Truth.**

testing patterns — from leadership emergence theory, one of 23 fairly common patters observed in the development of leaders. The pattern involves three aspects: test, response, resultant action. Two sub-patterns occur. The success pattern, also called the positive testing pattern, involves test, positive response, and expansion. The failure pattern, also called the negative testing pattern, involves test, negative response, and remedial action.

testing, negative pattern — The negative testing/ remedial pattern describes God's use of the testing cluster of items (integrity check, obedience check, word check, faith check, ministry task) to point out lack of character traits through a three step process which includes:

1) presentation of a test of character through a given incident in life experiences,

2) a failure response in which the leader either does not perceive the incident as God's dealing and makes a poor choice or a failure response in which the leader deliberately chooses to go against inner convictions or that which pleases God's desires in the situation,

3) remedial action by God which tests again the leader on the same or similar issue, restricts the leader's development until the lesson is learned, or disciplines the leader.

testing, positive pattern — The positive testing/ expansion pattern describes God's use of the testing cluster of items (integrity check, obedience check, word check, faith check, ministry task) to form character in a leader via a three step process:

1) presentation of a test of character through a given incident in life experience,

2) response of the leader first to recognize the incident as God's special dealing with him/her and then the positive response of taking action which honors inner convictions and God's desires in the situation,

3) expansion in which God blesses the positive response by confirming the inner conviction as an important leadership value and by increasing the leader's capacity to influence or situation of influence.

That Day — a phrase used by Paul especially in Php and both 1,2Ti (same concept somewhat phrased differently in 1,2Th) to describe the fact that there will be leadership accountability for a lifetime of ministry before God some day. See also Heb 13:17.

Glossary

time-line (leader)	a horizontal display of a leader's life broken up into developmental phases which use labels to identify the major development in a phase. This time-line can serve then to integrate all kinds of findings about a leader over his/her lifetime.
time-line (leadership)	a horizontal display of the six Biblical leadership eras which lists the basic times involved and describes the sub-phases or intermediate leadership times as well as the key leaders and labels for macro-lesson.
tongues	technically called kinds of tongues. One of the 19 spiritual gifts. It belongs to the Power Cluster. The gift of tongues refers to a spontaneous utterance of a word from God in unknown words (to the individual giving the word) to a group of people. **Its Central Thrust Is Speaking A Spontaneous Message In An Unknown Language.**
Training Methodology	a Pauline leadership value seen in 2Co. *Leaders must be concerned about leadership selection and development.*
Transforming Ministry	a Pauline leadership value seen in 2Co. *Followers who are increasingly being set free by the Holy Spirit and who are increasingly being transformed into Christ's image ought to be the hope and expectation of a Christian leader.*
True Competence (its ultimate source)	a Pauline leadership value seen in 2Co. *A leader's ultimate confidence for ministry must not rest in his/her competence but in God the author of that competence.*
True Credentials (competency and results)	a Pauline leadership value seen in 2Co. *A leader should be able to point to results from ministry as a recommendation of God's authority in him/her.*
True Judgment Criterion	a Pauline leadership value seen in 2Co. *Leaders should value people in terms of their relationship to God in Christ and not according to their outward success in the world* (even in the religious world).
Ultimate accountability	a Pauline leadership value seen in 2Co. *Leaders actions must be restrained by the fact that they will ultimately give an account to God for their leadership actions.* See **Articles**, *Day of Christ—Implications for Leaders, Motivating Factors for Ministry.*
ultimate contribution	a focused life concept; one of 4 focal issues; An ultimate contribution is a lasting legacy of a Christian worker for which he or she is remembered and which furthers the cause of Christianity by one or more of the following: setting standards for life and ministry; impacting lives by enfolding them in God's kingdom or developing them once in the kingdom; serving as a stimulus for change which betters the world; leaving behind an organization, institution, or movement that will further channel God's work; the discovery of ideas, communication of them, or promotion of them so that they further God's work. 13 categories have been identified. Paul indicates a 14—that of giving to the poor. See **Article**, *A Focused Life*.
Unequally Yoked	a Pauline leadership value seen in 2Co. *Christian leadership must not be dominated by relationships with unbelievers so that non-Christian values hold sway.*

Glossary

union life	a phrase which refers both to the fact of the spiritual reality of a believer joined in spirit with the resurrected Spirit of Christ and the process of that union being lived out so that the person is not dominated by sin in his/her life. Synonym: exchanged life, replaced life, deeper life, victorious life, normal Christian life. Paul comprehensively explains this kind of life in Romans 1-8. He models it in Philippians. He also shows its power in his own life in 2 Corinthians.
upward burden	that aspect of burden which senses not only the responsibility for a ministry because it comes from God but also the accountability for that ministry to God. Paul especially demonstrates this in 1,2Co. See also accountability.
vested gifts	a concept from leadership emergence theory. Leaders operate repeatedly over a lifetime with certain gifts. These are called vested gifts. There is the implication of development and use of the gift (see 2Ti 1:6 fn 8). Most of the word gifts are vested gifts. See also non-vested gifts.
vicarious confession	sometimes called identificational repentance, this concept involves the confession of sins past by a present day leader as if he/she had committed those sins. The confession is done on the behalf of people in the past who did not confess this sin. The result is the on-going work of God, which may have been blocked due to this unrepentant sin. See Daniel 9 for an excellent application of this concept.
*word check	from leadership emergence theory. One of 51 process items that God uses to shape a leader. A <u>word</u> <u>check</u> is a process item which tests a leader's ability to understand or receive a word from God personally and to see it worked out in life with a view toward enhancing the authority of God's truth and a desire to know it.
word gifts	a category of spiritual gifts used to clarify and explain about God. These help us understand about God including His nature, His purposes and how we can relate to Him and be a part of His purposes. These include: teaching, exhortation, pastoring, evangelism, apostleship, prophecy, ruling, and sometimes word of wisdom, word of knowledge, and faith (a word of). All leaders have at least one of these and often several of these.
*word of knowledge	one of the 19 spiritual gifts. It is primarily in the *Power Cluster* but can be in the Word Cluster and Love Clusterde pending upon what is revealed. The *word of knowledge gift* refers to the capacity or sensitivity of a person to supernaturally perceive revealed knowledge from God which otherwise could not or would not be known and apply it to a situation. **Its central thrust is Getting Revelatory Information.**
*word of wisdom	one of the 19 spiritual gifts. It is primarily in the Power Cluster but can be in the Word Cluster and Love Cluster depending upon what is revealed. The **word of wisdom gift** refers to the capacity to know the mind of the Spirit in a given situation and to communicate clearly the situation, facts, truth or application of the facts and truth to meet the need of the situation. **Its central thrust is Applying Revelatory Information.**
writer	a label given to the ultimate contribution of a Christian leader who captures ideas and reproduces them in written format to help and inform others. e.g. Paul, Luke, John.

Bibliography

(Bratcher, Robert G. et al)
    n.d.   **Good News Bible—Today's English Version**. New York: American Bible Society.

Clinton, Dr. J. Robert
    1977   **Interpreting The Scriptures: Figures and Idioms**. Altadena, Ca: Barnabas Publishers.

    1986   **A Short History of Leadership Theory**. Altadena, Ca: Barnabas Publishers.

    1986   **Coming to Conclusions On Leadership Styles**. Altadena, Ca: Barnabas Publishers.

    1987   **Reading on the Run—Continuum Reading Concepts**. Altadena, Ca: Barnabas Publishers.

    1988   **The Making of A Leader**. Colorado Springs, Co: Navpress.

    1989   **Leadership Emergence Theory**. Altadena, Ca: Barnabas Publishers.

    1993   *Getting Perspective—By Using Your Unique Time-Line* included in **LETReader.pdf** (available at www.BobbyClinton.com website). Altadena, Ca: Barnabas Publishers.

    1993   **Leadership Perspectives**. Altadena,Ca: Barnabas Publishers.

    1993   **The Bible and Leadership Values**. Altadena, Ca: Barnabas Publishers.

    1995   *Gender and Leadership*. included in **BibleLeadership.pdf** (available at www.BobbyClinton.com website). Altadena, Ca: Barnabas Publishers.

    1995   *The Life Cycle of A Leader* included in **LETReader.pdf** (available at www.BobbyClinton.com website). Altadena,Ca: Barnabas Publishers.

    1997   **Reading On The Run—Continuum Reading Concepts**. Altadena, Ca: Barnabas Publishers.

Clinton, Dr. J. Robert   (the following are yet unpublished but anticipated in the next two to five years):

Volume I. Leadership Articles from the Apostolic Books: 1,2 Timothy, Titus

Volume II. Leadership Articles from Other Pauline Epistles: 1,2 Corinthians, Philippians, Philemon,

Volume III. Leadership Articles from the Gospels—John, Mark

Volume IV. Leadership Articles from The Earlier Pre-Kingdom Leadership (Moses and Joshua): Deuteronomy, Joshua

Volume V. Leadership Articles Concerning the Formation of Kingdom Leadership: 1,2 Samuel, Part I

Volume VI. Leadership Articles Concerning the Formation of Kingdom Leadership: 1,2 Samuel, Part II

Volume VII. Leadership Articles from the Kingdom Leadership Era: Jonah, Habakkuk, Obadiah

Volume VIII. Leadership Articles from the Post Kingdom Era: Daniel, Haggai, Nehemiah, Malachi

Volume IX. Leadership Articles from the Acts, Part I
Volume X. Leadership Articles from the Acts, Part II

Clinton, Dr. J. Robert and Dr. Richard W.
    1991   **The Mentor Handbook—Deatiled Guidelines and Helps for Christian Mentors and Mentorees**. Altadena,Ca: Barnabas Publishers.

    1993   **Unlocking Your Giftedness—What Leaders Need To Know To Develop Themselves and Others**. Altadena,Ca: Barnabas Publishers.

Doohan, Helen
    1984   **Leadership in Paul**. Wilmington, Del.: Michael Glazier, Inc.

De George, Richard T.
    1985   **The Nature and Limits of Authority**. Lawrence, Kan. : University Press of Kansas.

Gerlach, L.P. and Hine, V.H.
    1970   **People, Power, Change: Movements of Social Transformation**. New York: Bobbs-Merrill Co.

Goodwin, Bennie
    1978   **The Effective Leader—A Basic Guide to Christian Leadership.** Downer's Grove, IL: InterVarsity Press.

Greenleaf, Robert K.
    1977   **Servant Leadership: A Journey Into the Nature of Legitimate Power and Greatness**. New York: Paulist Press.

Harris, R. Baine, editor; bibliography by Richard T. De George
    1976 **Authority : A Philosophical Analysis.** University, Ala. : University of Alabama Press

Hersey, Paul and Ken Blanchard
    1977   **Management of Organizational Behavior—Utilizing Human Resources**. Englewood Cliffs, N.J.: Prentice-Hall, 1977.

Kraft, Charles H.
    1979   **Christianity and Culture**. Maryknoll, N.Y.: Orbis Books.

Kuhn, Thomas
    1974   **The Structure of Scientific Revolutions**. Chicago: University Press.

Glossary

Machiavelli, Nicolo (version translated by W.K. Marriott)
    1952   **The Prince**. Chicago: Encyclopedia Britannica.

Nee, Watchman
    1948   **Spiritual Authority.** Fort Washington, Pa. : Christian Literature Crusade. (various versions are available today, translated by Kaung, Stephen).

Stanley, Paul and J. Robert Clinton
    1992   **Connecting—The Mentoring Relationships You Need to Succeed in Life**. Colorado Springs, Co: Navpress.

Strong, James
    1890   **The Exhaustive Concordance of the Bible** (with Dictionaries of the Hebrew and Greek Words). Nashville: Abingdon Press.

(Taylor, Ken did original version; other Bible scholars the new version)
    1996   **Holy Bible—New Living Translation**. Wheaton, Il: Tyndale house Publishers, Inc.

Tippett, A. R.
    1972   **Solomon Island Christianity**. Pasadena: William Carey Library.

Woolman, John
    1961   **The Journal of John Woolman, and a Plea for the Poor**. New York: Corinth Books.

Wrong, Dennis
    1979   **Power—Its Forms, Bases, and Uses**. San Francisco, CA: Harper and Row.

BARNABAS PUBLISHER'S MINI CATALOG

Barnabas: Encouraging Exhorter — Dr. J. Robert Clinton & Laura Raab

Connecting: The Mentoring Relationships You Need to Succeed in Life — Dr. J. Robert Clinton

Fellowship With God — Dr. J. Robert Clinton

Figures and Idioms (Interpreting the Scriptures: Figures and Idioms) — Dr. J. Robert Clinton

Having A Ministry That Lasts: By Becoming a Bible Centered Leader — Dr. J. Robert Clinton

Hebrew Poetry (Interpreting the Scriptures: Hebrew Poetry) — Dr. J. Robert Clinton

A Short History of Leadership Theory — Dr. J. Robert Clinton

Isolation: A Place of Transformation in the Life of a Leader — Shelley G. Trebesch

Joseph: Destined to Rule — Dr. J. Robert Clinton

The Joshua Portrait — Dr. J. Robert Clinton and Katherine Haubert

Leadership Emergence Theory: A Self Study Manual For Analyzing the Development of a Christian Leader — Dr. J. Robert Clinton

Leadership Perspectives: How To Study The Bible for Leadership Insights — Dr. J. Robert Clinton

Coming to Some Conclusionson Leadership Styles — Dr. J. Robert Clinton

Leadership Training Models — Dr. J. Robert Clinton

The Bible and Leadership Values: A Book by Book Analysis — Dr. J. Robert Clinton

The Mentor Handbook: Detailed Guidelines and Helps for Christian Mentors and Mentorees — Dr. J. Robert Clinton

Parables—Puzzles With A Purpose (Interpreting the Scriptures: Puzzles With A Purpose) — Dr. J. Robert Clinton

Reading on the Run: Continuum Reading Concepts — Dr. J. Robert Clinton

Samuel: Last of the Judges & First of the Prophets–A Model For Transitional Times — Bill Bjoraker

Selecting and Developing Those Emerging Leaders — Dr. Richard W. Clinton

Starting Well: Building A Strong Foundation for a Life Time of Ministry — Dr. J. Robert Clinton

Strategic Concepts: That Clarify A Focused Life – A Self Study Guide — Dr. J. Robert Clinton

The Making of a Leader: Recognizing the Lessons & Stages of Leadership Development — Dr. J. Robert Clinton

Unlocking Your Giftedness: What Leaders Need to Know to Develop Themselves & Others — Dr. J. Robert Clinton

A Vanishing Breed: Thoughts About A Bible Centered Leader & A Life Long Bible Mastery Paradigm — Dr. J. Robert Clinton

Webster-Smith, Irene: An Irish Woman Who Impacted Japan (A Focused Life Study) — Dr. J. Robert Clinton

Word Studies (Interpreting the Scriptures: Word Studies) — Dr. J. Robert Clinton

(Book Titles are in Bold and Paper Titles are in Italics with Sub-Titles and Pre-Titles in Roman)

BARNABAS PUBLISHERS

*Unique Leadership Material that will help you answer the question:
"What legacy will you as a leader leave behind?"*

*"The difference between leaders and followers is perspective. The difference
between leaders and effective leaders is better perspective."
Barnabas Publishers has the materials that will help you find that
better perspective and a closer relationship with God.*

BARNABAS PUBLISHERS
Post Office Box 6006 • Altadena, CA 91003-6006
Fax Phone (626)-794-3098

www.ingramcontent.com/pod-product-compliance
Lightning Source LLC
Chambersburg PA
CBHW080451170426
43196CB00016B/2763